BRITISH POLITICAL CRISES

BRITISH POLITICAL CRISES

The Rt. Hon.
Sir Dingle Foot, Q.C.

WILLIAM KIMBER · LONDON

First published in 1976 by
WILLIAM KIMBER & CO. LIMITED
Godolphin House, 22a Queen Anne's Gate,
London SW1H 9AE

© Sir Dingle Foot, 1976
ISBN 0 7183 0194 3

Typeset by Watford Typesetters
and printed in Great Britain by
The Garden City Press Limited
Letchworth, Hertfordshire, SG6 1JS

CONTENTS

Preface   9

Acknowledgements   13

I   1886   15

II   1916   45

III   1922   84

IV   1931   115

V   1940   156

Biographical Notes   193

Select Bibliography   211

Index   215

LIST OF ILLUSTRATIONS

Facing Page

Sir Dingle Foot, Q.C.   *Godfrey Argent*   32
Isaac Foot during the Bodmin Election Campaign
        Radio Times Hulton Picture Library   33
William Ewart Gladstone   64
Joseph Chamberlain   64

Between pages

Winston Churchill with Major Archibald Sinclair in 1916
        Radio Times Hulton Picture Library   64–5
Lord Balfour with Winston Churchill in 1915
        Radio Times Hulton Picture Library   64–5
David Lloyd George with H. H. Asquith in July 1924
        Beaverbrook Library   64–5
Lloyd George with Asquith at Paisley *Beaverbrook Library*   64–5

Facing Page

Andrew Bonar Law leaving the Carlton Club in 1922
        Radio Times Hulton Picture Library   65
Lloyd George with his daughter Megan in 1928
        Beaverbrook Library   96

Between pages

Ramsay MacDonald and his family in 1907   96–7
Philip Snowden, on Labour's first Budget Day
        Radio Times Hulton Picture Library   96–7
Ramsay MacDonald leaving No 10 on 23rd August 1931
        Radio Times Hulton Picture Library   96–7

Facing Page

Stanley Baldwin with Sir Austen Chamberlain
        Radio Times Hulton Picture Library   97
Sir Herbert Samuel at the Geneva Disarmament Conference   *Dr Erich Saloman*   97

Facing Page

Stanley Baldwin and Neville Chamberlain arriving for the
Economic Conference on 13th August 1931
Radio Times Hulton Picture Library   128

The first Cabinet meeting of the National Government
Radio Times Hulton Picture Library   129

Ramsay MacDonald giving a statement to the press on 3rd
October 1931   *Radio Times Hulton Picture Library*   129

Philip Snowden arriving for a Cabinet meeting after the
Ottawa conference *Radio Times Hulton Picture Library*   160

Ramsay MacDonald at Downing Street on 30th September
1932   *Radio Times Hulton Picture Library*   160

The Ottawa delegates on their way to Canada
Radio Times Hulton Picture Library   160

The British War Cabinet in 1939
Radio Times Hulton Picture Library   161

Leslie Hore-Belisha *Radio Times Hulton Picture Library*   161

Neville Chamberlain at No 10 on 10th May 1940
Radio Times Hulton Picture Library   192

Sir Kingsley Wood, Winston Churchill and Anthony Eden
Radio Times Hulton Picture Library   192

Mr and Mrs Winston Churchill taking up residence at No
10 Downing Street in 1940
Radio Times Hulton Picture Library   193

Mr and Mrs Neville Chamberlain in St James's Park on
10th May 1940   *Radio Times Hulton Picture Library*   193

*The author and publishers would like to thank the staffs of the House
of Lords Records Office, the Beaverbrook Library and the Radio
Times Hulton Picture Library, and Mrs G. Howlett for their help in
providing the illustrations for this book.*

PREFACE

In this book I endeavour to describe five moments of crisis in British political history. In each case I have tried to give an impression of the underlying causes, the prevailing atmosphere, the clash of personalities, and above all the consequences that ensued. On every one of the five occasions the course of events was entirely changed by a single incident.

On 31st May 1886 fifty-five Radicals in Committee Room 15 decided to vote against the Second Reading of the Home Rule Bill. In so doing they brought about the continuing tragedy of hatred and violence in Ireland, of which the end is not yet in sight. They also caused the departure of the Whigs from the Liberal Party and the postponement of radical social reform for over twenty years.

When, on 5th December 1916 the Liberal Prime Minister Asquith yielded to the persuasions of McKenna, Runciman and others and went back on his agreement with Lloyd George to set up a small war committee, he brought about a two-fold result. The first was that the war ended in victory instead of defeat or stalemate. The second was the permanent destruction of the Liberal Party as a major force in British politics.

Then on 19th October 1922 the meeting at the Carlton Club signalised the end of the Coalition, the fall of Lloyd George and the enthronement of mediocrity over the next eighteen years. Standards of political behaviour may have improved. The quality of statesmanship certainly did not.

On 23rd August 1931 Ramsay MacDonald went to the Palace to hand in the resignation of the Labour Cabinet. He emerged half an hour later with the King's permission to form a National Government. It may be argued that something of the kind was inevitable and that the Labour Administration could not have continued without disaster. But the effect on Parliamentary life, and indirectly on the policies the new Government was able to pursue were, to say the least, unfortunate to an extent never before contemplated. This enabled the

9

Chamberlain Government to carry out its policy of unemployment and deflation at home and appeasement abroad with no serious Parliamentary challenge.

Finally, on 8th May 1940 no-one could doubt the significance of the occasion. It is impossible to suppose that the Chamberlain Government would have prosecuted the war to a successful conclusion. The ultimate victory of the West against the Axis powers was only made possible in the 'No' lobby of the House of Commons.

I have been able to draw to some extent on my own recollections. My father, Isaac Foot, sat as Liberal Member for Bodmin in five Parliaments, albeit for a total of only eight years. He and my mother were strong Asquithians and shared to the full the general Liberal conviction that, in replacing Asquith Lloyd George committed an act of gross betrayal. At the age of sixteen I attended the Liberal meeting at Queen's Hall on 25th January 1922, and heard the immensely impressive speeches of Asquith and Grey. It really seemed as if the Liberals were coming back. This impression was confirmed when, in the following month, my father won a sensational victory at the Bodmin bye-election and entered the House of Commons for the first time. The General Election of 1922 was a bitter disappointment.

During the middle 'twenties I was an undergraduate at Oxford. My brother Hugh (now Lord Caradon) was at Cambridge. We both took an active part in the activities of our University Liberal Clubs. Throughout this period Liberalism made a considerable appeal to politically-minded undergraduates. But it was the Liberalism of the Summer Schools and not the arid doctrines of *laissez-faire* and rigid economies favoured by the principal Asquithians. And the Liberalism of the Summer Schools was in effect the Liberalism of Lloyd George. One of my political mentors was C. F. G. Masterman. He had bitterly opposed Liberal reunion. But now he admitted that, 'When Lloyd George returned to the Liberal Party, ideas returned also.' So it came about that the young Liberals in the 'twenties accepted Lloyd George's leadership with great enthusiasm and when, after the General Strike, Asquith publicly excommunicated Lloyd George the young Liberals were overwhelmingly for Lloyd George.

When we returned home for the vacation and explained our attitude our parents were considerably distressed. But in 1929 my father, who had narrowly lost his seat in the 'Red Letter' election of 1924, returned to the House of Commons under Lloyd George's leadership. Although he would have been reluctant to admit it, he yielded to the magic. Each weekend we were regaled with Lloyd George's speeches on the floor of the House of Commons or at Party meetings, or with snatches of his conversation. My mother, on the other hand, stayed in Cornwall and her views remained unaltered.

During the Parliament of 1929–31 I acted as my father's secretary at the House of Commons. On most evenings during the summer of 1931 I repaired to the National Liberal Club. There I received an account of what had happened at Westminster during the day. On the formation of the National Government my father was appointed Secretary for Mines, and held this post until, with other Liberal leaders, he resigned in September 1932 because of the Ottawa Agreements. He described in full the feeling of the Liberal Party and in particular the struggle with Hore-Belisha as he formed the Liberal National Party. On one occasion there was a Party meeting at which it appeared that Hore-Belisha had a majority. If there had been a vote he might have carried a resolution hostile to the Liberal Ministers. But my father succeeded in moving the adjournment of the meeting and the danger was averted.

From 1931 until 1945 I was Liberal Member for Dundee. It was a two-member seat and my colleague was a strong Conservative, Miss Florence Horsbrugh. Those were the days of extreme industrial depression in Dundee. There were many thousands of unemployed; indeed the percentage never fell below 17% and was generally higher. In many cases unemployment lasted not for days or weeks but for years. Dundee was mainly dependent on the jute industry. The wages were extremely low and determined by a Trade Board. A boy on leaving school at fourteen would enter a jute mill on a boy's wage. When he became eighteen it was necessary to pay him a man's wage. He would then be dismissed and might face years of unemployment. In these circumstances the imposition of the Household Means Test to which I refer in Chapter 4 had a particularly widespread effect in Dundee. For the first three years after the 1931 election ninety per cent of my constituency correspondence referred to the Means Test, and those who I interviewed on my visits to the city almost all came to protest about their assessments by the Public Assistance Committee. For these reasons I have particularly vivid recollections of the Debates on the Means Test and unemployment. I recollect in particular, Churchill's outburst against Chamberlain on 12th February 1933 (see Chapter 4).

There is one respect in which I have tried to put the record straight. From 1935, when Sir Archibald Sinclair became Liberal leader, there was the closest understanding between him and Winston Churchill. On

some occasions, as I record in Chapter 5, Liberals could choose a subject for debate. They could do so by putting down an Amendment to the
Address or by choosing one of three-and-a-half Supply Days. On Sinclair's insistence these opportunities were used, after 1935, to raise
aspects of national defence. On more than one occasion this gave
Churchill his opportunity to make some of his historic attacks on the
Chamberlain Government. This was the result of the close understanding between the two men. There is, however, no record of it in
Churchill's *Gathering Storm*, or, as far as I am aware, in any other
contemporary history.

I was, of course, present at all the Debates which I describe, and in
particular at the Norway Debate and the Division of 8th May 1940. I
was in the 'No' lobby when, at the very last minute, just as the doors
were about to be closed, the young Tory Members made their final
decision and marched into the lobby. They were all, or nearly all, in
uniform, and to me it appeared, although I was afterwards informed
that it was not so intended, that they were marching four abreast in
military formation. The effect was dramatic in the extreme.

When the Churchill Government was formed I was appointed Parliamentary Secretary to the Ministry of Economic Warfare, a post
which I held until the end of the Coalition in 1945. I was not, of course,
a Cabinet Minister. Nevertheless, I saw the Cabinet minutes and from
time to time in the absence of my chief (first Hugh Dalton, then Lord
Selborne) I would be summoned to attend a meeting. I thus had several
opportunities of observing Churchill's conduct of Cabinet business.

ACKNOWLEDGEMENTS

I have drawn freely on the various published works and in particular on J. L. Garvin's *Life of Chamberlain*, Philip Magnus's *Gladstone*, Roy Jenkins's *Asquith* and Dr Trevor Wilson's *Downfall of the Liberal Party*. I have acted throughout in the spirit of the introduction to the *Barrack Room Ballads*:

> 'When 'Omer smote 'is blooming lyre,
>   He'd 'eard men sing by land and sea :
> An' what he thought he might require
>   'E went an' took   the same as me'.

The technique is the same although, I admit, the result is different.

My thanks are due to Mr A. J. P. Taylor for permission to use the Beaverbrook Library, and to the Countess Lloyd George for giving me her recollections of 1911 and to Miss Hilde Sloane for information regarding Hore-Belisha.

I would also like to thank the following for permission to quote from material within their copyright : Mrs George Bambridge and Messrs Eyre Methuen Ltd. for permission to quote from Kipling's *Barrack Room Ballads*; Messrs John Murray Ltd. for *Gladstone* by Sir Philip Magnus; Messrs J. M. Dent & Sons, and James Nisbet & Co. Ltd. for *Prophets, Priests and Kings* by A. G. Gardiner; Messrs Macmillan London and Basingstoke, for *Life of Joseph Chamberlain* by J. L. Garvin and *Lord Randolph Churchill* by Winston Churchill; Mrs Dorothy Cheston Bennett and Messrs Eyre Methuen Ltd. for *Clayhanger* by Arnold Bennett; Messrs David Higham Associates for *The Supreme Command* by Lord Hankey; Messrs William Collins (Sons) Ltd. for *Asquith* by Roy Jenkins, *The Downfall of the Liberal Party* by Trevor Wilson, *The Decline and Fall of Lloyd George* by Lord Beaverbrook and *Diaries and Letters of Harold Nicolson* edited by Nigel Nicolson; Messrs Eyre and Spottiswoode (Publishers) Ltd. for

The Unknown Prime Minister by Robert Blake and *Reginald McKenna – A Memoir* by Stephen McKenna; Messrs Hutchinson & Co. for *The Yield of the Years* by Sir Guy Gaunt, and to Mr Julian Amery and Messrs Hutchinson & Co. for *My Political Life* by Leo Amery; Messrs Victor Gollancz for *I Fight to Live* by Lord Boothby; Messrs Secker & Warburg Ltd. for *The Tragedy of Ramsay MacDonald* by L. McNeill Weir; Messrs Hamish Hamilton for *The Life of Lord Birkett of Ulveston* by Hertford Hyde (© 1964 by Hertford Hyde, Hamish Hamilton); The Hamlyn Publishing Group for *Great Contemporaries* and *The Aftermath* by Winston Churchill.

CHAPTER I

1886

AT ONE O'CLOCK in the morning of 8th June 1886 the House of Commons voted on the Bill for Irish Home Rule. It was defeated by 343 to 313. In retrospect it can hardly be disputed that this was the most disastrous vote in British Parliamentary history. The Bill did not propose the complete separation of Britain and Ireland. The Westminster Parliament was still to maintain complete control over foreign affairs and defence. All that was envisaged was that the Parliament at Dublin, which had existed up to 1800 should be recreated and resume responsibility for Irish domestic affairs. This would have satisfied Parnell and the Irish Members. It would also have averted ninety years of continuing bitterness and bloodshed.

But the vital decision was not taken on the floor of the House. It was reached eight days earlier, on 31st May, in Committee Room 15. The meeting consisted of the Radical dissenters, 55 in all. They were to decide whether to abstain or whether to vote against the Bill. How far they realised the importance of their choice there is no way of knowing. In fact they determined the future of the Liberal Party and changed the whole course of British politics.

In retrospect the issue seems clear enough. Was the Dublin Parliament to be restored in accordance with the manifest wishes of the Irish people? It appeared far less simple at the time. Was it right to surrender to violence? What was to be the position of the Loyalists in Ulster? Would not the Dublin Parliament begin a process which would end in complete secession? Ought Irish Members continue to sit at Westminster? These were some of the problems which troubled the consciences of the 55 Members as they assembled in the Committee Room. Joseph Chamberlain presided. At first he embarked on what appeared to be a dispassionate survey of the alternatives. They must 'Walk out' or 'Vote against'. He did not reveal his own preference. But then the decisive moment was reached. He read a letter from John Bright.

Bright's prestige was enormous. Together with Cobden he had led the agitation for the repeal of the Corn Laws. Thereafter he had become a major prophet of Victorian Liberalism. In his 'Angel of Death' speech he had denounced the useless slaughter in the Crimea. In the American Civil War he, almost alone among leading English politicians, had supported the North, and Abraham Lincoln had acknowledged the debt owed by the United States to 'one John Bright of England'. To Radicals and Nonconformists he seemed the embodiment of all political virtues.

Although he had expressed his misgivings in private correspondence with Gladstone, he had made no pronouncement on Home Rule. But now his letter was read :

> 'My present intention is to vote against the second reading. Not having spoken in the Debate, I am not willing to leave my view of the Bill or Bills in any doubt. But I am not willing to take the responsibility of advising others as to their course. If they can content themselves with abstaining in the Division I shall be glad. They will render a greater service by preventing the threatened dissolution than by compelling it, if Mr Gladstone is unwise enough to venture upon it.'

This decided the issue. The vote was taken. Only three of the fifty-five Members favoured support for the Second Reading. Thirteen were for abstention, thirty-nine agreed to vote against the Bill. The result in the House of Commons could thereafter be in no doubt.

The division in the Liberal ranks was never repaired. Prior to 1886 the Party represented a broad-based, albeit somewhat uneasy, alliance. One element consisted of the Whig aristocracy supported by a considerable number of lesser country gentlemen. On the other wing were the radicals, who were largely republican in sentiment and who advocated sweeping measures of social reform. How long this strange combination would have continued is impossible to estimate. It might not long have outlived Mr Gladstone. But it was effectively shattered by the division on Irish Home Rule.

Nothing in British political history compares with the amazing ascendancy of Mr Gladstone. The impression which he made on everyone who heard him was immense.[1] On 15th April 1940 the 18 Liberal Members of Parliament gave a dinner in the House of Commons to Mr Lloyd George. The occasion was to mark the fiftieth anniversary of his election for Caernarvon Boroughs. The Liberal leader, Sir Archibald Sinclair, proposed the toast. In reply Mr Lloyd George did not make a

---

[1] In 1872 in the preface to the 2nd edition of *The English Constitution* Bagehot wrote '. . . Mr Gladstone's personal popularity at the last election was such as has not been seen since the times of Mr Pitt and such as may never be seen again.'

set speech. Instead, for over an hour he allowed his mind to wander over the past. He referred to the battle over health insurance; the People's Budget of 1909, and the divisions in 1916 over the conduct of the war. But throughout the speech he kept reverting to Gladstone. He said:

'Everyone of us is at the mercy of his biographers. Disraeli was fortunate. Moneypenny and Buckle wrote one of the best biographies in the English language. Gladstone's life, on the other hand, was written by John Morley at a time when Morley himself was burned out. The result is that many people today regard Gladstone as a dull, stuffy figure. No-one so regarded him when he was alive.'[1]

Lloyd George then went on to describe how, as a young Member of Parliament, he had heard Gladstone wind up the debate on the Second Home Rule Bill in 1893. It was the only occasion when he had seen chairs placed on the floor of the Chamber. Everyone knew that there would not be a single absentee. He described how Gladstone, then aged 83, ended with a tremendous ten-minute peroration on Irish history and all that Ireland stood for in the world. When he sat down the eighty Irish Members rose together and cheered for minutes on end. Then, as one man, they trooped out of their seets and stood in a phalanx on the floor before the Prime Minister. They went on cheering, and it was necessary for the Speaker to suspend the sitting. Lloyd George said that this was the most amazing scene that he had ever witnessed in his fifty years at Westminster. But there was no mention of it in Morley's book.

Lloyd George, in retrospect, may have exaggerated the occasion; nevertheless the scene had remained in his mind over half a century as the outstanding episode in his recollection. It illustrated the impact which Gladstone made on everyone who heard him.

How can his career be explained? He was the son of Sir John Gladstone, a West Indian slave holder, and his maiden speech in Parliament was in defence of slavery. At the Oxford Union he had opposed the Reform Bill. He was against removing the disabilities of the Jews or allowing the admission of the Nonconformists to the Universities. At his first election for Newark in 1832, he promised to resist 'that growing desire for change' which threatened to produce 'along with partial good a melancholy of mischief'. His earlier political outlook was cloistered and reactionary. When he was an undergraduate at Oxford he heard a working man exclaim: 'Damn all foreign countries. What has old

[1] I quote from memory.

England to do with foreign countries?' He recorded this outburst in his diary with the observation, 'This is not the first time I have learnt an important lesson from a humble source.'

Yet from the middle fifties of the century onward his whole outlook underwent a complete and staggering metamorphosis. It is a common phenomenon for politicians to grow more conservative in later years. As their spiritual arteries harden they go from Left to Right. Gladstone is one of the very few examples of the opposite process. In addressing the electors of Midlothian in 1886 he declared that he found arrayed against him 'in profuse abundance, station, title, wealth, social influence, the professions, or the large majority of them – in a word the spirit and power of class and the dependants of class'. He said that for the past sixty years the classes had 'fought uniformly on the wrong side'. And after his defeat in the election he referred to 'the singular fact that for a long series of years, depending mainly on broad considerations of justice and humanity, wealth station and rank had been wrong and the masses had been right'. How appalled by these sentiments the young Mr Gladstone would have been!

He was obviously a man of immense physical vitality. This is a factor which biographers and historians generally tend to overlook or underestimate. Sir Philip Magnus has recorded how in 1882, when Gladstone was 73, Lord Granville consulted Gladstone's doctor, Sir Andrew Clarke, about the Prime Minister's health. Sir Andrew told him that Gladstone was not only sound from head to toes but built in the most beautiful proportions he had ever seen of all the parts of the body to each other – head, legs, arms and trunk all without a flaw, like some ancient Greek statue of the ideal man. H. G. Wells describes him as 'a white-faced, black-haired man of incredible energy, with eyes like an eagle's, wrath almost divine and the finest baritone voice in Europe.'

It is possible that the transformation began in the middle sixties. Until 1865 he sat in in the House of Commons as one of the Burgesses for the University of Oxford. Then he was defeated. Undoubtedly he felt deeply wounded by this reverse. Seemingly, however, the wound did not take long to heal. On the following night he addressed 6,000 people in the Free Trade Hall at Manchester, opening with the words: 'I am come amongst you and I am come . . . unmuzzled.' On the same evening he addressed an audience of 5,000 in Liverpool.

Thus began his career as the greatest platform orator in British history. All the accounts agree that he had a magnetic effect on an audience. Mr Francis Birrell[1] has suggested that this is the explanation

[1] *Gladstone*: Duckworth, 1944.

of his career: he found that he had this tremendous sway over the electors; therefore the electors were a good thing and there ought to be more of them. Hence his consistent support for extensions of the franchise.

Contrary to the general impression which is probably the result of Morley's biography, he had a keen sense of the ridiculous and a considerable wit. When Disraeli promoted his Secretary, Montague Corry, to the House of Lords as Lord Rowton, Gladstone observed that nothing comparable had been seen since Caligula made his horse a consul. One example of his humour is to be found in his description of his final interview with Queen Victoria. He had been four times her Prime Minister. Yet the Queen could not bring herself to say a word of appreciation. Gladstone's comment was to compare himself with the mule which he had ridden in Sicily in 1831 : 'I had been on the back of the beast for many scores of hours. It had done me no wrong. It had rendered me much valuable service. But it was in vain to argue. There was the fact staring me in the face. I could not get up the smallest shred of feeling for the brute. I could neither love nor like it.'

He had very definite limitations. His views on 'retrenchment' were carried to the point of absurdity. Thus in 1886 he somewhat reluctantly agreed with Joseph Chamberlain that Jesse Collings should be appointed an Under Secretary. Collings was then a hero in Liberal eyes. His slogan of 'Three acres and a cow' had swept the rural constituencies at the election. It was he who moved the amendment in the House of Commons on this subject which brought about the fall of the Salisbury Government. Yet Gladstone at once insisted that his salary as an Under-Secretary should be reduced from £1,500 to £1,200 a year. Chamberlain was understandably furious and Gladstone was constrained reluctantly to give way.

Sir Philip Magnus[1] has written of Gladstone that 'he understood passion well but sentiment hardly at all.' Hence his attitude towards the Sudan and the death of General Gordon. Sir Philip writes :

> The patriotic youth of the nation felt that its interests were no longer safe in Gladstone's hands; it was inexcusable that he should have found no words of praise for all the Nile Army had endured in vain.

and Lord Wolseley wrote to the Queen in March 1885 : 'A few cheering words to these soldiers . . . would have cost him nothing.'

But the passion was never lacking. It first showed itself in 1851, when

---

[1] *Gladstone: A biography*: John Murray, 1954.

he despatched his letter to Lord Aberdeen on the Government of Naples:

> It is the wholesale persecution of virtue . . . it is the awful profanation of public religion . . . it is the perfect prostitution of the judicial office . . . it is the savage and cowardly system of moral as well as physical torture. This is the negation of God erected into a system of Government.

and of course there was his historic condemnation of Turkish atrocities in the Balkans:

'Let the Turks now carry away their abuses in the only possible manner, namely by carrying off themselves. Their Zeptiehs and their Nudirs, their Bimbashies and their Yuzbachis, their Kaimakams and their Pashas, one and all, bag and baggage, shall, I hope, clear out from the province they have desolated and profaned. This thorough riddance, this most blessed deliverance, is the only reparation we can make to the memory of those heaps on heaps of dead; to the violated purity alike of matron, of maiden and of child . . . There is not a criminal in a European gaol; there is not a cannibal in the South Sea Islands, whose indignation would not arise and overboil at the recital of that which has been done, which has too late been examined, but which remains unavenged; which has left behind all the foul and all the fierce passions that produced it, and which may again spring up in another murderous harvest, from the soil soaked and reeking with blood, and in the air tainted with every imaginable deed of crime and shame . . . No Government ever has so sinned; none has proved itself so incorrigible in sin or, which is the same, so impotent for reformation.'

The chief antagonist of Home Rule was Joseph Chamberlain. Apart from Gladstone himself, he was beyond question the outstanding figure in British politics during the last two decades of the nineteenth century. Their two careers represented a complete antithesis. Gladstone, as has already been said, moved from Right to Left. The transmogrification of Chamberlain was the precise opposite. He entered Parliament in 1876 as the enemy of privilege, no matter whether it took the form of rank of wealth. He and his close friend Sir Charles Dilke were avowed republicans. They did not expect to see the monarchy last more than a few years, and they were both the exponents of a new radicalism whose aim was completely to transform the condition of the people. They supported the Liberal Party because they detested Disraelian Toryism. But they were scarcely less opposed to the Whigs. It was only with the

utmost hesitation that Chamberlain consented in 1880 to join Gladstone's Government with its preponderance of Whig nobles. He
frequently wondered whether he had made the right decision.

If Chamberlain and Dilke had remained as Liberal leaders, the
course of political history must have been entirely different from what
actually occurred. One or other of them would have succeeded Gladstone in the leadership. The influence of the Whig nobles and land-
owners must have steadily diminished. The social programme carried
out by the Liberal Government thirty years later under the inspiration
of Lloyd George might have been enacted in the 1880s. The Labour
Party might never have emerged as a separate force. But Dilke's career
was destroyed in the Divorce Court in 1885. Although he continued in
Parliament for another twenty years he never recovered. Chamberlain
remained as the only possible successor to Gladstone. With his remarkable qualities, he must have been one of the greatest Prime Ministers.
But his whole career, and indeed the whole course of British politics,
was entirely altered by the Irish controversy of 1886.

Joseph Chamberlain was a man of immense determination. At the
same time he always knew with the utmost clarity what his objectives
were. As a young man he had been extremely successful as a screw
manufacturer in Birmingham. He had been pre-eminent in local government, and as Mayor immensely successful. Towards the end of his
life Mr A. G. Gardiner wrote of him as follows :[1]

Mr William Watson has told us how, in the blackest days of the
[Boer War] struggle, he went one evening into the smoking room of the
Devonshire Club, of which Mr Chamberlain was a member. In a corner,
smoking a cigar and reading a book, sat the Colonial Secretary, in-
different to all around him. Mr Watson left, and went to dinner. Re-
entering later he found Mr Chamberlain in the same place, still smoking,
still reading. Returning to the Club late at night from an engagement,
he entered the smoking room. The figure in the corner seat was unmoved, still smoking, still absorbed in his book. It is the stillness of a man
who never doubts himself, takes his own reading of the public pulse
and then acts with a swiftness and momentum without planning the
reason. His view of the public is of a mob charged with electricity; waiting for a man to fuse it and direct the lightnings. The one fatal defect
in a leader is indecision. To hesitate is to be lost – to doubt is to fail.
Mr Balfour, lost in the complexities of this incalculable world, who was
on all sides doubting of things, convinced of the futility of action, stands
at the helm nerveless and abstracted, involved in a deep that has no
end. Mr Chamberlain leaps to the wheel and crashes full steam ahead

[1] *Prophets, Priests and Kings*: Wayfarer's Library, J. M. Dent, 1914.

through the storm, sometimes to reach the happy hills, sometimes to find the gulfs that have washed him down.

His philosophy is simple – give the people a confident lead and they will follow, a catchword and they will adopt it as a creed, a personality and they will not bother about the argument. 'What I have said I have said. Do I contradict myself? I give no explanation, offer no apologies. I have no yesterdays, carry no old clothes. I am not a slave to other men's theories or to my own past . . .'

This pride of will and this scorn of men had been the source of his power, but they are the key also of his failure. They have led him into grave miscalculation of other men and other forces. He believed he could throw Gladstone and carry the Liberal Party with him. He broke the Party, it is true, broke it for twenty years, but it re-emerged with his policy triumphant and with him as its chief and bitter foe. He believed, as the famous interview with Campbell-Bannerman shows, that he could 'bluff' the Boers. And again he miscalculated the forces against him and met his Moscow. He believed he could raze out the memory of the war and stampede the country with a new cry. He misjudged the intelligence of his countrymen and met his Waterloo. All the journey is marked with the mighty 'debris' of pride.

He entered Parliament after a by-election on the week before his fortieth birthday. His reputation had preceded him and he took his seat in an atmosphere which he himself described as 'strange, unsympathetic, almost hostile'. The prejudice against him was confirmed by his failure to remove his hat before taking the oath. The chief door-keeper whispered in his ear. It was noticed that the cool novice uncovered 'but not confusedly and not at once'.[1] 'At least', said Disraeli, 'he wears his eye-glass like a gentleman.'

Almost at once he became a major figure on the political scene. During the last half-century 'temperance' has ceased to be a principal issue. It was different during the later years of Victoria's reign and in the first quarter of the twentieth century. The problem of drunkenness among the working classes occupied the attention of every social reformer. This was one of the products of the Industrial Revolution. Whisky was 3d a dram and beer 2d a pint. The working man became drunk on Saturday night 'because it was the shortest way out of Manchester'. Winston Churchill has recorded how, when he stood for Dundee in 1908, he was struck by the 'bestial drunkenness' which disfigured the life of the town. On Saturday night the industrial worker began the evening with a double whisky as a 'chaser'; this was followed with several pints of beer.

[1] J. L. Garvin, *Life of Chamberlain* Volume 1 pp. 230, 231 : Macmillan & Co., 1932.

To an extent which is now wholly forgotten, drink and licensing figured in political programmes. The Liberals drew their support in large part from nonconformity, and nonconformists reacted in the strongest manner against the evils of drunkenness. The remedy, as they believed, lay in one form or another of statutory restriction. They advocated complete prohibition, local option (i.e. local prohibition determined by ballot); Sunday closing and the restriction of licensing hours. Not unnaturally these measures did not commend themselves to the brewers. Consequently, there grew up a close alliance between the Tory Party and 'the Trade'. A strange paradox ensued. The Liberals with their free church supporters were the advocates of personal freedom at home and abroad. They were the enemies of repression whether in the Balkans or in Ireland. Yet, as their opponents inevitably pointed out, there was one freedom which they denied – at least to the working man – the freedom to drink.

This was one of the first issues with which Chamberlain was concerned after his entry into Parliament. In 1877, accompanied by Jesse Collings, he visited Sweden. He came back deeply impressed with the Gothenburg system, under which the sale of strong spirits was placed under municipal control. On 13th March, he addressed the House of Commons for nearly an hour and sat down amidst loud and continued applause from all sides.

His theme was that since the drink traffic could not be wholly suppressed, it must be regulated. Alcohol must no longer be sold for private profit. The trade must be taken out of private hands and given over to municipal authorities. It was a theme which continued for many years, though for better or worse, it never attracted the support of most temperance advocates.

Next he created the Caucus. It arose out of the electoral system initiated by the Act of 1867. In an attempt to provide a rudimentary form of proportional representation, provision was made for three-member seats in which each elector had no more than two votes. Thus it was hoped that minorities would secure their due representation. On this basis Birmingham, with its Liberal majority, might have returned only four or five out of seven Members. It was, however, apparent to the Liberal organisers that such a catastrophe might be avoided. If the Liberal vote could in each ward be given according to instructions, the whole seven seats could be retained. The exercise was carried out by a supreme organiser, Mr Joseph Schnadhorst. It was wholly successful. At the General Election of 1880 the Liberals in Birmingham carried all seven seats. The triumph of the Caucus became another subject of major controversy. Chamberlain was accused of introducing American methods into British politics.

His career between 1880, when he joined the Gladstone Government, and 1885 is unparalleled. Many Cabinets include disparate types, some cautious and some adventurous. Despite the doctrine of Cabinet solidarity, no contemporary observer has much doubt as to where the division lies. It can, however, never have been more apparent than during Gladstone's third administration. During the last two years, Chamberlain increasingly emerged as the enemy of privilege and class distinction. Thus in March 1883, Lord Salisbury visited Birmingham and denounced the Caucus and its 'machinating demagogue that was meant to make the House of Commons itself the pliant tool of a tyrannist organisation.' Chamberlain replied on the following day in a speech which rang through the land :

'Lord Salisbury constitutes himself the spokesman of a class – of a class to which he himself belongs, who toil not neither do they spin [great cheering], whose fortunes, as in his case have originated by grants made in times gone by for the services which courtiers rendered Kings [renewed cheers] and have since grown and increased while they have slept by levying an increased share on all that other men have done by toil and labour to add to the general wealth and prosperity of the country.'

The phrase 'who toil not neither do they spin' created an immense sensation. Chamberlain was denounced as 'Robespierre revealed'. Lord Salisbury declared that this was 'the Jacobin theory pure and simple'. The Queen was furious. Mr Gladstone was displeased. But Chamberlain had become, as it seemed, the undoubted leader of radical England.

His greatest achievement as President of the Board of Trade was the Merchant Shipping Act. This dealt with the evil of 'coffin ships'. During the preceding twenty years the British Mercantile Marine, and the profits made by ship owners, had immensely expanded. Vessels went to sea inadequately equipped but heavily insured. If they reached the end of their voyage the profit was considerable; if they sank it was hardly less. There was an annual death rate of 3,500 British sailors lost at sea. Chamberlain's Bill, aimed at suppressing overloading, undermanning, defective construction and over-insurance, met with furious opposition. No more determined lobby has ever been organised at Westminster. The shipowners, some of them Liberals, did everything in their power to drum up opposition. Chamberlain had little support in the Cabinet. The Bill had to be withdrawn. But he defended it in August 1885, in a speech at Hull which added enormously to his reputation. The town was covered with placards acclaiming him as 'your coming Prime Minister'. Hull was a seaport, and its senior Member was a Whig who had opposed the Bill. It was a speech which, as Garvin has remarked,[1] no man then living could excel. 'It should be read sometime by any who have forgotten or have never known how Joseph Chamberlain could speak.'

'I found in the first place that every year more than 3,000 lives were lost at sea; that in some years this total amounted to 3,500 and even more. Death is always a pathetic thing; but death when it comes under circumstances of such horror and when it comes in the shape of a violent end to existence, is still more tragic and pathetic. And it was not only the men whose lives were lost whose fate you have to consider. What is the fate of their families who are left without resource, struggling against destitution when the breadwinner is removed? The next point which struck me was this, that the proportion of this loss of life to the men employed was something extravagant and almost horrible . . . actually 1 in 56. But what does it matter, whether it is 1 in 56 or 1 in 60 or one in 100? It is a loss of life absolutely unparalleled in any other trade, deplorable in itself, and which ought not to be endured by a civilised people.

'Then I went on naturally to the next point of the enquiry. I tried to discover how far this loss of life was preventable . . . I found the extraordinary fact that in a great number of cases, I am not certain that it might not be so in the majority of cases, the owners whose vessels went to the bottom, the bones of whose crews whitened the sands   these men suffered no loss and might even in some cases make a profit.

'I thought that this was a state of things which loudly called for remedy. I for one was not prepared to take the responsibility of standing with folded hands doing nothing to remove a source of so much misery and suffering to so many of my fellow-countrymen.'

In May 1885, Gladstone reluctantly announced that he would renew the Coercion Act for Ireland. A few days later he further announced his intention to introduce a scheme of State land purchase. On the issue of coercion Chamberlain and Dilke tendered their resignations, which they agreed to suspend for a short time. On 8th June the Irish Nationalists combined with the Conservatives to overthrow the Government. The adverse vote was 264 to 252. Gladstone resigned next day and Lord Salisbury was constrained to form a minority administration which lasted for the next seven months. During this time Chamberlain deli-

[1] *Life of Chamberlain.*

vered a series of speeches which shook Victorian England. These were in support of the 'unauthorised programme' which contained seven objectives:

(1)   Free primary education;
(2)   Full local government for the counties;
(3)   Home-Rule-All-Round, on equal terms for the different nationalities of the United Kingdom, leaving the Imperial Parliament unimpaired in composition and authority as the supreme legislature of a common realm;
(4)   Financial reform, partly by graduated taxation, moderately applied – through death duties and house duties, not income tax – partly by levying on unearned increment, in order to lighten the pressure of indirect taxation on the people and to pay for better housing and other social measures.
(5)   Land reform, chiefly to give the labourer a stake in the soil and to create again a race of smallholders – not excluding larger holdings – by the steady action of local authorities equipped with compulsory powers for land purchase at an equitable price;
(6)   Disestablishment of State Churches in England, Scotland and Wales.
(7)   Manhood suffrage and payment of Members.

To the Victorian establishment, from the Queen downwards, these proposals appeared to threaten the foundations of Church and State Their fears were amply confirmed by the tone of Chamberlain's speeches. Here are two examples:

'If we cannot convince our allies of the justice and reasonableness of our views, then, with whatever reluctance, we must part company, we will fight alone; we will appeal unto Caesar; we will go to the people from whom we come and whose cause we plead; and, although the verdict may be delayed, I, for my part, have not one shadow of doubt as to the ultimate decision. We have been looking to the extension of the franchise in order to bring into prominence questions which have been too long neglected. The great problem of our civilisation is still unsolved. We have to account for and to grapple with the mass of misery and destitution in our midst, co-existence as it is with the evidence of abundant wealth and teeming prosperity. It is a problem which some men would put aside by reference to the eternal laws of supply and demand, to the necessity of freedom of contract, and to the sanctity of every right of property. But, gentlemen, these phrases are the convenient cant of selfish wealth.'

'Politics is the science of human happiness, and the business of a statesman and of politicians is to find out how they can raise the general condition of the people; how they can increase the happiness of those who are less fortunate among them. What are the facts of the case? I sometimes think that we are so used to poverty and to its consequences that we forget it or neglect it. Yet surely there is some reason to doubt the perfection of our system when in this, the richest country in the world, one in thirty of the population at every moment are unable to obtain the means of subsistence without recourse to the parish, and one in ten at the same time are on the verge of starvation.'

On 1st October, Labouchère wrote in *Truth*:

Mr Chamberlain's advent to power may be regarded as certain. He has at various times declared himself for the disestablishment and disendowment of the Church, for the abolishment of the House of Lords, against further Royal Grants, for local self-government in the widest sense, for limitation of landed estates; for the taxation of ground land lords in towns, and for State aid and interference in behalf of the weak against the strong, and has shown that these are not vague words destined to catch votes, but are views that he is not inclined to surrender for place or power.

Here then was the situation as it appeared at the end of 1885. Mr Gladstone, it was generally supposed, was nearing retirement. Indeed, he himself so intended. There could be only one successor. Then, under a Chamberlain administration, the whole of society would be transformed. So it would almost certainly have happened if it had not been for Ireland.

Ever since the Reform Bill Irish grievances had been constantly raised at Westminster. Two of the greatest Parliamentary orators during the thirties and forties were Shiel and O'Connell. Every year a motion was introduced in favour of the Irish self-government, and every year it was voted down. Ireland suffered from an alien Church and an alien landed aristocracy. One of Gladstone's principal achievements in his first Administration (1868 to 1873) was the disestablishment of the Irish Church. But the economic and social grievances remained.

In 1870, the first measure was passed for protection of Irish tenants. It empowered the Courts to revise exorbitant rents. This measure proved ineffective, expecially when, in the middle seventies, a great agricultural depression began. Prices catastrophically fell. Thousands of Irish tenants could no longer pay their rents and were unmercifully evicted. The result, not surprisingly, was a wave of violence directed against

landlords, their agents and their properties. The British Government
found itself in a dilemma which has frequently recurred, and not only
in Ireland. When suspects were accused of agrarian crimes no-one
would come forward to give evidence against them and, even where
such evidence could be obtained, juries would refuse to convict.

In these circumstances, successive British Governments felt constrained to pass Coercion Acts providing for imprisonment without
trial. Examples can be found in the Act of 1881 – 'For the better
Protection of Person and Property in Ireland'. It provided that any
person declared by warrant of the Lord Lieutenant to be reasonably
suspected of treason or of any act of violence or intimidation tending
to interfere with or disturb the maintenance of law and order might be
legally detained as directed by the Lord Lieutenant and should not be
discharged or tried by any court without the direction of the Lord
Lieutenant. It was further provided that 'such warrant should be con-
clusive evidence of all the matters therein contained and the legality
of the arrest and detention.'

To Liberals, such legislation presented a horrible dilemma. They
were the traditional champions of freedom and the rule of law. Gladstone himself had denounced the Neapolitan prisons and spoken of the
Sudan as 'a nation rightly struggling to be free'. The idea of coercion
was abhorrent both to Whigs and to Radicals. Yet so long as Ireland
was governed from Westminster, there appeared to be no escape. As
early as 1871 when Gladstone released some political prisoners, Disraeli
had charged him with 'shaking property to its foundations, consecrating
sacrilege, condoning treason, making Government ridiculous and sow-
ing the seeds of Civil War'. In the Parliament of 1880 there was no
escape from Irish affairs. Parnell and his followers set out completely
to disrupt the business of the House of Commons. For a time they were
largely successful. Hours and days of Parliamentary time were con-
sumed by Irish speeches 'sometimes' said Gladstone, 'rising to the level
of mediocrity.' Eventually the Standing Orders were drawn up providing for the closure of debate.

The Liberal Government introduced a Bill compelling Irish landlords in certain circumstances to compensate the tenants whom they
evicted. It is significant that 20 Liberal Members voted against it and
others abstained. Lord Lansdowne, an English Peer, and a great Irish
landowner, was Under-Secretary for India. He resigned his office in
protest against the Bill. These events are significant; they mark the
beginning of the defection of the Whigs. The Bill was rejected by the
House of Lords by an overwhelming majority. The Coercion Act was

carried. It was accomplished, however, by a new Land Bill, which established for Irish tenants what came to be known as the three 'Fs' – Fair rents, Fixity of security of fixture and the right to sell their holdings. Another great Whig, the Duke of Argyll, resigned from the Cabinet.

It is not necessary to trace in detail the events of the next few years. The Irish Nationalists tried to wreck the Act by persuading tenants not to apply to Rent Tribunals. In a speech at Leeds Gladstone denounced Parnell, declaring that the 'resources of civilization are not yet exhausted.' Parnell was arrested and held in prison. There followed in 1882 the 'Kilmainham Treaty' under which Parnell was released. He agreed to support the Land Act in return for the introduction of a Bill which would expand benefits of the Act to tenants who were in arrears with their rent. It is significant that the understanding with Parnell was negotiated on Gladstone's behalf by Joseph Chamberlain. He used two intermediaries : one was Justin Macarthy, the other was Captain O'Shea, who, as it afterwards appeared, was the husband of Parnell's mistress. The main responsibility, however, for arriving at these terms, lay with Chamberlain.

We are now presented with one of the strangest phenomena in political history. On this occasion and throughout the next four years, Chamberlain was the unvarying advocate of Irish conciliation. He was a believer in devolution for all parts of the United Kingdom, and strongly favoured a Council to deal with Irish affairs. He detested coercion. In May 1885, Gladstone announced that he intended to renew some parts of the Coercion Act. This was the occasion when Chamberlain and Dilke tendered their resignations.

It was perhaps inevitable that Gladstone should decide in favour of a separate Irish Parliament. He had favoured the cause of nationalism in Italy, in the Balkans and in the Sudan. How could he fail to sympathise with the nationalist aspirations of the Irish? He finally reached his decision during a cruise of the Norwegian fiords in August 1885. Gladstone was immensely attracted by the Norwegians living in a small but free and democratic country.

He was confronted with a problem of leadership. Undoubtedly Ireland was uppermost in his thoughts. A Party leader, however, is always at the mercy of circumstances. He cannot sit back like an academic and determine his own priorities : they are invariably determined for him. Gladstone's problem was a familiar one which has often recurred before and since – how to maintain at least the appearance of cohesion between the two wings of his Party.

Every Party, and especially every Left-Wing Party is a coalition of forces, and there is a never-ending struggle as to which shall prevail. This form of conflict has never been more acute than inside the Liberal Party from 1880 to 1886. On the one side were Dilke, Chamberlain and the Radicals, on the other were the Whigs. These included not, indeed, the whole, but a very large part of the landed aristocracy. The most striking figure in Trollope's political novels is the Duke of Omnium. He is enormously wealthy, he has vast estates, he exercises vast political patronage and in many Parliamentary constituencies his endorsement guarantees elections. But he is a Whig and therefore a member of the Liberal Party. He is regarded with jealous disapproval by the minor Tory gentry.

The Whigs believed in freedom : they had destroyed the rotten boroughs and carried out the great Reform Bill which enfranchised the middle classes. In alliance with Bright and Cobden they had supported Peel and had abolished the Corn Laws. They were the heirs of Fox and Brougham; their ancestors had brought about the glorious revolution and had opposed the royal pretensions of George III.

There was, however, another side to their philosophy. It was by no means illogical. In economic matters they believed almost completely in *laissez-faire*. Indeed, Dicey the editor of *The Observer*, wrote in 1885 : '*Laissez-faire* was our motto, and to that motto I, for one, adhere still.' Governments should not interfere with the working of the market or determine the relationship between employer and worker or landlord and tenant. Especially the latter. The Whigs, it has been said, defended property in the name of liberty. It was therefore natural for them to oppose the unauthorised programme.

At the same time they increasingly disliked the Government's Irish legislation. Every measure designed to allay the discontents of the Irish peasantry necessarily involved interfering with the rights of landlords. Thus we find in 1880 the Cabinet equally divided. The Whig nobles were on one side and the Radicals (including Chamberlain) on the other.

Gladstone's own instinctive sympathies were undoubtedly with the Whigs on all matters except Ireland. But he intended to avoid a breach during his lifetime. Writing to Chamberlain in September, he accepted that a split was likely 'in the far or middle distance' but that he would have nothing to do with it. To Hartington, the Leader of the Whigs, he wrote that if they were men of sense 'the crisis will not be yet'. His address to the electors at Midlothian was a masterpiece of ambiguity. The main issue in the counties was the position of rural labourers on the land. The Radicals campaigned on the theme first proclaimed by

Jesse Collings of three acres and a cow. Gladstone stated in his address
that he would rejoice if legislation on such matters as entail land transfer
and registration, possibly on primogeniture 'or other means in themselves commendable' should lead to a large extension in the number
'directly interested in the position and produce of the soil.' These melli-
fluous phrases could not altogether hide the deep rift between the two
wings. During the election Labouchère wrote to Chamberlain :

> We have been losing for a very clear reason. You put forward a good
> radical programme. This would have taken. But no sooner had you put
> it forward than Hartington and others denounced it. The Grand Old
> Man proposed that any question should be shunted to the dim and dis-
> tant future, and that all should unite to bring him back to power, with
> a coalition Ministry – in fact the old game which had already resulted
> in shilly-shally. I think the inhabitants of the towns have shown their
> wisdom in preferring even the Conservatives to this . . . Our hope now
> is 'the cow' and here too I am afraid that the Whigs will have poured
> cold water on all enthusiasm . . . milk may be good for babies but Whig
> milk will not do for electors.

In October Chamberlain was Gladstone's guest at Hawarden. It was
the only occasion when the two stayed under the same roof. Garvin has
described the astonishment with which Chamberlain received the invitation.[1] It appears that the visit was suggested by a young aristocratic
Liberal MP, George Russell, who had become one of Chamberlain's
devotees. He himself stayed at Hawarden and discussed Chamberlain
with Gladstone. He expressed the opinion that Chamberlain did not
mean to dethrone Gladstone from the Liberal leadership, and probably
felt that he could not do so if he wished, but he himself meant to prevent
Lord Hartington from succeeding to the leadership when Gladstone
should surrender it. He then suggested that his host should ask Chamberlain to come to Hawarden and talk it out with him. He records :

> My host could not have looked more amazed if I had suggested
> inviting the Pope or the Sultan; but my persuasions prevailed over his
> reluctance to mix political with private life, and the invitation was
> duly despatched and accepted.

Chamberlain arrived on 7th October and stayed for two days. On the
first day they walked in the woods and discussed chiefly the Irish question. Next day they sat in the library (where, apparently, Chamberlain
was not allowed to smoke) and discussed other issues. They differed

---

[1] J. L. Garvin, *Life of Chamberlain* : Volume 2 p. 105.

over compulsory purchase by local authorities of land for small holdings and allotments. Otherwise there does not seem to have been any acute difference, least of all on the Irish question. In a letter to Lord Granville describing the exchange, Gladstone wrote :

> All these subjects I separated entirely from the question of Ireland, on which I may add he and I are pretty well agreed; unless upon a secondary point, namely, whether Parnell would be satisfied to acquiesce in a County Government Bill, good so far as it went, maintaining on other matters his present general attitude. We agreed, I think, that a prolongation of the present relations of the Irish Party would be a national disgrace, and the civilised world would scoff at the political genius of countries which could not contrive so far as to understand one another as to bring their differences to an accommodation.

Chamberlain's account, written to Dilke on the following day, was as follows :

> I am not quite certain what was Mr G's object in sending for me. I suppose he desired to minimise our conditions as far as possible. He was very pleasant and very well with no apparent trace of his hoarseness.
>
> He spoke at considerable length on the Irish question – said he was more impressed with the advantages of the central council scheme and had written strongly to that effect to Hartington.

Some years later Chamberlain recorded that, assuming the Liberals with a majority over the Irish and Conservatives combined, their policy should be to offer a Land Bill and a Local Government Bill without saying anything about Home Rule. Apparently Mr Gladstone did not offer much criticism of these proposals but suggested that perhaps the Conservative Government would be prepared to go in the direction of Home Rule. Nothing was said about the current negotiations being carried on with the Irish Party by Herbert Gladstone and Labouchère.

It was a strange meeting. The two men parted without any real understanding on the Irish question. Gladstone never revealed to Chamberlain the extent of his conversion to Home Rule. On his side, Chamberlain never made clear the extent of his opposition. If indeed their minds were made up, neither can be acquitted of sheer dissimulation. This seems improbable. The explanation would appear to be that neither Gladstone nor Chamberlain had arrived at a final decision on Home Rule.

Their minds never really met. As Garvin has pointed out, Chamberlain was absorbed by one thing, the British social question; Gladstone by another, the Irish national question. But it may be that the real

The Author

Isaac Foot with supporters during the Bodmin Election campaign in 1924

significance of the occasion is to be found in the last paragraph of Chamberlain's later memorandum :

> Almost at the close of the interview Mr Gladstone said 'I think I ought to tell you that it is not my intention to remain much longer in public life. I have, as you know, long wished to retire. I have been induced by the representations of yourself and my other colleagues to remain at the head of the Party much longer than I wished or intended. I have carried you through the Franchise Bill and I am now going to stand at your head for the General Election, but as soon as you are fairly started in the new Parliament and in a very few months, I propose to hand over the leadership to Hartington. . . .
>
> I did not think at the time that he was likely to maintain his expressed intention to resign, but it seemed to me indirectly a proof that he did not contemplate a Home Rule programme, with which, of course, any suggestion of resignation would have been entirely inconsistent.

It is a matter of sheer surmise, but it may be this marked the parting of the ways. Only Gladstone's supreme prestige had kept together the Whigs and the Radicals. Chamberlain had every reason to look forward to the succession when Gladstone retired. But now Gladstone had made it clear that in his view the mantle should descend upon the leader of the Whigs. Who could say that his wishes would not prevail?

But there was another possibility. Gladstone might continue. He had expressed his intention to resign to Chamberlain, who may in this matter have been a better judge of Gladstone's temperament than Gladstone himself, and did not believe him. What were the prospects if he continued? After his return to Birmingham, Chamberlain wrote to Russell that nothing could have been socially more pleasant than the visit, but politically it had been a failure, since Gladstone would not budge an inch towards the unauthorised programme. If I were to resist, said Chamberlain, 'the very stones would cry out'. Russell's opinion was that after this acute disagreement Home Rule was only the signal and the occasion for a severance which was inevitable.

The General Election took place in November. Addressing the electors at Midlothian, Mr Gladstone clearly contemplated the possibility of Home Rule. After a verdict for 'the honourable maintenance of the unity of the Empire' he continued : 'To stint Ireland in power which might be necessary or desirable for the management of matters purely Irish would be a great error.' He appealed for a majority totally independent of the Irish vote. His hope was disappointed. On 7th October, Lord Salisbury made a speech at Newport, clearly intended to conciliate

Parnell and his followers. He took credit in the fact that the Conservative Government had refused to renew the Crimes Act and he appeared to exonerate boycotting in Ireland. The result was soon apparent. In November Parnell issued a manifesto. In effect, the Irish vote in British constituencies was handed over to the Conservative Party. It was a fateful decision which diverted the whole course of Irish history.

There has never been any General Election comparable in its results to 1885. Since then, the electoral map of England (as contrasted with Scotland and Wales) has shown a fairly consistent pattern. The industrial and mining towns have, as a general rule returned first Liberal and then Labour Members. Apart from the West Country and East Anglia, the counties have been true blue and have returned, for the most part, an unbroken succession of Conservative Members. 1885 was wholly different. The boroughs, influenced by the Irish vote, swung to the Conservatives. In the counties the farm labourers were newly enfranchised; to the universal amazement, they marched to the polls in support of Liberal candidates. It seemed like a revolution. Ever since the Reform Bill, the rural constituencies had been largely the preserve of the landed aristocracy, whether Whig or Tory. In so far as their writ did not run, the influence of the squire and the parson was paramount. Now it was assumed that the rural labourers, who had hitherto shown no apparent interest in political issues, would follow the traditional pattern. This expectation was completely falsified by what was described as 'the revolt of Hodge'. The universal amazement among the Tory gentry may be compared to a recent phenomenon – the intense surprise with which the Smith regime in Rhodesia observed the African reaction to the Pearce Commission's inquiry.

So far as can now be discerned, there were two causes. One was the Radical programme of three acres and a cow. The other was the still overwhelming popularity of Mr Gladstone. Morley refers to 'An ardent agrarian reformer', who later became a conspicuous unionist, who wrote to Gladstone in July of the great rural gatherings which he had attended. 'One universal feature of these meetings is the joy, affection and unbounded applause with which your name was received by these earnest men. Never in all your history had you so strong a place in the hearts of the common people as you have today. It required to be seen to be realised.'

The rural constituencies redressed the balance in the boroughs. Nevertheless, the effect of Parnell's intervention was to produce almost a dead heat between the Liberals on the one side and the combined votes of Conservative and Irish Members on the other. The Liberals numbered 333, the Conservatives 251 and the Parnellites 86. Of particular significance were the results in the Irish constituencies. Parnell carried 85 and the Conservatives 18. In the whole of Ireland not a single Liberal was returned.

There can be little doubt that it was the Irish results which brought about Gladstone's final decision. There was no longer any room for compromise. Ireland was completely divided between the supporters of Parnell and the small minority of Ulster Members. The choice now lay between Home Rule and indefinite coercion; there was no third alternative. But Gladstone did not at once announce his conversion. How much better it seemed to him if a measure of Home Rule were passed by a Conservative Government! This would avoid the otherwise insuperable obstacle of the House of Lords, which would almost certainly have rejected a Liberal Bill but might be expected to accept a Conservative *volte-face*. Gladstone therefore conveyed to Salisbury his willingness to support him in a scheme of moderate Home Rule. The Conservative Cabinet, who were mostly unaware of Salisbury's negotiations with the Irish before the election, turned down the offer. Winston Churchill, in his *Life of Lord Randolph Churchill*[1], describes their reaction :

> His letter was treated with contempt. No other word will suffice . . . 'His hypocrisy', wrote a Minister to whom this letter had been shown, 'makes me sick'. In the Tory Cabinet there was but one opinion. He was 'Mad to take office'; and if his hunger was not 'prematurely gratified' he will be forced into some line of conduct which would be discreditable to him and disastrous'.

This passage illustrates the malignant hatred with which Gladstone at this time was regarded by his opponents. Salisbury, whose actions in these critical months would be hard to defend, reneged on his secret agreement with Parnell. It was emphasised in the Queen's Speech that there could be no change in the principle of Legislative Union. Then it was announced that the Government intended to bring in a new Coercion Bill.

On 17th December, Gladstone's son, Herbert Gladstone, flew what came to be known as the Hawarden Kite. He conveyed to the Press in London that his father 'was working at' a scheme for Home Rule. It is now generally accepted that he acted without Gladstone's knowledge and that what he intended was merely a confidential briefing and not for publication. But the news broke and the sensation was enormous.

[1] *Lord Randolph Churchill*: Macmillan, 1906.

Everyone now knew what to expect. Gladstone issued a disclaimer to the effect that the statement was not an accurate representation of his views, but a speculation upon them, and that it had not been published with his knowledge or authority. This ambiguous pronouncement merely confirmed the prevailing impression. The Whigs were horrified. Chamberlain was furious, though according to Dilke he did not see his way to oppose Gladstone. The Conservatives determined to oppose at all costs. Lord Randolph Churchill wrote to Salisbury regarding a conversation with Labouchère. The letter included the following passage :

> Lastly I communicated to him that even if the Government went out and Gladstone introduced a Home Rule Bill, I should not hesitate, if other circumstances were favourable, to agitate Ulster even to resistance beyond constitutional limits; that Lancashire would follow Ulster and would lead England; and that he was at liberty to communicate this fact to the GOM.

The return to coercion was announced on 26th January 1886. Gladstone immediately decided to overthrow the Government. He went to call upon Sir William Harcourt and announced his decision.

Harcourt said, 'What! Are you prepared to go forward without either Hartington or Chamberlain?'

Gladstone answered 'Yes'.

An amendment to the Address stood upon the notice paper in the name of Jesse Collings, the champion of 'three acres and a cow'. It regretted the omission from the Gracious Speech of measures for benefiting the rural labour. The debate lasted only six hours. At one o'clock in the morning on 27th January the House divided. The Irish Members voted with the Liberals and the Government were defeated by 331 votes to 257. But what was of the utmost significance was not the actual figures but the cross-voting and the abstentions. Over 70 Liberals abstained. Eighteen Liberals voted with the Government. They included Lord Hartington, G. J. Goschen and Sir Henry James. Lord Hartington declared that he could not accept the implications of the amendment and this was undoubtedly his genuine view. Nevertheless, all those who dissented from their leader clearly had Home Rule in mind. This was the beginning of the Whig defection. The Government resigned. Gladstone proceeded to form his third administration.

This was a unique occasion. As a general rule, when a Party returns to office, after a spell in opposition, Westminster is crowded with willing recruits. Even the most jaundiced critics of the incoming Prime Minister suddenly discern his outstanding qualities or, at the very least, are prepared to put the national interest first. They are all, or almost all, willing to serve. The only refusals come from those who are offered minor office incommensurate, as they consider, with their abilities and their record of Parliamentary achievement. The complacent satisfaction of the new Ministers as they face the burdens of office is only counterbalanced by the bitterness of those who have been passed over.

Not so in 1886. Half the Whigs refused to serve. They included Lord Hartington, Lord Derby, Lord Northbrook, Lord Selborne and Lord Carlingford, who had all been members of Gladstone's last Cabinet. The other refusals were from the Duke of Argyll, Sir Henry James, G. J. Goschen and John Bright. The influence of Bright extended far beyond that of the Whigs, and undoubtedly his attitude contributed in large measure to the ensuing defeat of the Government.

Home Rule might still have been carried but for a personal tragedy. Dilke, in Gladstone's own words, was 'unavailable'. He was involved in divorce proceedings which attracted the attention of the whole country. Thereafter he was even thought to be in danger of a trial for perjury. This was a major tragedy for himself and for the Liberal Party. He was a man of outstanding capacity and Disraeli had prophesied in 1879 that he would be Prime Minister. Many observers ranked him higher than Chamberlain. But he was also Chamberlain's close friend and confidante and, had he been in the Cabinet, he might well have persuaded Chamberlain to take a different course.

In dealing with Chamberlain himself, Gladstone committed a major error. First he offered him the Admiralty, which was refused. Then, according to Dilke, Gladstone asked him what he wanted. Chamberlain replied 'the Colonies'. Gladstone answered, 'Oh! A Secretary of State.' Chamberlain was naturally angry and refused the Board of Trade. Reluctantly he accepted the Local Government Board.

This may well have been the final cause of the breach. Gladstone appointed to the Colonial Office his old and loyal friend Lord Granville, an amiable mediocrity, who had been Foreign Secretary for six months in the former Liberal Government. Chamberlain, thoroughly disgruntled, administered for a short time the work of his new Department. He appears to have occupied a position of complete detachment. According to Lord Randolph Churchill, with whom he was now in close association, he did not even speak to John Morley, the Irish Secretary, during his last six weeks in office.

The final breach took place in the Cabinet on 26th March. Gladstone announced his decision. There was to be a Resolution in the House of Commons approving the establishment of a legislature in

Dublin with power over strictly Irish affairs. Chamberlain asked : 1) whether the Irish representation was to cease at Westminster; 2) whether the power of taxation, including customs and excise, was to be given to the Irish Parliament; 3) whether the appointment of the judges and magistracy was to vest in the Irish Authority; and 4) whether the Irish Parliament was to have authority in every matter not specially excluded by the Act constituting it, or whether it was only to have authority in matters specially delegated to it by statute. Gladstone, it appears, answered each question with an uncompromising affirmative.

Chamberlain said, 'Then I resign' and accompanied by Sir George Trevelyan left the room.

Home Rule divided the Liberals in the country as well as in Parliament. In Arnold Bennett's *Clayhanger*[1] there is a vivid description of the effect on father and son in the grim atmosphere of the Five Towns. First he describes the reaction of the youthful Edwin Clayhanger as he read the report of Gladstone's speech on the Second Reading of the Home Rule Bill :

'I'm going this road,' said Darius, when they were safely out of the Bank, pointing towards the Sytch.
'What for?'
'I'm going this road,' he repeated, gloomily obstinate.
'All right', said Edwin cheerfully, 'I'll trot round with you.'
He did not know whether he could safely leave his father. The old man's eyes resented his assiduity and accepted it.
They passed the old Sytch Pottery, the smoke of whose kilns now no longer darkened the sky. The senior partner of the firm which leased it had died, and his sons had immediately taken advantage of his absence to build a new and efficient works down by the canal-side at Shawport – a marvel of everything save architectural dignity. Times changed. Edwin remarked on the desolation of the place and received no reply. Then the idea occurred to him that his father was bound for the Liberal Club. It was so. They both entered. In the large room two young men were amusing themselves at the billiard table which formed the chief attraction of the naked interior, and on the ledges of the table were two glasses. The steward in an apron watched them.
'Aye !' grumbled Darius, eyeing the group. 'That's Rad, that is ! That's Rad ! Not twelve o'clock yet !'
If Edwin with his father had surprised two young men drinking and playing billiards before noon in the Conservative Club he would have been grimly pleased. He would have taken it for a further proof of the

[1] Methuen & Co., 1910.

hollowness of the opposition to the great Home Rule Bill; but the spectacle of a couple of wastrels in the Liberal Club annoyed and shamed
him. His vague notion was that at such a moment of high crisis the two
wastrels ought to have had the decency to refrain from wasting.

'Well, Mr Clayhanger,' said the steward, in his absurd boniface way,
'you're quite a stranger.'

'I want my name taken off this Club,' said Darius shortly. 'Ye understand me! And I reckon I'm not the only one, these days.'

The steward did in fact understand. He protested in a low, amiable
voice, while the billiard-players affected not to hear; but he perfectly
understood. The epidemic of resignations had already set in, and there
had been talk of a Liberal–Unionist Club. The steward saw that the
grand folly of a senile statesman was threatening his own future prospects. He smiled. But at Edwin, as they were leaving, he smiled in a quite
peculiar way, and that smile clearly meant 'Your father goes dotty, and
the first thing he does is to change his politics.' This was the steward's
justifiable revenge.

'*You* aren't leaving us?' the steward questioned Edwin in a half-
whisper.

Edwin shook his head. But he could have killed the steward for that
nauseating suggestive smile. The outer door swung to, cutting off the
delicate click of billiard balls.

At the top of Duck Bank Darius silently and without warning mounted the steps of the Conservative Club. Doubtless he knew how to lay
his hand instantly on a proposer and seconder. Edwin did not follow
him.

But reaction in Society was violent in the extreme. Sir Philip Magnus
quotes[1] from a letter written to Sir Dighton Probin, v.c., a member of
the Prince of Wales's Household, to Sir Henry Ponsonby, the Queen's
Secretary:

> Don't talk to me about Gladstone. I pray to God that he may be
> shown up as a lunatic at once and thus save the Empire from the des-
> truction which he is leading her to. If he is not mad he is a Traitor.
>
> I am worried about Lord Spencer. I have always looked upon his
> being an honest Englishman and a gentleman . . . but he has fallen into
> that traitor's clutches and is lending a helping hand to a fearful civil
> war . . . a man of that sort advocating communism shakes my belief in
> anything mortal.

The attitude of the Conservative Party is shown by Lord Randolph
Churchill's address in the following June to the electors of South
Paddington:

[1] *Gladstone: A Biography.*

'Mr Gladstone has reserved for his closing days a conspiracy against the honour of Britain and the welfare of Ireland more startlingly base and nefarious than any of those other numerous designs and plots which, during the last quarter of a century, have occupied the imagination . . . this design for the separation of Ireland from Britain . . . this monstrous mixture of imbecility, extravagance and political hysteria, is furnished by its author with the most splendid attributes and clothed in the loftiest language . . . but united and concentrated, genus of Bedlam and Colney Hatch would strive in vain to press a more striking issue of absurdity.

'For the sake of this . . . farrago of superlative nonsense, business other than that which may be connected with political agitation is to be impeded and suspended . . . all useful and desired reforms are to be indefinitely postponed, the British Constitution is to be torn up, the Liberal Party shivered into fragments.

'And why? For this reason and no other . . . to gratify the imagination of an old man in a hurry.'

Gladstone introduced the Home Rule Bill on 8th April amidst intense excitement both in Parliament and outside. In spite of torrents of rain, his supporters cheered him from Downing Street to New Palace Yard. We are told by Morley that Princes, Ambassadors, great Peers, High Prelates, thronged the Lobbies. The House of Commons was packed as never before. From daybreak onwards Members came to secure their seats and every seat was marked before noon. Extra benches were placed on the floor of the House from the Mace on to the bar. Gladstone spoke for nearly three and a half hours, and recorded in his diary: 'Voice and strength and freedom were granted to me in a degree beyond what I could have hoped, but many a prayer have gone up for me, and not, I believe in vain.'

The first reading was allowed to pass unopposed and the second reading began on 15th May. The debates on the Bill occupied sixteen days. As nearly always happens with a great theme, the level of speeches was consistently high. Parliamentary debates vary according to the subject-matter. When Members are engaged in purely procedural wrangles or are only concerned to score points off the other side, or beat off criticism, the House not infrequently descends to what Disraeli called 'the dreary drip of desultory declamation.' But when the subject-matter is of first-class importance, and an historic decision is to be arrived at, the House of Commons nearly always rises to the occasion. The outstanding example was, of course, the Norway Debate in 1940 which brought about the fall of the Chamberlain Government. But all accounts of the Home Rule Debate in 1886 show that it was conducted on the highest level.

The most extraordinary contributions came from Chamberlain himself. To the universal amazement he advocated a Federation on the Canadian model. Britain was to become a Federal State. Since this would have involved the creation of a subordinate Parliament in Dublin, it was difficult to see where the fundamental difference lay. Indeed, on 16th April he wrote a friendly letter to Gladstone stating that the difference in the Cabinet had 'lessened considerably' and hoping that they might be further reduced before the second reading was begun. Whether in fact he ever wavered may be doubted, for it was Chamberlain in the end who brought about the defeat of the Bill. The result had already been decided, not on the floor of the House, but in Committee Room 15.

Now there could be only one result. When Gladstone rose on the night of 7th June to wind up the Debate, he must have known that he faced almost certain defeat. Nevertheless, for over three hours, he delivered a speech of immense power.

The final passage could scarcely have been equalled in any Parliamentary debate :

'We have given Ireland a voice : we must all listen for a moment to what she says. We must all listen – both sides, both Parties, I mean as they are, divided on this question – divided, I am afraid, by an almost immeasurable gap. We do not undervalue or despise the forces opposed to us. I have described them as the forces of class and its dependants : and that as a general description – as a slight and rude outline of a description – is, I believe, perfectly true. I do not deny that many are against us whom we should have expected to be for us. I do not deny that some of whom we see against us have caused us by their conscientious action the bitterest disappointment. You have power, you have wealth, you have rank, you have station, you have organization. What have we? We think that we have the people's heart; we believe and we know that we have the promise of the harvest of the future. As to the people's heart, you may dispute it, and dispute it with perfect sincerity. Let that matter make its own proof. As to the harvest of the future I doubt if you have so much confidence, and I believe that there is in the breast of many a man who means to vote against us tonight a profound misgiving, approaching even to a deep conviction, that the end will be as we foresee, and not as you do – that the ebbing tide is with you and the flowing tide is with us. Ireland stands at your bar expectant, hopeful, almost suppliant. Her words are the words of truth and soberness. She asks a blessed oblivion of the past, and in that oblivion our interest is deeper than even hers.

'My Right Hon. Friend the Member for East Edinburgh (Mr Goschen) asks us tonight to abide by the traditions of which we are the heirs. What traditions? By the Irish tradition? Go into the length and breadth of the world, ransack the literature of all countries, find, if you can, a single voice, a single book, find, I would almost say, as much as a single newspaper article, unless the product of the day, in which the conduct of England towards Ireland is anywhere treated except with profound and bitter condemnation. Are these the traditions by which we are exhorted to stand? No; they are the sad exception to the glory of our country. They are a broad and black blot upon the pages of its history; and what we want to do is to stand by the traditions of which we are the heirs in all matters except our relations with Ireland, and to make our relations with Ireland to conform to the other traditions of our country. So we trust our traditions – so we hail the demand of Ireland for what I call a blessed oblivion of the past. She asks also a boon for the future; and that boon for the future, unless we are much mistaken, will be a boon to us in respect of honour, no less than a boon to her in respect of happiness, prosperity, and peace. Such, Sir, is her prayer. Think, I beseech you, think well, think wisely, think, not for the moment, but for the years that are to come, before you reject this Bill.'

No more powerful appeal can ever have been made to the House of Commons. But the result was already determined. Ninety-three Liberal and Radical Members, led by Hartington and Chamberlain, voted in the 'No' Lobby. The Bill was defeated by a majority of 30. At the ensuing General Election the Liberals were swept from power. 316 Conservatives and 70 Liberal Unionists were returned, as against 191 Gladstonian Liberals and 85 Irish Nationalists. The farm labourers almost completely reversed their attitude of the previous year. They voted solidly Conservative. Gladstone's cheerful comment to his son was, 'Well, Herbert, dear old boy, we have had a drubbing and no mistake.' But he was wholly unrepentant and devoted the next six years of his life to the continuing advocacy of Home Rule.

The division between Liberals and Liberal-Unionists was to prove irreparable. It did not at first appear so. Members on both sides sought to heal the breach. Chamberlain himself proclaimed in December that, 'We Liberals are agreed upon 99 points of our programme: we only disagree upon one . . .' He held a meeting known as the 'Round Table'. Chamberlain was accompanied by Trevelyan. On the other side were

Harcourt, Herschell and Morley. But Chamberlain would not budge. In a letter sent to an American acquaintance and published in *The Times* he declared:

> Once granted that Ireland is entitled to be considered as a nation and not as a member of a nation or a State within a nation, then you must follow this to its logical conclusion and give them the rights of a nation, including separate taxation, foreign relations and military forces.

The Round Table held three meetings. Any prospect it might have had of achieving agreement was destroyed by Chamberlain himself. He wrote an article for a Belfast newspaper which appeared in every other newspaper throughout the land. His critics had reproached the Liberal Unionists for postponing Liberal legislation, and especially Welsh disestablishment. Chamberlain was furious:

> Whether the process occupied a year or a century 'poor little Wales' must wait until Mr Parnell is satisfied and Mr Gladstone's policy adopted. They will not wait alone. The crofters of Scotland and the agricultural labourers of England will keep them company. Thirty-two millions of people must go without much-needed legislation because three millions are disloyal.

This was the end. There was never again any real prospect of Liberal reunion. Reluctantly but inevitably the Liberal Unionists were drawn into the Conservative orbit. The first and most lasting result of the Home Rule Bill was the final secession of the Whigs. As has already been shown, they had grown increasingly restive ever since 1880, chiefly over legislative interference with the rights of Irish landlords. To them the rural policies of Chamberlain were anathema. Nevertheless they had played a vital role. In 1883 Hartington wrote:

> I admit that the Whigs are not the leaders in a popular movement, but Whigs have been able, as I think, to the great advantage of the country, to correct and guide and moderate those popular movements.

Many, if not all of them, might have continued in this role. But Home Rule created an irreparable breach and the character of the Liberal Party, and of Parliament itself, was fundamentally changed. The long term result was that British political parties came to be increasingly organised on a class basis. Of course there were still rich men in the Liberal Party and they have not been unknown in the ranks of Labour, but in the main the property classes have been overwhelmingly Conservative. This was apparent to Gladstone himself. On 28th October 1892, he sent a memorandum to the Queen on the growing danger of class war. He explained that the views of Liberal Ministers were hardly understood and, as he believed, imperfectly known in the 'powerful social circles with which Your Majesty has ordinary personal intercourse'. He continued :

> The leading fact to which I would point is the widening of the gap or chasm which . . . separates the upper and most powerful from the more numerous classes of the community. The evil has been aggravated largely by the prolongation and intensity of the Irish controversy. . . . For the first time in our history we have seen, in the recent election, a majority of the House of Commons, not indeed very large, but also not a very small one, returned against the sense of the entire peerage and landed gentry and of the vast majority of the upper and leisured classes. The moderate Liberal [and by 'moderate' Liberal Mr Gladstone means such a person as Lord Grenville or Lord John Russell] has not quite become, but is becoming, a thing of the past. There is to a large extent not only a readiness but a thirst for conflict with the House of Lords.

Unlike the Whigs, the Radicals did not secede in a body. Many of them, including Dilke and Labouchère, remained inside the Liberal Party. But Dilke's career had been destroyed in the Law Courts and there was no-one to replace Chamberlain. Nothing more was heard of the 'Unauthorised Programme'. So it came about that the Radical impulse disappeared and was not revived until 1908 when Lloyd George said he would 'wage inexorable warfare against poverty'. The achievements of the Liberal Government in the realm of Old Age Pensions and National Insurance would almost certainly have been anticipated before the turn of the century if Chamberlain had succeeded Gladstone as Prime Minister. The Labour Party might never have replaced the Liberals. These matters were determined on 31st May 1886, in Committee Room 15.

CHAPTER II

1916

THE 4th DECEMBER 1916, was the most fateful date in the history of British political parties. Sometime during the afternoon, at 10 Downing Street, Mr Asquith took a decision of enormous consequence. He went back on the undertaking he had given to Lloyd George on the previous day, namely, to set up a committee of three to run the war. In so doing, he not only brought to an end his own career as Prime Minister; he destroyed the Liberal Party as one of the alternative parties of Government. Thereafter, the Liberals became a party of the fringe. They could in some degree influence opinion; they could, in certain circumstances, hold the balance in the House of Commons; a few of their leaders might serve in coalition Governments formed at times of real or imagined emergency. But never again was there to be a Liberal administration – to the immense loss of the nation and the world. These momentous consequences all flowed from the events of the Monday afternoon. They would almost certainly have been avoided if Asquith had kept faith with Lloyd George.

The downfall of the Liberal Party is the principal tragedy of British politics in modern times. It had been predominant in British politics for seventy years – ever since the repeal of the Corn Laws. During that time there were only twenty years when there was a Tory majority in the House of Commons. During the second half of the 19th century (save in relation to Irish Home Rule) Gladstonian Liberalism entirely prevailed. Free trade was established, apparently forever. The restricted franchise of the Reform Bill was replaced by universal manhood suffrage; aristocratic and ecclesiastical privilege were swept away and patronage was brought to an end; universities were thrown open to Jews and nonconformists; purchase of commissions in the Army was abolished; entry into the Civil Service was made conditional upon competitive examination; school education was made universal. In 1895, when Lord Rosebery resigned, the gulf between rich and poor was still

45

enormous; but the foundations of a democratic egalitarian society had been laid by half a century of Liberal reformism.

The history of the last Liberal Government is even more remarkable. By any standard it was one of the most successful – if not the most successful – peacetime administration in British political history. It laid the foundations of the Welfare State. After many years of controversy, old age pensions were enacted. In the teeth of bitter Conservative opposition and (in the initial stages) in spite of some unpopularity, National Insurance came into being for the sick and the unemployed. Taxation was reformed by the introduction of supertax. Above all, the battle with the House of Lords ended in a resounding triumph.

No one can now look back on the years 1906 to 1914 without acknowledging the immense achievements of the Liberal Government. This was not surprising; it was literally a Government of all the talents. The average level of ability on the Front Bench can never have been higher. Asquith, Lloyd George, Churchill, Haldane, Reading and Grey – they were all men of pre-eminent capacity. No one questioned the ability of McKenna and Runciman. And in the second rank were Herbert Samuel, a supremely competent administrator, and the outstanding political writer of his time, Charles Masterman.

The scales were most unevenly weighted. The Conservatives had at their disposal the subtle intelligence of Balfour and the brilliant rhetoric of F. E. Smith. Otherwise Bonar Law, however competent, was not an inspiring leader. Austen Chamberlain and Walter Long were respected pillars of the Establishment. So far, therefore, as political talent was concerned, there was a very considerable disproportion. It is not too much to say that the balance lay overwhelmingly on the Liberal side.

In the constituencies, the Liberals were securely entrenched. The majority of the industrial workers voted Liberal. Scotland and Wales were Liberal strongholds. In the nonconformist areas of the West Country and East Anglia they were well in the lead. It is true that Labour support was growing and as a result of the compact in 1905 between Lord Gladstone and Ramsay MacDonald, Labour took control of some 30 to 50 seats. But these were dependent on the cooperation of Liberal voters and the Labour Party, though occasionally rebellious, was still an auxiliary of the Liberals. There is no compelling reason to believe that this partnership would not have lasted.

If therefore, war had been avoided, it is at least probable that the pattern of the last eighty years would have continued. The balance on the Left might gradually have shifted towards Labour and Labour leaders, following the example of John Burns, would no doubt have been included in Liberal administrations. Of course there would have been an occasional reaction, as in 1874, resulting in a few years of Conservative rule. These, however, would have been the exceptions. Britain would have continued along the course of social democracy.

In the event, everything was changed. The Labour Party became the embittered enemy of the Liberals. Between them the two could still command, at almost every election a majority of the voters. But during 36 years out of the 54 years following the war, the Tories had a majority in the House of Commons. They owed this predominance almost entirely to the rift between Liberalism and Labour. These were the momentous consequences of a single, tragic decision on 4th December 1916.

Historians of the First World War have emphasised the personal failings of Mr Asquith as a war leader. But they sometimes fail to appreciate his immense standing as Prime Minister and the devotion which he inspired among his followers. Thus, at the Bar and in politics, his had been a career of almost unbroken success. He had entered Parliament as Member for East Fife in 1886. He was without influence in the days when family connexions were still of great importance. He had no private means and was wholly dependent upon his professional earnings. Yet within a very few years he had become one of the leading figures at the English Bar. His cross-examination of the *Times* Editor in the Parnell Inquiry was a classic example of forensic skill. He became the youngest member of Mr Gladstone's last Cabinet in 1892, and achieved immediate ministerial success.

During the ensuing ten years of Conservative rule, his standing in Parliament and the country steadily grew. This was still the age of the public meeting, when great crowds assembled to hear political leaders and when their speeches were fully reported in the national and local Press. In 1903, Joseph Chamberlain embarked on his tariff reform campaign. He addressed packed audiences in all the great cities of the Midlands and the North. Asquith followed his example and became his principal antagonist. He was not a great emotional orator such as Gladstone or Lloyd George but he was the master of incisive speech and lucid argument. There were no false points and no loose ends. This was a controversy which precisely suited him. In speech after speech, the protectionist argument was ruthlessly hammered and destroyed. He was undoubtedly assisted by the fact that this was a period of growing industrial activity when Chamberlain's prophesies of disaster seemed manifestly unrealistic. There can, however, be no doubt that he won the nation-wide debate.

It seems clear in retrospect – though it was not so at the time – that the divided and ageing Conservative Government, weakened by successive resignations, must have lost the General Election of 1905. But no one foresaw the greatest landslide in British political history.

Of course there were other issues which undoubtedly influenced the electors. The Education Act of 1902 had antagonised the non-conformists and led to 'passive resistance' against the payment of rates for Church schools. The Taff Vale judgment[1] had roused the Trades Unions as never before. The cry of 'Chinese slavery' arising from the employment of indentured Chinese labour on the Rand undoubtedly had a powerful effect, and there was an inevitable reaction against the Khaki Election of 1900. When Campbell-Bannerman denounced 'methods of barbarism' in the South African concentration camps, undoubtedly he evoked a considerable response. But Free Trade versus Tariff Reform remained the greatest single issue. The verdict was overwhelming and Asquith was the main architect of victory.

When therefore Campbell-Bannerman died in 1908, Asquith inevitably became Prime Minister. His mastery was complete. He did not himself inspire most of the great Liberal reforms of the next six years, although as Chancellor of the Exchequer he sponsored old age pensions and initiated the differentiation between taxation of earned and unearned income. Nor was he the originator of the successful struggle with the House of Lords. These were the personal achievements of Lloyd George, with the powerful support of Churchill and Masterman. But Asquith was the ideal chairman of his brilliant Cabinet. No one questioned his imperturbable authority and he had one attribute which is rare in public life. He was completely devoid of personal jealousy and wholly loyal to his colleagues. This outstanding characteristic was to have a far-reaching result. At the time of the Marconi Inquiry, Lloyd George and Rufus Isaacs were exceedingly vulnerable. They might well have been driven out of public life. Asquith threw his mantle over them.

From 1909 when the Lords rejected the 'People's Budget', until 1912 when the Parliament Act was placed upon the Statute Book, the role of the House of Lords was the principal issue in British politics. In retrospect, we can only marvel at the folly of the Conservative Peers. For years they had arrogated to themselves the right to amend or reject Liberal legislation. Thus they had thrown out the second Home Rule

---

[1] Courts held for the first time that Trades Unions were liable in damages for actions done by their individual members in furtherance of industrial disputes.

Bill in 1894 and shown themselves hostile to Liberal social legislation from 1906 onwards. When a Conservative Government was in office, they relapsed into a state of perpetual acquiescence. But no Liberal Government could be certain of carrying any of its legislation – except in the realm of finance. Ever since the 1860s it had been an established convention that taxation was a matter solely for the Commons and that the Lords would not interfere. Now in 1909, goaded beyond endurance by Lloyd George's land taxes, they threw out the Finance Bill. In so doing, they brought about the defeat of their own Party at two ensuing General Elections and the permanent erosion of their own powers. Before the Budget, the by-elections had been running strongly in favour of the Opposition, and Conservative leaders anticipated a 1905 landslide in reverse. Now the Liberals were presented with a first-class constitutional issue which could hardly have been better calculated to rally their failing support in the country.

Even so, the situation called for statesmanship of a high order. If after a General Election the Lords were still recalcitrant, they could only be coerced by the creation, or the threatened creation, of 500 new Peers. This prospect was regarded with general aversion, save by the 500 prospective nominees – and their wives. But it involved Royal acquiescence. This, according to the Opposition, meant bringing the Crown into politics. Feelings were deeply stirred. Lord Esher was a former Whig and a personal confidante of King Edward. In December 1909, writing of the Government's intention to raise the matter before the General Election, he said :

> I cannot conceive a more monstrous proposal, and even now I cannot believe that responsible Ministers, anxious as they must be to sustain the Monarchy, will be determined to make such a request to the Crown.

Asquith never lost his complete mastery of the situation. The Liberals, in alliance with the Labour Party and the Irish Members, won the general elections of January and December, 1910 by majorities of 124 and 126. Even so, the Lords would not give way. The time had come for the final card to be played. The King was informed that it would now be necessary to create Peers in sufficient numbers to overcome the diehard opposition. He indicated that he was prepared to act on this advice. The decision was conveyed to the Opposition leaders in a personal letter from the Prime Minister. The news was received by the Conservative Party with unbridled fury. When on 24th July 1911, Asquith rose to speak, there was a scene unprecedented, and indeed unparalleled, in Parliamentary history. Speeches are often interrupted in the House

of Commons by bursts of real or simulated anger. But never before or since has a Prime Minister, rising to make a statement of great importance, been denied any hearing whatsoever. On this occasion the Conservative Members led by Lord Hugh Cecil were determined that not a word should be uttered. They maintained a chorus of shouts and jeers for over an hour while Asquith stood dignified and contemptuous at the despatch box. Eventually he resumed his seat. As the tumult died away, an Irish Member rose to his feet. He pointed to the Tory howlers with the words : 'And these are the gentlemen of England.'

Such an occurrence could only enhance Asquith's prestige with his own followers and indeed it could hardly have stood higher in 1914. There was of course, the menacing problem of Irish Home Rule and Ulster resistance. Then as now, there was no ideal solution. When Conservative leaders, notably F. E. Smith, preached resistance in Ulster, they might indeed have been prosecuted for sedition. But, as Asquith has pointed out in his memoirs, a Belfast Jury would certainly have acquitted. As it was, a settlement was very nearly reached at the Buckingham Palace Conference in 1914. As Churchill informed the House of Commons eight years later, the only final obstacles were 'the dreary steeples of Fermanagh and Tyrone'. When after the Curragh Colonel Seely, the Secretary of State for War, resigned his post, Asquith himself took the steam out of the situation by himself taking over the War Office. The problems were not solved but it is difficult to see how anyone else could have done better.

The position which Asquith occupied at the outbreak of the war was therefore one of unrivalled strength and authority. This was due to his own special qualities. In 1912 Lloyd George confided to Lord Riddell[1] :

> He is like a great counsel in whom solicitors and clients have faith. The party feel that when a matter is in his hands, he will see it through satisfactorily. He has splendid judgment, and, as a rule, deals with great and small subjects in council and in the House of Commons in an imperturbable manner. It remains to be seen, however, how he will conduct himself, if he has to fight a losing cause.

A year later he added this assessment :

> He is a big man. He never initiates anything, but he is a great judge. He brushes aside all small points and goes straight to the heart of the subject. I prefer to discuss a big project with him rather than with anyone else. That is one of the troubles in the House of Commons. He stands so much above the other side and dominates the situation.

[1] *Lord Riddell's War Diary* 1914-1918 : Nicholson & Watson, 1933.

This is confirmed by other observers.

In 1915, a year after the beginning of the war, Mr. A. G. Gardiner wrote :

> It is the custom of his enemies to speak of him simply as an intellectual machine. 'He talks like a barrister from a brief,' said Mr Chamberlain bitterly in those memorable days of the Protectionist revival when Mr Asquith pursued him from place to place and blew his case to the winds. . . . But if his mind works within a more limited circumference than that of Fox or Gladstone, it is within that range marked by a rare integrity of purpose and performance. No man is more scrupulously loyal to his word, more exact in the fulfilment of his engagements. It is not enough to fulfil the letter : he must fulfil the spirit. It is not the judgment of others that he fears; but the judgment of his own mind. He can stand abuse and slander and misrepresentation with cold and silent disdain, for he has that type of mind which is more at ease when it is attacked than when it is flattered.

These assessments emphasise Asquith's intellectual mastery and the integrity of his character. What they do not reveal is the deep personal affection with which he was regarded not only by his close associates, but by his followers in Parliament and in the country. As Campbell-Bannerman lay dying he described Asquith as a 'wonderful colleague, so loyal, so disinterested, so able, the greatest gentleman I have ever met'. And when in 1916 he ceased to be Prime Minister, Sir Maurice Hankey (later Lord Hankey) who was Secretary to the Cabinet, wrote[1] to him in the following terms :

> Dear Mr Asquith,
>
> I cannot let the present occasion pass without writing to give some expression to the overwhelming regret and deep emotion with which I am filled by the prospect of the severance, temporary though I hope and believe it to be, of the official ties which have bound me to you for nearly nine years, during close on 5 of which I have been in direct and personal association with you as Secretary of this Committee.
>
> The one slight alleviation is that the personal and individual, as apart from the official, ties, which have grown up under the stress and strain of war, are too strong to be broken. The fact that you have given me so generously your friendship and confidence has been a continual source of pride and happiness to me, and I can say from the bottom of my heart has made the heaviest tasks light.
>
> . . . The country at present has only a slight conception of what it owes to your courage, nerve, tact, unswerving straightness, incredible patience, and indomitable perseverance. History however, will record

[1] *The Supreme Command* 1914-18: Allen & Unwin, 1961.

it, and when the appropriate time comes I shall not fail to give my own testimony . . . If in this last and most hateful crisis I have offered advice or taken any step, which you think was mistaken, I have at least never been animated by any other sentiment than personal devotion to you, which to me has been synonymous with devotion to the true interests of the country.

I only hope that the day may not long be postponed when I may once more be privileged to serve you again in an official capacity, and in the meantime, if ever opportunity occurs for me to serve you and yours, you may rely on my personal devotion and affection.

This affection was not confined to the writer. In 1920, after two years' absence from the House of Commons, he won a famous by-election at Paisley. It would be difficult to exaggerate the wave of thankfulness and loyalty among Liberals everywhere. They wept with joy. When he drove from his London home to take his seat, great cheering crowds lined the streets. At least until 1926, when he himself appeared to divide the Liberal Party, he never lost his capacity to inspire devotion among the Liberal rank and file. Sometimes it was 'this side idolatry'.

A great deal has been written about his failure as a war leader. It is said that by 1916 he was clearly losing his grip. If so, this may well have been due to two events. There has now been revealed[1] the astonishing story of his relations with Miss Venetia Stanley. Throughout the first eighteen months of the war, he wrote to her almost every day revealing the most intimate Cabinet secrets. Even the code name of a forthcoming military operation was confided to her. When she informed him of her decision to marry E. S. Montagu, he wrote in anguish :

'. . . never since the war began had I such an accumulation (no longer shared !) of anxieties . . . one of the most hellish bits of these most hellish days was that you alone of all the world – to whom I have always gone in every moment of trial and trouble, and from whom I have always come back solaced and healed and inspired – were the one person who could do nothing, and from whom I could ask nothing. To my dying day, that will be the most bitter memory of my life . . .

I am on the eve of the most astounding and world-shaking decisions – such as I would never have taken without your counsel and consent. It seems so strange and empty and unnatural : yet there is nowhere else that I can go, nor would I, if I could.'

This was followed by a personal tragedy in September 1916. His brilliant son, Raymond, was killed in action. There were of course many

[1] *Asquith*, Roy Jenkins: Collins, 1964.

parents who sustained similar losses. But this must have been incredibly hard to bear. Raymond had seemed in every way qualified to inherit his father's mantle. His career at Balliol had been even more outstanding. He carried off the Craven & Ireland prizes which had eluded his father. He also was President of the Union. Among other gifts, he was an outstanding writer of light verse. He was about to become a Member of Parliament. Who could have doubted that here was a future Prime Minister? The tragedy of Raymond's death was often recalled by Asquith's admirers after the breach in 1916. They said of Lloyd George that he 'stabbed Asquith in the back while he was mourning over the grave of his son'.

These tragedies may have contributed in part to Asquith's loss of authority. But in any event, it is difficult to believe that he would have survived as Prime Minister. The very qualities which had made him a successful Prime Minister in days of peace became positive defects in war. His imperturbability; his indestructible patience; his magnanimity towards his colleagues and subordinates – these had been immense assets to himself and his Party from 1908 until 1914. But when in modern times, a nation embarks upon a great war, all values change overnight. A tranquil disposition is no longer an asset but a misfortune. Ripe administrative experience, acquired in peace time, can be a positive disaster. The whole tempo of life in Government changes overnight. Decisions which normally would require mature considerations must be made in a space of days or hours or even minutes. No doubt it is admirable in normal times that statesmen should relax, whether it be at the dinner or bridge tables, or as helmsmen. But a Minister engaged in the actual conduct of a war can never completely relax. To succeed he must possess the utmost physical and mental resilience. He cannot depend in the same way as in peace upon his senior Civil Servants. They are almost by definition capable and experienced. But here again peace-time methods and peace-time experience may be positive handicaps as soon as war begins. Above all, he must possess a perpetually enquiring mind.

These were the qualities which Asquith lacked and which Lloyd George possessed to an extent which has never been excelled. Thus, it almost inevitably happened that, as the war proceeded, there was mounting criticism of the Prime Minister. The shell shortage probably did more than anything else to weaken confidence in the Government. Probably nothing damaged the Government as much as Asquith's seemingly complacent assurance in his speech at Newcastle. No doubt he was misled by Kitchener and Sir John French. But the question

presents itself : should he have been misled? In the third volume of
the life of Churchill,[1] Mr Martin Gilbert quotes a letter which Churchill
wrote to Asquith on 7th February 1915 :

> More than three weeks ago you told me of the vital importance of
> Servia. Since then nothing has been done, and nothing of the slightest
> reality is being done. Time is passing. You may not yet feel the impact
> of the projector. But it has already left the gun and is travelling along
> its road towards you. Three weeks hence you, Kitchener, Grey, will all
> be facing a disastrous situation in the Balkans : and as at Antwerp, it
> will be beyond your power to retrieve it. Unless we are prepared to run
> a risk and play a stake the Balkan situation is finished fatally for us.

In the original draft of this letter a final sentence read : 'Surely in
your position you cannot be content to sit as a Judge pronouncing on
events *after* they had taken place'.

This of course is precisely what a judge does. His function is to discern
past events and to decide which party was right and who was wrong.
Asquith, as Lloyd George had himself acknowledged, brought into
politics the highest judicial quality. In war-time, it was entirely out of
place.

As the war proceeded, the volume of criticism grew. Mounting criticism
became increasingly directed at No 10 Downing Street. Lord Riddell
and Frances Stevenson have both recorded how in 1915, Bonar Law
suggested to Lloyd George that he should supplant Asquith as Prime
Minister. Lloyd George categorically refused. Now, however, Mr
Gilbert has recorded how on 31st January 1916, Lloyd George, Bonar
Law and F. E. Smith repaired to Max Aitken's headquarters at St
Omer, where Churchill awaited them. There was full and complete
agreement that Asquith 'had to be got rid of at all costs'.

This view was certainly not shared by the great majority of Asquith's
Liberal followers in the House of Commons, or indeed, by his fellow
Liberal Ministers other than Lloyd George. But it was widely held by
the general public. It sometimes happens that phrases are hung around
a statesman's neck. Mr Lloyd George in later years was never allowed
to forget his invocation of 'a land fit for heroes to live in'. Mr Harold
Wilson must frequently have regretted his remark after the devaluation
of the pound to the effect that 'The pound in your pocket has not been
devalued'. Mr Heath must rue the moment when he declared that
prices would be contained 'at a stroke'. But no statesman has ever been

---

[1] *Churchill*, Heinemann Ltd, 1971.

damned by a phrase to the same extent as Asquith. Before the war, in a perfectly normal Parliamentary reply, he had advised a questioner to 'wait and see'. Moreover, his apparently sybaritic manner of life became a matter of general comment. Mr George Robey initiated a song which became familiar throughout the land :

> In Parliament today
> They all are in a stew
> For they don't know what to say
> And they don't know what to do.
> Then up gets Mr Asquith
> And in a manner calm
> Says 'Another little drink
> Wouldn't do us any harm.'

Since the outbreak of war, Mr Lloyd George had undergone a transformation. Up to 4th August 1914, he had appeared the least warlike figure imaginable. Apart from a brief spell in the Yeomanry as a very young man, he had displayed not the slightest interest in the art of war. His reputation had been achieved at the turn of the century as the leader of the pacifists and the pro-Boers. The outstanding episode of his early career was when disguised in a policeman's coat and helmet, he was rescued from a furious jingo crowd in Birmingham Town Hall. In the House of Commons he made his name by attacking the war and its chief protagonist, Joseph Chamberlain.

On one occasion he recalled how, when hostilities began, Chamberlain had appealed to the God of Battles. He then pointed out however since our armies in the field had been beset by floods and droughts and pestilence, in fact by all the natural disasters which lawyers describe as 'acts of God'. And then he added in a stage whisper : 'Perhaps that is the answer to the Rt. Hon. gentleman's appeal'.

During the years of Liberal supremacy, his attitude remained much the same. It is true that in 1911 he issued a stern warning to the German Government over Agadir. But it does not appear that he was ever greatly concerned by the growth of German power on land or at sea. All Chancellors of the Exchequer (including Churchill himself) have resisted demands of the Service Departments. None have done so with greater determination than Lloyd George. There was a prolonged battle first with McKenna and then with Churchill, over the naval estimates. No doubt this was due in part to his preoccupation with social reform. The resources of the State would, he believed, be far better employed in redressing social inequality than in building up great armaments.

This divergence of outlook was, however, not solely due to his passion for social reform. His attitude represented the deeply ingrained convictions of a large part, probably the majority, of the Liberal Party. This went back to John Bright, in the days of the Crimean war, when he had declaimed to a spellbound House of Commons 'The Angel of Death is abroad in the land. You may almost hear the beating of his wings'.

The spiritual successors of Bright were profound isolationists. They distrusted all foreign entanglements. They regarded the whole military establishment with intense distrust. Although they in August 1914 must have all reluctantly accepted the need to go to war, this attitude continued. It has never been better described than in a letter to *The Times* of 30th May 1916, by Lord Hugh Cecil:

> Those steady Liberals by tradition and temperament dislike war. They dislike it, not only as we all do, on account of its horrors and burdens, but because they conceive it to be dangerous to civil and political liberty. They distrust and dread all that war makes necessary, 'large infringements of the liberty of the subject, extensive military service, a general subordination of domestic questions to the more fundamental ones involved in war'. These things create an atmosphere which is to them like that of a room with a smoky chimney, unpleasant and almost suffocating.

Until August 1914, this would exactly have described the politics of Lloyd George. How, then, did he become one of the greatest War Ministers of all time? The particular explanation, I believe, is to be found in two facets of his character. In the first place he was entirely single-minded. He always had one overriding objective. From 1908 to 1914 it was 'to wage implacable warfare against poverty'. From 1914 to 1918, having convinced himself of the justice of the war, victory became the sole objective. From approximately 1928 until 1936 he was concerned with defeating unemployment. His greatest error was at Berchtesgaden in 1936, when he carried away a momentarily favourable impression of Hitler. This was because Hitler was carrying out in Germany precisely the policy of national development which Lloyd George was advocating for Britain.

Secondly, he had a unique gift for discerning the essentials of every situation. His questing mind was never content to accept official attitudes or orthodox doctrines. In 1925 he was the only leading statesman to challenge the return to the Gold Standard. Four years later he led the Liberal Party into the General Election of 1929 on a full Keynesian programme. When in 1939 Chamberlain gave the Polish pledge, Lloyd George (incredible as it may now seem) was the only speaker in the House of Commons debate who pointed out that this guarantee was worthless without Russian support. It was this particular quality of discerning essentials which served him as a War Minister.

He had one other considerable advantage. He could and did use to the full the abilities of others. When he moved into Downing Street the staff was extended to the basement and the garden. This was the famous 'Garden Suburb'. It included Waldorf Astor, Philip Kerr, W. G. S. Adams, David Davies, Sir Joseph Davies, Cecil Harmsworth and later Edward Grigg. Colonel Hankey became the first Secretary of the War Cabinet. The assistant secretaries included Sir Ernest Swindon, Sir Mark Sykes, Leo Amery and William Ormsby Gore. No more powerful team can ever have been assembled.

But these administrative achievements, great as they were, formed only part of the story. His earlier Liberal attitude continued right up to 4th August. When it came to the declaration of war, he was one of the most hesitant members of the Cabinet. If it had not been for the German invasion of Belgium, he would almost certainly have joined Morley, Burns and Trevelyan in resigning from the Government. Yet once the decision was taken he became a transformed character. To an extent only paralleled by Chatham in the eighteenth century and Churchill in the Second World War, he became the embodiment of the will to win.

This became clear when at the Queen's Hall on 19th September he made the most powerful speech of his career. It is a supreme example of his unique gift of pictorial speech :

'I know a valley in North Wales, between the mountain and the sea. It is a beautiful valley, snug, comfortable, sheltered by the mountains from all the bitter blasts. But it is very enervating, and I remember how the boys were in the habit of climbing the hill above the village to have a glimpse of the great mountains in the distance, and to be stimulated and freshened by the breezes which came from the hilltops, and by the great spectacle of their grandeur.

'We have been living in a sheltered valley for generations. We have been too comfortable and too indulgent – many, perhaps, too selfish – and the stern hand of Fate has scourged us to an elevation where we can see the everlasting things that matter for a nation – the high peaks we had forgotten, of Honour, Duty, Patriotism, and, clad in glittering white, the great pinnacle of Sacrifice, pointing like a rugged finger to heaven.

'We shall descend into the valleys again; but as long as the men and women of this generation last, they will carry in their hearts the image of those great mountain peaks whose foundations are not shaken, though Europe rock and sway in the convulsions of a great war.'

It was this which Masterman described as 'the finest speech in the history of England'.

The events leading up to the change of Government in December 1916 have been frequently described. It is sometimes suggested that, if Bonar Law had shown to Asquith the written views of his Conservative colleagues, the upshot might have been different, or Bonar Law himself might have accepted the King's invitation to form a Government. The suggestion sometimes appears to be that it was only as a result of mis-calculation and intrigue that Lloyd George took Asquith's place.

But this does far less than justice to the reputation which Lloyd George had acquired both inside Government circles and beyond. On 4th March, 1915, F. S. Oliver wrote to his brother in Canada:

> The only two men who really seem to understand that we are at war are Winston and Lloyd George. Both have faults which disgust one peculiarly at the present time, but there is a reality about them, and they are in earnest, which the others aren't.

And there was the verdict of Sir Hubert Llewellyn Smith transferred from the Board of Trade to the Ministry of Munitions, who wrote in 1916 that Lloyd George 'had a passion to win the war which none of the other members of the Cabinet seemed to understand'.

In his book *Great Contemporaries*,[1] Sir Winston Churchill wrote:

> Mr Asquith was probably one of the greatest peace time Prime Ministers we ever had. His intellect, his sagacity, his broad outlook and civic courage contained him at the highest eminence in public life. But in war he had not those qualities of resource and energy, of prevision and assiduous management, which ought to reside in the executive. Mr Lloyd George had all the qualities which he lacked. The nation, by some instinctive almost occult process, had found this out.

Among the Asquith papers is a letter written on 5th December, the day of the breach, by Lord Robert Cecil. Though never a fanatical Tory like his brother Hugh, Lord Robert was nevertheless a Conservative Member of Parliament and a bearer of one of the most famous names in English history. No one could have had less sympathy with the rabble-rousing Lloyd George of pre-war days and his bitter attacks on the landed aristocracy. Yet on 5th December, the day of the final

[1] Thornton Butterworth, 1937.

breach, he wrote to Asquith asking if he would accept office in a Lloyd George Ministry. He continued :

Do not think that I underrate the magnitude of the sacrifice I am suggesting. But at this time it is really of vast importance that you should do so. Nothing else can preserve the unity of the country and the respect of Europe. . . . Your decision may make all the difference between success and failure in the war. I mentioned the matter to my Unionist colleagues and every one of them [Balfour was away] warmly agreed with me.

Precisely who the colleagues were, we do not know, and no reference to this meeting appears in any of the published accounts of these days. But the significance of the letter is obvious. The point had been reached where Lloyd George was recognised, both in Parliament and outside, as the indispensable war leader. The metamorphosis was complete.

The story leading up to the final breach has been more than amply covered by diarists and historians. 1916 had been a disastrous year for the Allies. The Somme offensive had ended in November. The British casualties were no less than 415000 and yet, to quote J. A. Spender :[1]

'The long drawn-out agony . . . had to the outward eye resulted only in pushing the enemy a few miles back to another set of impregnable trenches and fortifications.'

Few if any observers realised the weaknesses of the enemy. The effects of the blockade were not yet apparent, nor was it understood that, as Ludendorff afterwards recorded, the German Army had been fought to a standstill and was utterly worn out.

It was in these circumstances that Lloyd George determined on the formation of a new 'Inner War Committee' consisting of no more than four Members. On 21st November over lunch, he told Colonel Hankey that its Members should be Carson, Bonar Law, Arthur Henderson (to conciliate Labour) and himself. In effect, the proposal was that these Ministers, without departmental duties, should take over the supreme direction of the war. Asquith would remain as Prime Minister and as the Government's chief spokesman in the House of Commons, but the day-to-day running of the war would rest with the Committee. Hankey records in his diary that Lloyd George had delivered his ultimatum practically threatening to resign unless the War Committee was reconstituted with himself as Chairman and demanding that Carson should have a place in the Government and Balfour leave the Admiralty. The entry for the following day contains the following passage :

[1] *Life of Herbert Henry Asquith, Lord Oxford and Asquith,* by J. A. Spender and Cyril Asquith : Hutchinson, 1932.

During the day the political crisis became very serious. The morning papers contained a great deal of information obviously inspired by Lloyd George. I suggested a solution to the P.M. but it was not well received. I lunched at 10 Downing Street. But very shortly after lunch, the P.M. left by motor for Walmer Castle. It was very typical both of his qualities and of his defects, of his extraordinary composure and of his easy-going habits.[1]

He then records how he met Bonar Law who intended to call a meeting of Unionist Cabinet Members on the following day and that he would probably send a letter of resignation. Bonham Carter was dispatched to Walmer to bring Asquith back next morning. Hankey continues :

I walked home with Lord Reading. We both agreed that the whole crisis is intolerable. There is really very little between them. Everyone agrees that the methods of the War Committee call for reform. Everyone agrees that the P.M. possesses the best judgment. The only thing is that Lloyd George and Bonar Law insist that the former and not the P.M. must be the man to win the war. The P.M. however, quite properly, says that if he is not fit to run the War Committee he is not fit to be Prime Minister. The obvious compromise is for the P.M. to retain the presidency of the War Committee with Lloyd George as Chairman and to give Lloyd George a fairly free run for his money. This is my solution.

It was this solution which was in effect agreed on the following day.

On the Sunday morning *Reynold's News*, a radical newspaper, published a front page story on the dissensions within the Government. Rarely, if ever, can an article in the press have produced such momentous results. The headlines were 'Will the Coalition Cabinet break up?' 'Lloyd George to resign'. It included the following passages :

Talk of reconstruction has been heard on every side for some time. But few people are prepared for the important announcement we make today that Mr Lloyd George has intimated to the Prime Minister his intention to resign his post as Secretary of State for War ...

The cause of the resignation may be briefly stated to be : Mr Lloyd George has arrived at the definite conclusion that the methods of dilatoriness, indecision and delay which characterised the action of the present War Council are such, in his opinion, as to endanger the prospects of winning the war ...

It is anticipated that Mr Lloyd George's reasons for resignation will be issued to the Press this evening, and the country will be able to form

[1] *The Supreme Command* 1914-1918.

their own judgment in the matter. It is possible, though not at the moment probable, that Mr Bonar Law may throw his lot in with Mr Lloyd George and Lord Derby is believed to be contemplating the same course . . .

Mr Lloyd George's failure to induce the Government to move in time to prevent the tragic reverse in Rumania is no doubt the final fact that operated with the Secretary of State for War in coming to his decision. It is no secret, however, that he has not been at all happy for a considerable period. He had the consciousness that his efforts to secure a more vigorous prosecution of the war had not received such support which he had the right to expect. The trouble which he had to induce the Government to take steps for obtaining the necessary men for reinforcing our Army at the front is still fresh in public memory. His strenuous battle for greater production of ammunitions never quite received that encouragement which he had a right to expect and the persistent and in some cases malignant personal attacks made upon him in the Liberal Press no doubt undermined to a considerable extent his influence for a time with the working classes . . .

It must also not be forgotten that after he had succeeded in bringing about a settlement of the troubles over the Irish difficulty, the Cabinet threw him mercilessly over without any real explanation so far as the public were concerned.

Asquith met Bonar Law on the Sunday afternoon. He was left with the possibly erroneous impression that the Conservative leaders were in revolt against him. Earlier on the same day the Unionist Ministers had assembled at Bonar Law's house. They were greatly incensed by the article which had appeared in *Reynold's News*.

Accounts vary as to what took place at this meeting. According to Lord Beaverbrook, who was in the next room and to whom Bonar Law recounted what had happened, the Conservative Ministers with the exception of Bonar Law himself, were entirely hostile to Lloyd George. According to Curzon, they were determined to bring about the fall of Asquith and the installation of Lloyd George in his place. The mystery will never be resolved but they passed the following Resolution :

We share the view, expressed to the Prime Minister by Mr Bonar Law some time ago, that the Government cannot go on as it is.

It is evident that a change must be made, and in our opinion the publicity given to the intentions of Mr Lloyd George makes reconstruction from within no longer possible. We therefore urge the Prime Minister to tender the resignation of the Government.

If he feels unable to take that step, we authorize Mr Bonar Law to tender our resignation.

The meeting broke up at three o'clock. Bonar Law went to 10 Downing Street. Here again, no one will ever know precisely what was said. We have on the one hand the account of Lord Beaverbrook, who was throughout Bonar Law's confidante and on the other that of Lord Crewe, which was confirmed by Asquith. It is quite clear that Asquith never saw the Resolution, although Bonar Law had it in his pocket. In his Memorandum (quoted by Mr Robert Blake[1]) Bonar Law states:

> I forgot to hand him the actual document. The Prime Minister was not only greatly shocked but greatly surprised by our communication and asked me to treat it as if it had not been made until he had had an opportunity of discussing the matter with Lloyd George.

The opportunity soon came. There was a telephone call from 10 Downing Street to Bolton Heath Place. Lloyd George came up to London. At the War Office he received a summons to No 10. There can be no doubt that agreement was reached. In a letter next morning Asquith stated:

> The suggested arrangement was to the following effect:
> The Prime Minister have supreme and effective control of war policy. The Agenda of the War Committee will be submitted to him; its Chairman will report to him daily; he can direct it to consider particular topics or proposals; and all its conclusions will be subject to his approval or veto. He can, of course at his own discretion, attend meetings of the Committee.

Lloyd George replied: he fully accepted in letter and spirit this summary of the suggested arrangement – 'subject, of course, to personnel'. It appeared therefore that agreement had been reached. This was certainly the impression formed by Montagu, who dined with Asquith that evening. At 11.45 an announcement was issued from No 10 Downing Street:

> The Prime Minister with a view to the most effective prosecution of the war, has decided to advise His Majesty the King to consent to a reconstruction of the Government.

Evidently Asquith himself thought that agreement had been reached. That night he wrote to a friend:

> I was forced back [from Walmer] by Bongie[2] and Montagu and Rufus[3] to grapple with a 'Crisis' – this time with a very big C. The

[1] *The Unknown Prime Minister*: Eyre and Spottiswoode, 1955.
[2] Sir Maurice Bonham Carter, Asquith's secretary.
[3] Rufus Isaacs.

result is that I have spent much of the afternoon in colloquing with Messrs Ll George and Bonar Law, and one or two minor worthies. The 'Crisis' shows every sign of following its many predecessors to an early and unhonoured grave. But there were many Wigs very nearly on the green.[1]

Next day everything changed. A leading article in *The Times* appeared to show complete insight into all that had been decided. We now know that it was written by Geoffrey Dawson without any communication with Lloyd George. But not unnaturally, the worst conclusions were drawn. Even so, the agreement might have been carried out. It might well have been entirely successful. Asquith would have remained at the head of the Administration and it is unlikely that he would have exercised, save on rare occasions, his power to intervene or his right to attend meetings of the Committee. The day-to-day conduct of the war would have been under the presiding genius of Lloyd George. The partnership between the two men might well have continued and with it the ascendancy of the Liberal Party.

At 12.30 Asquith had audience with the King and submitted the resignations of all his colleagues. After lunch at No 10 he went to the House of Commons. Bonar Law came to see him in his room and asked whether he was still in favour of the arrangement agreed upon the previous day. According to Beaverbrook, Asquith replied that he was 'not so keen on the War Council plan as he had been'. He stated that all his colleagues, Liberal and Conservative, seemed to be against it and that Lloyd George 'was trafficking with the Press'. Asquith was then called to the Front Bench where he proposed that the House should adjourn until Thursday while the Government was reconstituted. Immediately thereafter, he returned to 10 Downing Street. Bonar Law followed him and, according to Beaverbrook, found Grey, Harcourt and Runciman waiting outside the Cabinet Room, with the Premier inside. He was duly admitted but found McKenna closeted with Asquith. He made it clear that if the agreement regarding the War Council was not adhered to, he would break with Asquith.

After Bonar Law had left, Asquith met the Liberal Ministers: Grey, McKenna, Harcourt, Runciman and Samuel. The most significant name in the list is that of McKenna. No full account of these interviews exists. Nevertheless, it may be surmised with near assurance that McKenna took a principal part in persuading Asquith to renege on his agreement with Lloyd George. He had always been on bad terms with Lloyd George. At the time of the Marconi affair, McKenna took the

[1] From Roy Jenkins: *Asquith.*

view, which he strongly urged upon Asquith, that the two erring Ministers should have resigned. His nephew, Stephen McKenna, has written of him[1] :

> Until the mellowed last quarter of his life, McKenna enjoyed --
> perhaps in two senses of the word – a reputation for prompt censorism
> when confronted with standards of conduct, ways of thought and forms
> of expression that were not his own. Disagreement with an opinion,
> moreover, tended to create suspicion of those who entertained it . . .
> some of McKenna's critics detected a tendency to associate economic
> heresy and political liberalism with intellectual collapse or original sin.

The breach between the two men had grown. McKenna, like many other Liberals, reacted against Lloyd George's advocacy of conscription, and as Chancellor of the Exchequer his concern was with economic rather than military considerations. Lloyd George wanted seventy divisions; McKenna did not believe that the nation could possibly afford more than fifty. There is no complete narrative of the meeting and the result might well have been the same even if McKenna had not attended. Among those present, this rigid unsympathetic character was undoubtedly the most hostile to Lloyd George. He must bear, though not alone, the responsibility for the advice which Asquith accepted. He therefore stands out as the principal architect of Liberal disaster.

The Liberal Ministers pledged themselves not to serve in a Bonar Law–Lloyd George administration. Asquith had received similar assurance from Curzon and other Tory Leaders.

On the following morning he wrote to Lloyd George. He insisted that the Prime Minister must be chairman of the new committee and that he alone would select its other members. He laid it down that Balfour must be a member and continue as First Lord of the Admiralty.

Lloyd George replied in a letter which should be quoted in full. It set out not only the reason for the breach but, in most vivid terms, his own attitude towards the conduct of the war.

> As all delay is fatal in war, I place my office without further parley
> at your disposal.
> It is with great personal regret that I have come to this conclusion.
> In spite of mean and unworthy insinuations to the contrary – insinua-
> tions which I fear are always inevitable in the case of men who hold
> prominent but not primary positions in any administration – I have felt
> a strong personal attachment to you as my chief. As you yourself said,

[1] *Reginald McKenna – a Memoir*, Eyre & Spottiswoode, 1948.

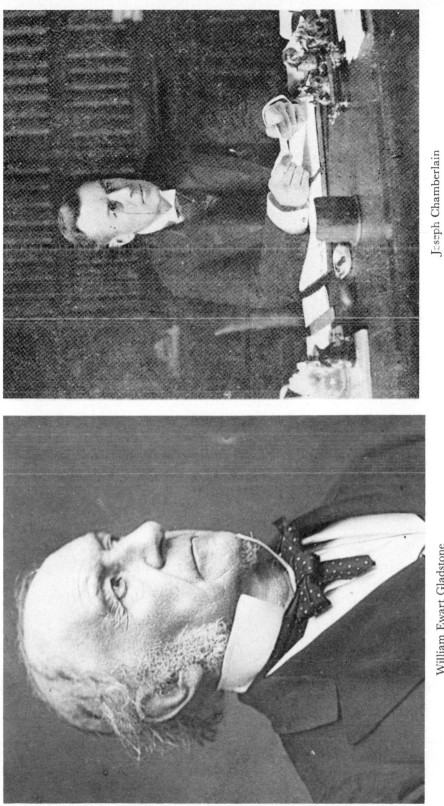

Joseph Chamberlain

William Ewart Gladstone

(*Left*) Winston Churchill in 1916, who at that time commanded the 6th Royal Scots Fusiliers, with Major Sir Archibald Sinclair, his second in command, and later during the Second World War the Secretary of State for Air

(*Right*) David Lloyd George with H H Asquith and Princess Priscilla Bibesco at Sutton Courtenay in July 1924, and (*below*) Lloyd George and Asquith on the same platform at Paislcy, 24th November 1923

(*Left*) Lord Balfour with Winston Churchill in 1915

Andrew Bonar Law leaving the Conservative meeting at the Carlton Club in 1922

on Sunday, we have acted together for ten years and never had a quarrel, although we have had many grave differences on questions of policy. You have treated me with great courtesy and kindness; for all that I thank you. Nothing would have induced me to part now except an over-whelming sense that the course of action which has been pursued has put the country – and not merely the country, but throughout the world, the principles for which you and I have always stood throughout our political lives – in the greatest peril that has ever overtaken them.

As I am fully conscious of the importance of preserving national unity, I propose to give your Government complete support in the vigorous prosecution of the War; but unity without action is nothing but futile carnage, and I cannot be responsible for that. Vigour and Vision are the supreme need at this hour.

On the afternoon of Wednesday, 6th December, a conference took place at Buckingham Palace. The King presided. It was attended by Asquith, Lloyd George, Bonar Law and Arthur Henderson. There is some conflict of evidence as to whether the prospect of a Balfour Premiership was canvassed. According to Lloyd George's recollection everyone was willing to serve except Asquith, who asked indignantly : 'What is the proposal? That I who have held first place for eight years should be asked to take a secondary position.'

Lord Stamfordham, the Kings Private Secretary, who drafted a memorandum on the conference, does not mention this observation. But in any event, it was agreed that Asquith should consider serving under Bonar Law and that if he refused, Lloyd George would endeavour to form a Government. Asquith returned to Downing Street where he met his Liberal colleagues and Henderson. Except for Henderson and Montagu, they were all opposed to entering a Bonar Law Government. At 7.30 that evening, Lloyd George accepted the King's Commission. Within twenty-four hours the new Government was formed. The atti-tude of Lloyd George is made abundantly clear from the diary of C. P. Scott[1], the Editor of the *Manchester Guardian*. His entry on Tuesday, 5th December reads as follows :

Tuesday December 5. Saw Lloyd George at War Office at 11.30. He was much angered and excited. Said he had just received a letter from the Prime Minister going back completely on his previous undertaking and that in consequence he had determined at once to send in his resignation (that is really his refusal to re-enter the Ministry) and he showed me the letter which was in the act of being typed by his secre-tary.

[1] *Political Diaries 1911–28*, Collins, 1970.

The *Manchester Guardian* supported Lloyd George. On 9th December L. T. Hobhouse, an eminent member of the Liberal Party, wrote to Scott referring to his leading article :

> I could not have taken the same line myself, but I hope, with trembling, that you are right. I admit (and I can find others who are not Georgian doing likewise) that it is impossible to defend the Asquith Government. To go on with it meant a certain defeat. Lloyd George I regard as kill or cure. He may land us in even worse disaster, or he may win. The point in his favour is that he will take decisions.

Anyone who has studied closely the events of 1916 must agree with this verdict. Yet – and this is perhaps the strangest feature of the whole affair – all the Liberal Ministers, with the single exception of Montagu, supported Asquith and refused to serve under Lloyd George. They can hardly have been unaware of Asquith's deficiencies or of the chronic failure to take decisions. They must have known of the feeling throughout the country in favour of Lloyd George as war leader. But considerations of personal and Party loyalty came first. By their action they brought about the permanent downfall of the Liberal Party.

Undoubtedly the country as a whole welcomed the change of Government. This was not the reaction among the Liberal rank and file. On 10th December, Geoffrey Howard wrote to Asquith :

> My information is that the Party in the country are almost solid behind you and will give you the most enthusiastic support in your leadership.

The legend grew, and became an article of faith, that Asquith had been the victim of an unutterably wicked intrigue. Indeed, Asquith himself later expressed the view that there had been 'A well organised, carefully engineered conspiracy' to turn him out of power. Of course it may well have been that Lloyd George aspired to be Prime Minister; this could indeed be said of almost every successful British politician. But the supporters of the conspiracy theory gave him no credit whatever for any patriotic motive. In their eyes he had been guilty of the blackest treachery and there was no mitigating circumstance.

This however was not the view of the general public. There can be no doubt that the change of Government was generally regarded with relief and indeed with enthusiasm. The popular reaction was expressed in a rhyming column which appeared in *John Bull* on the 16th December :

Glutted with two long years of war
Death sat upon his throne
Sated, yet hungering for more
He gnawed a fleshless bone.
Though bloated by the awful feast
Yet ever and anon
His hideous appetite increased
With that he fed upon.
To him a ghastly messenger
Than lightning flash more fleet
Sped up the gloomy hall and there
Fell prostrate at his feet;
'Hail, King of all things mortal ! Hear
The news to me consigned
The days of scarcity draw near
For Asquith has resigned.
Not yet perhaps the pinch you will feel
Indeed, though yet may be
Long months through which your ceaseless meal
May yield more plenteously
For Asquith's dilatory ways
Effects must leave behind –
The bloody legacy of days
Before he had resigned.'
Death cast the mumbled bone aside
And stirred upon his throne
'This is indeed bad news,' he cried
'The worst that I have known.'
'But may be who takes his place
My maw may long engorge
His minion raised a troubled face –
'Not, Sire, if it's Lloyd George.'

Asquith himself never publicly expressed himself with the same
bitterness as his followers. Nevertheless his actual feelings were fully
revealed five months later. In May 1917, after the United States had
entered the war, Lloyd George planned a reconstruction of his Government. He wished Asquith to become Lord Chancellor. The Lord Chief
Justice, Lord Reading, acted as the intermediary. He joined the Whit-
sun house party at Asquith's country residence. Asquith's papers con-
tain his own account of what took place between them. It includes the
following passage :

This (Monday) morning the Lord Chief Justice returned to the charge, with something more like a frontal attack. He said that he, and many others, regarded my active participation in the Government as essential, and he hinted that this was the view of the Prime Minister. I gathered that I could have almost any post I chose except that of the head of the Government.

I answered that I must use preferably plain language, since he had raised the subject. I was quite ready to go on giving the Government full support so long as they carried on the War in the proper spirit, and use my influence within my party, and in the country, in the same sense. But he and others had better understand clearly, and at once, that under no conditions would I serve in a Government of which Lloyd George was the head. I had learned by long and close association to mistrust him profoundly. I knew him to be incapable of loyalty and lasting gratitude. I had always acknowledged, and did still, to the full his many brilliant and useful faculties, but he needed to have someone over him. In my judgment he had incurable defects, both of intellect and character, which totally unfitted him to be at the head.

There is no reason to suppose that Asquith and his friends ever changed their opinion of Lloyd George – an opinion which was generally shared among orthodox Liberal politicians. And yet – and here is the supreme paradox – this man with his allegedly 'incurable defects' became the main architect of victory.

No one can measure the 'ifs' of history. But it is as certain as anything could be that, if Lloyd George had not become Prime Minister when he did, the result of the war would have been different. In 1917 Britain faced the prospect of final defeat at sea. As in the Second World War, the only battle she could never afford to lose was the battle of the Atlantic. On 1st February 1917, the Germans had declared unrestricted submarine warfare. The Kaiser stated: 'We will frighten the British flag off the face of the waters and starve the British people until they, who have refused peace, will kneel and plead for it.'

The threat very nearly became a reality. By the end of the month, 316,368 tons of British shipping had been sunk. The total for March was 350,000 tons. In April the figure was 526,447 tons. It was evident that this rate of loss could not be sustained. Admiral Sir Guy Gaunt, British Naval Attaché in Washington wrote in his diary[1]:

Up to the end of January, 1917, it was touch and go whether the U-boat campaign would do more harm than the whole of the German Army. More than 300,000 tons of British shipping had been sunk by

[1] *The Yield of the Years*: Hutchinson, 1940.

submarine. Our intelligence experts are agreed that Germany can starve us out by midsummer if this rate of destruction is maintained.

The situation was dramatically saved by the introduction of convoys. This, as everyone knows, was due to the personal insistence of the Prime Minister.

He was faced with the strongest professional resistance. In particular, the First Sea Lord was opposed. He argued that merchant vessels could not keep in line and that, even if they did, they presented an obvious target to the German submarines. But Lloyd George discovered that the convoy system was already in operation. A naval officer named Commander Henderson was already engaged in convoying coal barges across the channel with armed trawlers. The climax of this situation is vividly described in volume 36 of Lloyd George's *War Memoirs*[2] (page 1162):

It was clear that the Admiralty did not intend to take any effective steps in the direction of convoying. After first discussing the matter with Sir Edward Carson I informed the Cabinet that I had decided to visit the Admiralty and then take peremptory action on the question of convoys. Arrangements were made accordingly with the Board that I should attend a meeting to investigate with them all the means at present in use in regard to submarine warfare. I stipulated for the right to send for any officers, whatever their rank, from whom I desired information.

Apparently the prospect of being invaded in their own sanatorium galvanized the Admiralty into a fresh inquisition, and by way of anticipating the inevitable they further examined the plans and figures which Commander Henderson had prepared in consultation with Mr Norman Lesley of the Ministry of Shipping. They then for the first time began to realise the fact, which had been ignored by them since August, 1914 that the figures upon which they had based their strategy were ludicrous, and that therefore protection for a convoy system was within the compass of their resources. Accordingly, when I arrived at the Admiralty I found the Board in a chastened mood. We discussed the whole matter in detail. We agreed on its conclusions which I then reported to the Cabinet.

Never can a civilian Minister in wartime have been so strikingly vindicated. The convoy system proved more successful than even its most enthusiastic advocates could have foreseen. Between its adoption in the summer of 1917 and the end of the war in November 1918 more than 17,000 vessels arrived at, or left, British ports. Only 154 were sunk.

[2] Nicholson and Watson, 1933-6.

The other outstanding example of Lloyd George's mastery occurred in 1918. In March the Germans launched their greatest offensive. Owing to the Russian revolution they were able to concentrate almost the whole of their forces on the Western Front. The situation could only be saved by American manpower. There were only 300,000 American troops in France of which a third were non-combatant supply services The American General intended to wait until their own fully trained forces under American command could take the field. Lloyd George persuaded the United States Government that, in this moment of dire emergency, they should serve with the British and the French. President Wilson agreed to the despatch of 120,000 troops per month. But how were they to be transported? American shipping was then entirely inadequate for the task. It could only be accomplished by the British Mercantile Marine, already, as it seemed, stretched to the limit. But somehow it was done. On taking office, Lloyd George had appointed Sir Joseph Maclay, whom he had never met before, as Shipping Controller. He sent for him in March, 1918, and said: 'Can we do it?' Maclay promised to let him know by 6 o'clock in the evening. He did so. The American troops were brought across in the required numbers.

These are two outstanding examples of Lloyd George's genius as a war leader. They illustrate his special qualities to which reference has already been made – his questioning mind, his capacity, to discern the essentials of any situation and his remarkable flair in using the abilities of others. It is hardly conceivable that Asquith or any other political leader of that generation (with possible exception of Churchill) would have shown the same qualities or achieved similar results.

There was a further consequence of the change of Government in December 1916. During the last two years of the war, the Kaiser and at least some of his advisers were thinking in terms of a compromise peace. They were not alone. In Britain there were both Conservatives and Liberals who could foresee no decisive end to the tragic, bloody stalemate on the Western Front. In November 1916, Lord Lansdowne had published his famous memorandum. In effect, he saw no prospect of complete victory. He wrote:

> We are slowly but surely killing off the best of the male population of these times . . .
> But the financial burden which we have already incurred is almost incalculable . . .
> All this it is no doubt our duty to bear but only if it could be shown that the sacrifice will have its reward . . .

All of us must of late have asked ourselves how the war is ever to be brought to an end . . .

It seems as if the prospects of a 'knock-out' were, to say the least of it, remote.

Asquith did not believe that the time had come to make overtures to the Germans. But in a private note to Lansdowne he expressed his 'complete concurrence' with his views.

Here is another of the great 'ifs' of history. If the Government had not changed in December 1916, there might conceivably have been a compromise peace sometime in the following year. To say this is not to condemn Asquith and his Liberal colleagues. To a great many informed observers the Lansdowne argument must have seemed irrefutable. But the prospect of a compromise, if it ever existed, faded away when Lloyd George entered 10 Downing Street. One of the closest students of the British political scene during the last two years of the war was Prince Max of Baden. He was a Minister in the Kaiser's Government. From 1916 onwards he was the principal German advocate of a compromise peace. His two-volume memoir[1] contains his constant assessments of British political leaders. His judgment never wavered : Lloyd George was the principal 'Lord of the battle cry'. Thus he writes of peace feelers in 1917 :

> Whatever secret German feeler, whether it went by way of Spain, or by way of Pachelli, or by way of Rosen and Heemskert, led in the end to Lloyd George and Lloyd George wanted war.

His constant theme is that if only the Imperial Government would restore in full the integrity of Belgium, influential opinion in Britain would be divided, Lloyd George overthrown, and his place taken by a Lansdowne or Asquith administration. Whether he was right we shall never know, because the complete restitution of Belgium was consistently opposed on strategic grounds by the German Generals. But he was undoubtedly right in his assessment of Lloyd George.

Reference has already been made to the contrasted personalities of Asquith and Lloyd George and the attitude of most of the Liberal leaders. But the division in the Liberal Party from December 1916 onwards was not only a matter of personalities. It was deeper and more fundamental. On the one side there were those who, like Lloyd George, were determined to win the war at almost any cost.

Throughout these crucial years, Lloyd George was supported by the *British Weekly* which, more than any other publication, reflected the

[1] *Memoirs of Prince Max of Baden* : Constable, 1928.

views of British nonconformity. Its editor was Robertson Nicoll. Lord Riddell has recorded[1] a tribute which Lloyd George paid to Nicoll when he died in 1923. The two of them, Lloyd George said, 'with much bitterness' had made enemies because when they decided – reluctantly – to go into the war, they went in heart and soul, whereas other Liberals agreed to participate but sought to satisfy their anti-war proclivities by carrying on the struggle in a meagre and unsatisfactory way.

This difference of attitude is most clearly illustrated by the issue of conscription. Looking back over the gap of more than fifty years, it is difficult to understand the passion which it aroused. In the Second World War, compulsory national service was taken for granted by members of all parties. But throughout the First War there were many Liberal and Labour politicians to whom the very idea of compulsion was completely abhorrent. During the first coalition. Lloyd George was the outstanding conscriptionist and eventually he had his way. In the event, only Sir John Simon resigned from the Government. But it is quite clear that Asquith, Runciman and most of their Liberal colleagues only yielded to pressure and, if they had had their way, would have preserved the voluntary system.

On 18th September, 1915, Asquith wrote to Balfour stating that during the last few days he had received from 'the most trusted and representative man' of the Liberal rank and file 'a number of apparently spontaneous communications, and all in a sense a resolute and dogged opposition. It is no exaggeration to say that at this moment, the two most unpopular and distrusted men in the Party are Lloyd George and Mr Churchill.' Inevitably conscription came into force. The anti-conscriptionists were never reconciled to its operation. Apart from their loyalty to Asquith, they could never forgive Lloyd George the part he had played in bringing it about.

After his fall from power, Asquith discharged the formal duties of leader of the Opposition. Until May 1918 he scarcely ever sought to embarrass the Government. But the followers who sat behind him on the Opposition Benches necessarily included all the Liberal pacifists, those who would have accepted a compromise peace and those who, in Lloyd George's words, would carry on the struggle 'in a meagre and unsatisfactory way.' Hence the significance of the Maurice debate.

The controversy over this debate has never ended. It is sufficient here briefly to recall the the sequence of events. On 9th April, the Prime Minister assured the House of Commons that the British Army

[1] *Lord Riddell's War Diary, 1914–18.*

in France was considerably stronger on 1st January 1918 than on 1st January 1917. On 18th April he was asked whether in arriving at this estimate he was including the labour battalions and other non-combatant units. The Under Secretary for War replied that the combatant strength of the British Army was greater on 1st January 1918 than on 1st January 1917. This was correct so far as the whole Army was concerned but it was not correct of the Army in France.

General Maurice, a serving soldier, took the unprecedented step of writing to *The Times* to contradict the Government. It was he who, in his capacity as Director of Military Operations, had been responsible for supplying the figures. He now wrote that the total strength of the Army in France on 1st January 1917 was 1,299,000 and on 1st January 1918 was 1,570,000. The latter figure however included 300,000 unarmed British labourers and Chinese coolies which did not appear in the 1917 figures, while the fighting troops in 1918 were more than 100,000 weaker.

Asquith immediately tabled a private notice question. Bonar Law on behalf of the Government offered to set up a Court of Honour consisting of two judges to investigate the allegation. Strange as it now seems, this offer was rejected by Asquith and in the debate two days later he pressed for a Select Committee of the House of Commons. He was, of course, reminded of the unhappy precedent of the Marconi enquiry which had divided precisely along Party lines. To this he could make no adequate reply. Lloyd George was in his most devastating form. It is now clear that the figures which he quoted were incorrect. Frances Stevenson, later the Countess Lloyd George, has told the astonishing story of how the corrected figures were afterwards discovered in a red box by Lloyd George's private secretary, J. T. Davies, and that he destroyed the document. But at the time it appeared that Lloyd George had completely routed his critics. One passage may be quoted from his speech :

'We had a controversy which lasted practically for months over unity of command. This is really a sort of remnant of it. The national unity is threatened – the Army unity is threatened – by this controversy. Days have been occupied in hunting up records and minutes and proces verbaux, in interviews, and in raking up what happened during the whole twelve months in the War Cabinet. And this at such a moment. I have just come back from France. I met some generals and they were telling me how now the German [sic] are silently, silently preparing perhaps the biggest blow of the war, under a shroud of mist, and they asked me for certain help. I brought back a list of things they wanted done, and I wished to attend to them. I really beg and implore, for our common country, the fate of which is in the balance now and in the next few weeks that there should be an end of this sniping.'

Lloyd George was immediately followed by W. M. R. Pringle who was his most bitter critic on the Liberal benches. No one can read his speech without appreciating the intense hostility by which it was inspired. The tone may be gauged by the following :

'I would invite any honourable gentleman to tell us what is the secret which the Prime Minister has let us into. He discovered, for the first time, that he had been subject to attacks by the cocoa Press. Cocoa slops, I understand, he says it is – an element which used to be very congenial to him. It was grateful and comforting in the days of the land campaign, and even more grateful and comforting when the Right Honourable Gentleman had to answer before a Select Committee of this House, and before the Gentleman who now cheer him with such impartiality. It occurs to me that this may account for the Right Honourable Gentleman's objection to Select Committees. He has had a Select Committee into his veracity before.

He has had a report written upon it by his colleague the Minister of Blockade. It is on the records of this House.'

A Rt Hon Gentleman :

'Are we at war ?'

Mr Pringle :

'Yes, and I am discussing an alternative method to a proposal which the Government itself put forward for getting on with the war.'

After Asquith himself, no other Liberal leader spoke from the Opposition Front Bench. Nevertheless, the Liberals divided the House. *The Times* pointed out that this was the first occasion during the war on which the Opposition Whips had acted as tellers against the Government and the Opposition Front Bench had voted against it on an issue of confidence. Thus was drawn the line of demarcation. The split in the Liberal Party was complete. It was never to be completely healed.

It was not surprising that the Asquithian Liberals went down to unprecedented defeat in 1918. In the eyes of the electorate, they represented the defeatists. Britain might have lost the war or accepted a compromise peace. Lloyd George was fully vindicated by the German surrender. He was hailed, with complete justice, as 'The Man Who Won The War'. This does not of course excuse his excess of speech in the ensuing general election. Undoubtedly he pandered to the jingoist and revengeful mood of the electorate when he spoke of hanging the Kaiser and squeezing Germany until the pips squeaked. Nevertheless, he cannot be fairly criticised for holding the election or for maintaining the coalition. The existing Parliament had lasted for eight years, and it was inconceivable having regard to events from December 1916 onwards that Lloyd George should immediately abandon his Unionist colleagues and return to his association with the Liberals, many of whom had come to hate him and who would, had it lain in their power, have overthrown his Government at the time of the Maurice debate. Winston Churchill wrote[1] :

> To this Election I was a consulted and consenting party. I thought we had need of all the strength we could get to face the problems of bringing home and disbanding our armies which then numbered at home and abroad nearly 4 million men, of reconstructing our industry, and making the treaty of peace. Moreover, I had in the stress of war resumed intimate contact with the Conservative Party and with the friends of my youth. Having seen so many implacable party quarrels swept away by the flood, I was in no mind to go back and look for them. The idea of methodically fishing up and revitalizing the old pre-war party controversies, and of fabricating disagreements even where none existed, was absurd and abhorrent. I therefore swam with the stream. If I had taken the opposite course it would not have made the slightest difference to the events. But candour compels acknowledgement of this measure of responsibility.

The Asquithian Liberals were left with only 33 members, one or two of whom were of uncertain allegiance. Labour with 63 seats became the official Opposition. Yet the Liberals might have recovered. After the election there was an almost immediate swing of public opinion. Liberal candidates won sensational victories at West Leyton, Central Hull and Central Aberdeen. Asquith himself, as already recalled, was returned for Paisley amidst public rejoicing in 1920. Many people confidently foresaw a Liberal revival. It came as an immense disappointment that, at the General Election of 1922 after the fall of the coalition, only 60 Asquithian Liberals were returned.

What was the explanation? It can be traced to December 1916. Every major party is in large degree a coalition. This was certainly true of the Liberals before the First War. On the one side there were the spiritual heirs of Cobden and Bright. They believed in free trade, laissez-faire and 'retrenchment'; above all, in 'retrenchment'. In their eyes all taxation was deplorable. Their favourite quotation was from Gladstone : 'Let the money fructify in the pockets of the people'. It was always an article of faith with these Liberals (and continued to be so for many

[1] *The World Crisis : The Aftermath* : Thornton Butterworth, 1929.

years after the war) that all Government Departments were guilty of vast, wasteful and unnecessary expenditures and that the principal task of statesmanship was to prune their insatiable demands.

On the other hand there were the supporters of what *The Nation* called 'radical Liberalism'. These were the architects of social reform. Their aim was, to repeat Lloyd George's phrase, 'to wage implacable warfare against poverty'. In the teeth of violent opposition, they laid the foundations of the Welfare State. The leaders of this school of thought included Churchill, Masterman and, above all, Lloyd George. And between 1908 and 1914 it was they who prevailed. The contradiction between the two schools of thought was never wholly apparent to the Liberal rank and file, whether in Parliament or outside. Many of them continued to preach the doctrine of rigid departmental economy while at the same time extolling the new conceptions of social reform.

The effect of the wartime division was to deprive the official Liberal Party of its radical inspiration. Lloyd George was now the principal enemy. Churchill was aligned with him. So was Addison. Masterman was in the shadows. He had lost his seat in 1914 and only returned to Parliament for a brief nine months at the 1923 General Election.

Those who remained belonged for the most part to the first school of thought described above. In his book *The Downfall of the Liberal Party*[1], Dr Trevor Wilson has described how Runciman deplored attempts by the Liberals to outbid Labour and advocated rigid adherence to the principles of economic individualism, and how Sir John Simon declared that Government retrenchment was the most urgent and fundamental need of the country, for it lay at the root of social progress, industrial prosperity, security of employment, a high standard of living and domestic peace.

He further cites a speech by Sir Donald Maclean in July 1920. Maclean was at this time the hero of the Liberal rank and file in the country. Though no orator, he was a man of evident integrity. Between Asquith's defeat at East Fife in 1918 and his return for Paisley in 1920, he had acted as the leader of the 30 Liberal Members in opposition. No Liberal speech at any public meeting was complete without a reference to 'Donald Maclean and his gallant band'. But here is his declaration of faith in 1920 :

> He was often asked the question : 'What is your policy?' Personally
> he had nothing heroic to offer. He believed we should only get things
> adjusted nationally by the same lines of simple common-sense and

[1] William Collins, 1966.

homely wisdom that were applied to any private concern, and he was not going to compete with the Labour Party in making promises which he knew could not be fulfilled. We had been through a war and a convulsion, and the only way to get back to national health was by way of economy. We could not settle the world simply by saying we would nationalise everything. But in and through the ideals and principles of Liberalism a great deal could be done.

It is quite true that other voices were making themselves heard, in particular, the Manchester Liberals led by E. D. Simon and Ramsay Muir who gave up his academic career to engage in Liberal politics. Preaching more radical doctrines, they were responsible for the foundation of the Liberal Summer School which, during the 1920s and 1930s, met each summer at Oxford or Cambridge and which was to become a power house of Liberal ideas. They did not, however, arrive on the scene in time to transform the image of official Liberalism. The only doctrines for which the Party clearly stood at this time were free trade (which did not again become an issue until 1923) and draconian economy in the public services. It is therefore not difficult to understand why the Liberal revival, so confidently predicted in the months after the 1918 election, wholly failed to materialise in 1922. C. P. Scott records in his Diary for 6th December 1922 how he had breakfasted with Lloyd George who asked him what he thought of the results of the General Election. Scott replied that he thought it was a disaster for the Liberal Party worse, if possible, than that of 1918 because there was excuse for it. Lloyd George agreed.

The rest of the story can be very briefly recapitulated. Baldwin succeeded Bonar Law as Conservative Prime Minister. To almost universal astonishment, he made a speech at Plymouth on 26th October, 1923 calling for the establishment of protection. A General Election was declared. The immediate effect was to close the Liberal ranks. Asquith and Lloyd George were formally reconciled. During the campaign Lloyd George, accompanied by his daughter Megan, appeared on Asquith's platform at Paisley. The result of the election showed a considerable Liberal revival. They captured 158 seats. Even so, they fell short of Labour with 191 and the Conservatives with 258. It is also to be observed that they acquired their accession of strength on a purely negative appeal – the rejection of tariffs.

The new Parliament lasted for only nine months. It was Asquith's Indian Summer. His authority seemed unimpaired and he exhibited all his gifts of imperturbability, serene judgment and incisive speech. Undoubtedly it was his decision to turn out the Baldwin administration and install the first Labour Government. The shrieks of indignation from the propertied classes left him sardonically unmoved. His speech in the House of Commons was a masterpiece. So indeed was his final speech in favour of a select committee to enquire into the Campbell case. But it was his last in the House of Commons. At the ensuing general election – the Red Letter election – he was defeated at Paisley and only 42 Liberal Members were returned.

During this brief period, the rift appeared to be almost healed. Lloyd George had made no difficulty about serving under Asquith and following his lead. In the new Parliament, however, the antipathies immediately flared up again. Lloyd George was elected Chairman of the Parliamentary Party by 26 votes to 7 with 7 abstentions. Immediately the dissentients announced the formation of a 'Radical Group'. Ironically, the leader was Walter Runciman. Less than any prominent Liberal of his time he deserved to be styled a 'Radical'. But no one was misled. It was manifest that the only purpose of the group was to emphasise its detachment from Lloyd George.

Lloyd George's career then entered upon a new phase. The later 1920s were years of stagnation. This was in particular due to the decision of the new Conservative Government to return to the Gold Standard at the former parity – a decision which Lloyd George, almost alone among leading political figures, strenuously denounced. But it was under his inspiration that the Liberal Party became the party of ideas. Reference has already been made to the Liberal Summer School where lectures were given each year by such figures as Ramsay Muir, Walter Layton and H. D. Henderson. It was also under Lloyd George's inspiration that a series of studies were undertaken as to how the resources of the nation might best be used. First there was *Coal and Power* which proposed the nationalisation of mineral royalties. Then there was the *Green Book* ('the Land and the Nation') dealing with agriculture and the ownership of land. Finally there was the *Yellow Book* ('Britain's Industrial Future') which proposed for Britain the kind of programme later carried out in the United States by Roosevelt's New Deal.

Whether or not it deserved to do so, the *Green Book* misfired. It was launched at a great meeting at Killerton Park, the home of the Acland family in Devon. Seventeen thousand people stood in the rain. To the amazement of the audience and the consternation of some of those seated on the platform, Lloyd George proposed the outright nationalisation of the land. The central feature of his programme was that on a given date 'all land should revert to the Crown'. Thereafter, there would be no private ownership, but only cultivating tenure. A farmer who failed to make efficient use of his acres would be dispossessed. 'The dogs in the manger must be lifted out by the ears'.

The speech was only a beginning. A new organisation was set up entitled 'The Land and the Nation League'. It was financed by the Lloyd George Fund. A fleet of travelling vans was acquired, each with a platform at the back. There were hired speakers. There were also volunteers, largely consisting of undergraduates during their vacations. Thousands of meetings were held in the villages of England.

Whether the *Green Book* policy would ever have found acceptance is anybody's guess. It faded out because it proved too much for the Liberal Party. Apart from Sir Francis Acland, there was scarcely a single prominent Liberal who gave it his wholehearted support. Eventually Lloyd George was constrained to accept a compromise. A special Liberal conference was held in London in the following year. The proposal for outright nationalisation was dropped. It was, however, agreed that in future the State should have the first option on all land coming into the market. Even this compromise proposal went further than has ever since been attempted by any political party.

Asquith and the other Liberal leaders regarded the land campaign with extreme distaste. They resented the nation-wide propaganda in support of the programme which had not received (and which never did receive) official party endorsement. Their attitude was hardened by their resentment over the Lloyd George Fund. Lloyd George had made substantial contributions to the Party's election expenses in 1923 and 1924 and was to do so again in 1929. But he consistently refused to hand over control of his fund to the official Liberal organisation. He has often been criticised. It is not, however, altogether surprising that he should not have made over these vast resources to men who continued to regard him with extreme resentment.

These differences helped to explain the final act in the long drawn-out tragedy. In May 1926, the general strike, was in protest against the savage reduction in miners' wages. The official Liberal leaders, headed by Asquith and Grey, unreservedly condemned the strike and supported the Government in demanding unconditional surrender. In the absence of newspapers, Churchill produced the *British Gazette*. It published a message of support from Asquith and Grey. In the House of Commons Sir John Simon declared the general strike illegal – a view which was by no means universally shared in the Temple. Lloyd George had other views. He agreed with several leaders of the Churches who called for negotiations. At this time he contributed regular syndicated articles to the American Press. He used this medium to criticise the

Government more sharply and he criticised the strikers. And finally, he declined to attend a meeting of the Liberal Shadow Cabinet called for 10th May.

The story of May 1926 is curiously similar to that of December 1916. After the meeting had been held Asquith wrote to Mrs Harrison a letter comparable in tone to that he had addressed to Venetia Stanley on the Sunday evening ten years before.

> There was one notable absentee – Ll-G. – who was in the sulks and had cast in his lot for the moment with the clericals – Archbishops and Deans and the whole company of the various Churches (a hopeless lot) – in the hope of getting a foothold for himself in the Labour camp. He is already, being a creature of uncertain temperament, suffering from cold feet. So much so, that I have a message this morning from Miss Stevenson asking me to arrange for a joint meeting in July in Carnarvon which he and I are to address.

Clearly he did not at this moment contemplate an irreversible breach. He did not even suggest that he would refuse to attend the proposed joint meeting at Carnarvon. Here again, his attitude changed. Mr Roy Jenkins says that this was 'perhaps because of the representations of colleagues'. The surmise is almost certainly justified. Some of them met with Asquith on the 18th May. They suggested that Asquith should write a letter to Lloyd George and that it should be published. This was done. Asquith wrote :

> It was, in my own judgment, the primary duty of all who are responsible for Liberal policy, and certainly not least of all the Chairman of the Parliamentary Party in the House of Commons, at such a time to meet together for a free and full discussion, and to contribute their counsels to the common stock. Your refusal to do so I find impossible to reconcile with my conception of the obligations of political comradeship.

Twelve Members of the Shadow Cabinet followed up with a public condemnation of Lloyd George. The names are significant, they were : Lords Grey, Lincolnshire, Buckmaster, Buxton and Cowdray; Sir John Simon, Sir Donald Maclean, Sir Godfrey Collins; Runciman, Vivian Phillips, Geoffrey Howard and W. M. Pringle.

These were the men who had never forgiven Lloyd George for 1916.

The reaction of Liberals throughout the country was entirely different. For the most part they detested the continuing feud. They felt that the prospects of a Liberal revival were constantly impeded by the continuing divisions in leadership. There was also a growing feeling that the only leadership in the realm of policy was being provided by Lloyd George. Moreover, Asquith's acceptance of Conservative backing in the 1924 election in Paisley, made many Liberals uneasy. The roles were entirely reversed from coalition days. Now it was Asquith who was close to the Tories and Lloyd George their outspoken opponent.

It followed that Liberal organisations, national and local, refused to join in the excommunication. In effect, they swung over to Lloyd George. One of Asquith's principal adherents, a leading West Country Liberal, himself an Asquithian, stated : 'Before all this happened the Party was two-thirds Asquithian and one-third Lloyd Georgian. Now it is the other way round.'

Asquith's health gave way. On 12th June he had a minor stroke and was incapacitated for nearly three months. On 15th October he published his resignation in a letter to the heads of the English and Scottish Liberal Federation. On the same night he made his farewell speech at Greenock. Those who travelled with him from London included Grey, Simon, Runciman and Maclean. He ended his speech with the words : 'The new problems are not outside the ambit of the old faith. Look neither to the right nor to the left but keep straight on.' It was a moving occasion. The audience were in tears. The genuine, deep affection which Asquith inspired among his followers found its expression as they rose and sang 'Will ye no' come back again'.

Asquith died sixteen months later on 15th February 1928. After his Greenock speech he took no part in politics. Lloyd George became the unchallenged Liberal leader. This does not mean that his principal enemies were reconciled. For the most part they never were. They could not, however, challenge his obvious pre-eminence. Nor could they resist the flow of his ideas. The new radicalism of the Summer School was in the ascendant. It is significant that at this stage Lloyd George became reconciled to Keynes. This was typical of his approach to individuals. Lady Violet Bonham-Carter once said of him, 'He was without loyalty and without rancour'.

If there were anyone against whom he might have borne rancour, it was obviously Keynes; for it was Keynes who had written *The Economic Consequences of the Peace*. And in so doing largely destroyed the reputation of the coalition and of Lloyd George himself. From 1926 onwards it made no difference. Lloyd George and Keynes both reacted in horror against the Treasury orthodoxy of the day and the deflationary policies of the Conservative Government. Lloyd George's imagination was deeply inspired by the tragedy of the dole queues and the prolonged agony of the miners' strike. In 1925 Keynes wrote *Economic Conse-quences of Mr Churchill*.[1] This was immediately after the return of the Gold Standard. With reference to the miners' strike, he wrote :

> Like other victims of economic transition in past times, the miners are to be offered the choice between starvation and submission, the fruits of their submission to accrue to the benefit of other classes.

With this Lloyd George agreed, and it probably influenced his atti-tude towards the events of 1926. The task was to produce a credible alternative and to make it an electorial issue. There followed three years of incisive research and discussion inside the Liberal Party. The results were embodied in two publications. The first was *Britain's Industrial Future* (the *Yellow Book*). It marked a complete departure from *laissez-faire*. The authors included Keynes himself, Walter Layton, Philip Kerr, Hubert Henderson and Seebohm Rowntree. It dismissed as an anachronism the absolute distinction between private enterprise and public ownership. It proposed the rationalisation of industry under an Economic General Staff and the setting up of a ministry of industry to supervise industrial relations. These proposals would not be regarded as remarkable today. They represented a considerable advance in 1928.

The *Yellow Book* had a considerable appeal among economists and political enthusiasts. It was hardly designed to set the electorate ablaze. The deficiency was sought to be made good by the next publication *We Can Conquer Unemployment*. This was proclaimed by Lloyd George at a luncheon for Liberal candidates on 1st March 1929. In effect, it proposed an immense programme of national development. Men were to be employed in constructing roads and bridges, on housing, telephone development and electrical development.

Lloyd George declared : 'The work put in hand will reduce the terrible figures of the workless in the course of a single year to normal proportions, and will, when completed, enrich the nation and equip it for successfully competing with all its rivals in the business of the world. These plans will not add one penny to the national or local taxation.'

This programme was probably the most intelligent ever presented to a British electorate. It was comparable to Roosevelt's New Deal three years later. No one can now doubt that if it had been carried out the tragedy of unemployment during the 1930s would have been largely averted and Britain would have been infinitely better equipped. In 1929, however, before Keynesian ideas had become respectable, it was

[1] L. & V. Woolf.

regarded as heretical by the Conservatives and with morose suspicion by the Labour Party.

The General Election was to take place on 1st May. For the next three months the Liberals carried on an intensive campaign. They were encouraged by the two highly favourable by-election results. They placed 500 candidates in the field. During the last three years Lloyd George and his followers had made a strong appeal in the universities and the total included a high proportion of ardent young men and women eager to make all things new.

> Bliss was it in that dawn to be alive,
> But to be young was very heaven.[1]

These dreams were shattered on 1st May. The Liberal programme had not been without its effect. The number of Liberal votes in the country was increased by over a million. The Liberal total was five million as compared with eight million for each of the other parties. Owing however to the extreme injustice of the electoral system the Liberals secured only 59 seats.

The resulting situation will be dealt with in the next chapter. The verdict on the election of 1929 must be that it was the end of the 1916 tragedy. The Liberals deserved to succeed. They grasped more fully than either of the rival parties the essentials of the economic situation. They were not obsessed, as were many people in the Labour Party, with doctrinaire notions about public ownership as the panacea for all discontents. They were led by the outstanding political genius of their time. If they had managed to win, the calibre both of the Cabinet and of the majority Party in the House of Commons would almost certainly have been higher than could have been achieved by either of the other parties. It was too late. The division in their ranks had done them infinite harm. It had temporarily disappeared from the public view. But the Party had been too much weakened to permit of any genuine recovery. It had been effectively destroyed on 4th December 1916.

[1] Wordsworth: *The Prelude,* Book XI.

CHAPTER III

1922

'IT WAS A RICH, warm, night at the beginning of August when a gentleman in a cloak, for he was in evening dress, emerged from a club-house at the top of St James's Street and descended that celebrated eminence.' These are the opening lines of Disraeli's last novel *Endymion*.

It was to become more celebrated – or notorious – if the gentleman in evening dress had descended on 19th October 1922. He would no doubt have turned in at No 89. This is the habitation of the Carlton Club where, in one evening, the whole course of British politics was changed. By an overwhelming majority of 187 to 87 the Conservative Members of Parliament voted to withdraw from the coalition. It was a unique declaration of no confidence in the Prime Minister. Next day Lloyd George resigned and left 10 Downing Street, never to return. The verdict of history (or at least of a distinguished historian) has been pronounced by Professor Mowat[1]:

> Thus ended the coalition. And thus ended the reign of the great ones, the geniuses of the Edwardian era and of the war; and the rule of the pygmies 'of the second class brains' began, to continue until 1940. Lloyd George remained in public life, admired, distrusted, unused and stonily watched the country sink in the hopeless morass of depression and unemployment while lesser men frittered away Britain's power in the world.

'We have no one of their calibre now,' soberly remarked a high official in 1938.

In retrospect this judgment will be generally accepted. During the next eighteen years there was a premium on mediocrity. No-one who sat in Parliament during the twenties or thirties could have disputed the pre-eminence of two men – Lloyd George and Winston Churchill. They towered above their contemporaries. Yet, except for five disastrous

[1] *Britain between the wars* 1918-1940: Methuen, 1955.

years as Chancellor of the Exchequer, Churchill was a political outcast. Lloyd George was permanently domiciled in the wilderness.

How did it happen? In the General Elections of 1918 Lloyd George had been accorded the greatest vote of confidence ever obtained by a British politician. He was deservedly acclaimed as 'The Man Who Won The War.' The overwhelming majority of the Conservatives and Liberal coalitionists were elected under his mantle. As their opponents sardonically observed, it was only necessary to make one simple appeal to the electorate :

> My only plea
> Lloyd George for me
> Oh take me as I am.

In personnel the majority were not impressive. In the phrase attributed to Baldwin they consisted in large part of 'hard-faced men who looked as if they had done well out of the war', as indeed many of them had. The Election had been conducted in a spirit of sheer jingoism and revenge. The leaders of the coalition pandered to the prevailing mood. Lloyd George himself spoke of 'searching their pockets for the last farthing', and Churchill has written of his own election speeches 'I swam with the tide'. But their supporters went much further. The Conservative candidate for Hampstead proclaimed, 'We will make the enemy pay in money. We will make the enemy pay in blood. We will make the enemy pay in tears.' And at Cambridge Sir Eric Geddes proclaimed, 'We will get out of her all you can squeeze out of a lemon and a bit more. I will squeeze her until you can hear the pips squeak.' This was the appeal to which the electors responded. In the result the Coalition was returned with 484 Members made up of 338 Conservatives and 136 Liberals with 10 Labour Members. On the other side there were 60 Labour members and 26 Asquithian Liberals.

It was a defeat from which the Liberals never recovered, and it had a profound significance. The Labour total was not in itself particularly impressive. But Labour was now clearly established as the second Party in the State. The result was traumatic. The Labour leaders in Parliament were, almost without exception, unadventurous and pedestrian. But to many respectable citizens socialism portended 'red ruin and the breaking up of laws'. They had before their eyes the excesses of the Russian Bolshevik revolution. Moreover the years 1919–1920 were a period of extreme industrial unrest, including the formidable miners' strike. The foundations of society appeared to be threatened. The prospect of a Labour Government was indeed terrifying and must at all costs be avoided. It was this attitude which profoundly affected British politics during the next four years and which explains the final breach at the Carlton Club.

This, however, was not the only explanation. The Coalition underwent a series of misadventures at home and overseas. In large part these were undeserved. In spite of the 'hard-faced men' this was not a period of black reaction. The social services were improved. In the realm of education H. A. L. Fisher achieved a considerable advance by his Act of 1920. In spite of the Conservative predominance, the Coalition Liberals (unlike the Liberal Nationals of the thirties) had by no means abandoned their Liberal convictions. In the last year of the war and the early stages thereafter reform was in the air to an extent which is now generally forgotten. The Haldane Commission surveyed the whole machinery of Government on a scale which has never been repeated. The Bryce Commission produced a scheme for a democratically elected House of Lords. It is ironical to recall that only a few dissident Liberal votes avoided proportional representation.

Yet every Government is overtaken by events which it did not, and often could not, have foreseen and with which it is unfitted to deal by its own temperament or that of its supporters. The Administration of Neville Chamberlain might have been reasonably successful if it had only been concerned with domestic issues. The Labour Government of 1964 would have left a most impressive record if it had not been confronted on its first day with a balance of payments crisis. Of the Coalition Government it must be said that they never lost their nerve. As Lloyd George said in the House of Commons during the Abyssinia debate in 1937, they were never cowards. Yet they sustained a series of remarkable misadventures.

The first was the publication of a book. In November 1919, J. M. Keynes completed *The Economic Consequences of the Peace*. He was a distinguished academic economist. He had been attached to the Treasury during the war, and, until his resignation in June 1919, had been on the Staff of the British delegation at the Versailles Peace Conference. Unlike many economists, he had an outstanding mastery of the English language. His reputation in later years was enormous. It began with the publication of his book on Versailles.

Of course there are precedents. There are other books which have affected the course of history. The British libertarian tradition is in large part attributable to *Areopagitica*. The French Revolution might never have occurred if Rousseau had not written *Le Contrat Social*. The whole of Victorian political thinking was affected by Adam Smith's

The Wealth of Nations. The Economic Consequences had an effect
hardly less profound and, as Lord Boothby has pointed out, wholly disastrous. Given the principle of self-determination, the chief provisions
of the Treaty of Versailles were in no way unjust. Quite the reverse.
Alsace-Lorraine was restored to France as was Schleswig to the Danes.
Poland was re-created and Czechoslovakia became an independent
State. The dismemberment of the Austro-Hungarian Empire had been
brought about by the force of events.

None of this is acknowledged in Keynes's book. He was an economist
(albeit a most brilliant member of his species) and almost entirely concerned with monetary issues. There can, of course, be no doubt that the
demands for reparations made by the victorious European powers were
wholly unrealistic. Indeed, the Germans could not possibly have met the
demands specified in the Treaty. This amounted, over a period of forty-
eight years from the Armistice, to a total of no less than £780,000,000,
and Keynes was no doubt right in declaring that Germany could not
pay anything approaching this sum. Later in the book he refers to a
report to a German Economic Commission addressed to the Peace Conference by Count Brockdorff-Rantzau, on 13th May 1919. It ended
with the words, 'Those who sign this Treaty will sign the death sentence
of many millions of German men, women and children.' On this Keynes
makes the following comment :

> I know of no adequate answer to these words. The indictment is at
> least as true of the Austrian as of the German, settlement. This is the
> fundamental problem in front of us before which questions of territorial
> adjustment and the balance of European power are insignificant.[1]

This judgment was wholly falsified by events. Twenty years later questions of territorial adjustment and the balance of power were infinitely
more important than purely economic considerations. But in 1919 this
was not apparent. The book had a quite enormous impact. As inevitably
happens, its supposed conclusions came to be accepted by vast numbers
of persons who had never read it. That the Versailles Treaty was essentially unjust, and indeed wicked, became a widespread article of belief.
Lord Boothby has written[2] :

> I am not here concerned to defend, or to controvert, the economic
> arguments which Keynes marshalled and presented, with such supreme
> lucidity and skill. There is a good deal to be said on both sides. Of
> infinitely greater importance today is the political and historic signifi-

[1] *Economic Consequences of the Peace* : Macmillan, 1919.
[2] *I Fight to Live* : Victor Gollancz, 1947.

cance of 'The Economic Consequences' which was profound and disastrous. It established irrecoverably the strength of the Versailles Diktat,
which more than anything else, reduced the Western democracies to
paralysed impotence and enabled Hitler only 20 years later, to trample
the Continent of Europe underfoot.

This was the effect – undoubtedly disastrous – on history between
the wars. We are here concerned with its more immediate effects. Undoubtedly it seriously diminished the reputation of Lloyd George and
the Coalition Government.

Throughout this Parliament the principal Ministers speculated on the
future. Undoubtedly Lloyd George and his chief Conservative associates
toyed with the idea of 'fusion'. There was to be a new central Party in
which Liberals and Conservatives were to be for ever united. This was
sheer illusion. The Conservatives and Coalition Liberals had been
brought together by the quirk of circumstance. Their fundamental difference of outlook remained. This clearly appeared as early as June
1919. During the war there had been introduced a series of import
levies known as the McKenna duties. Even at the time, amidst the
clash of arms, they had been regarded with horror by stern and unbending Liberal free traders. Now it was proposed that they should be
continued in time of peace. The Coalition Liberals were presented with
an agonising decision. When the House divided only 35 of them supported the Government. Seventeen voted against, while about 60 abstained. Among the abstentionists were four prominent Members of the
Government – Churchill, Hewart, Montagu and McCurdy. As contrasted with the Liberal Nationals ten years later, the Coalition Liberals
were not prepared to sacrifice all their Liberal beliefs.

In the following year there occurred an event which revealed the
fundamental difference of outlook. On 30th April 1920, there took
place the Amritsar massacre.

There had been a state of acute unrest in the Punjab and, indeed, in
other parts of India. A British sergeant had been murdered at Amritsar.
A Miss Sherwood, a lady missionary, had been knocked down by blows
in the street and left for dead. General Dyer, newly arrived in Amritsar,
had distributed leaflets forbidding gatherings of more than four persons.
How far this was generally known was doubtful. On the day in question
a crowd of several thousands assembled in a great open space named
Jallianwallah Bagh. General Dyer, with a force of several hundred
soldiers, arrived on the scene. At this stage – whatever might have
happened later – the crowd were entirely orderly and were listening to
a lecture. Without any warning or order to disperse, General Dyer

ordered his troops to open fire. They fired 1,650 rounds. 379 people were killed and about 1,100 wounded. The crowd fled and congregated in the available exits. The firing continued into these concentrations. Thereafter General Dyer issued what was known as the Crawling Order. Indians passing this particular spot were compelled to do so on their hands and knees.

No single incident contributed more to undermine British rule in India. The Indian Government set up a commision of inquiry – the Hunter Commission. General Dyer gave evidence. He stated that, 'If his orders against holding a meeting were disobeyed, he was going to open fire', and he made it clear that his action was in no way an attempt to deal with an immediate threat to law and order. He stated :

'It was no longer a question merely of dispersing the crowd, but one of producing a sufficient moral effect, from a military point of view, not only on those who were present, but more especially throughout the Punjab. There could be no question of undue severity.'

The majority of the Hunter Commission held that he had committed a grave error. He had given the crowd no chance to disperse, and it was 'a mistaken conception of duty' for him to attempt a moral effect upon the Punjab. His Crawling Order unnecessarily punished the innocent as well as the guilty. The minority report produced by the three Indian members of the Commission condemned General Dyer in stronger terms.

This produced an almost frenetic reaction in the United Kingdom. Of course many people were appalled by the Amritsar massacre. What is more surprising, in retrospect, is that General Dyer commanded an immense volume of support. These differences were reflected in each House of Parliament. There was a furious debate in the House of Commons which took place on the 8th July 1920. Montagu, as Secretary of State for India, spoke with passion :

'If an officer justifies his conduct, no matter how gallant his record is – and everyone knows how gallant General Dyer's record is – by saying that there was no question of undue severity : if his means had been greater the casualties would have been greater, and that his intention was to teach a moral lesson to the whole of the Punjab, I say without hesitation, and I would ask the committee to contradict me if I am wrong, that it is the doctrine of terrorism. I would say further that when you pass an order that all Indians, whoever they may be, must crawl past a particular place, when you pass an order that all Indians, whoever they may be, must forcibly or voluntarily salaam an officer of His Majesty the King, you are enforcing racial humiliation. I say, thirdly, that when you take selected schoolboys from a school, guilty or innocent, and whip them publicly, when you put up a triangle, where an outrage which we all deplore and all India deplores has taken place, and whip people who have not been convicted, when you flog a wedding party, you are indulging in frightfulness and there is no other adjective which could describe it.'

And later in the debate Winston Churchill expressed himself in the same sense :

'. . . one tremendous fact stands out – I mean the slaughter of nearly 400 persons and the injury of probably three or four times as many at the Jallianwallah Bagh on the 13th April. That is an episode which appears to me to be without precedent in the modern history of the British Empire.'

These speeches made no appeal to the Conservative back-benchers. Their leading spokesman was Sir William Joynson-Hicks, later to become the Home Secretary in a Conservative Government. Referring to Montagu, he said :

'The speech which he has made this afternoon will have utterly destroyed any little shred of confidence which was left to him, not merely in the minds of the Indian Civil Servants, but in the minds of the British Army in India.'

And later he added :

'He asks whether there was anybody in this House who was prepared to say that General Dyer was right. I am. I am prepared to say so. I am backed up in this opinion by 80% of the Indian civilians and by 90% of the European population.'

In the Division Lobby the Government obtained 230 votes. But 129 Members supported Joynson-Hicks. Nothing could thereafter abate the hatred of Montagu on the Conservative back-benches. In March 1922, as will afterwards appear, he was compelled to resign. The Conservatives were delirious with joy.

The House of Lords took a different view. On 19th July, Viscount Finlay proposed a motion deploring the conduct of the case of General Dyer as 'unjust to the officer and as establishing a precedent dangerous to the preservation of order in the face of rebellion'. The first Government spokesman was Lord Sinha, himself an Indian, who was Under-Secretary of State for India. He emphasized that the crowd were unarmed and listening to a lecture, and included a large number of outsiders who were not even aware of the proclamation against public gatherings. Lord Birkenhead emphasized that General Dyer had directed that the fire should be concentrated where the numbers were thickest of those who were trying to escape. He demanded could anyone defend that, and he went on to quote from General Dyer's evidence, 'If I had had more weapons there would have been more casualties'.

This made no impression on the Conservative peers. Lord Hines delivered a savage attack on Gandhi as 'the responsible author of all these riots, all this agitation, all the violence and all the murders – not directly, I admit, but indirectly unquestionably'. Lord Ampthill declared : 'Let me say at once that I believe General Dyer was absolutely right in what he did, and I am among those who regard him with gratitude and admiration.' And Lord Salisbury declared in unmistakable terms the attitude of himself and his Conservative colleagues :

"The issue your Lordships are going to try tonight is whether, when officers who knew best the positions of great difficulty (and positions in which, if they had not done their duty, the most formidable consequences would have ensued) they are to be supported by the Government or not. That is the real issue. If you do not support this motion you will strike a great blow at the confidence of the whole body of officers throughout our Empire whose business it is to defend the cause of law and order and maintain your Government.'

Lord Finlay's motion was carried by 129 to 86. Nothing could more clearly reveal the fundamental differences between the parties. As nearly always happens – and there have been many other examples before and since – Conservatives stood for authority, Liberals for human rights. Between the two there could never be any lasting compromise. On this occasion it was clear that Coalition had not obliterated these fundamental differences. The Liberals, including Coalition Liberals, were appalled at the massacre. Conservatives were shocked by the treatment of General Dyer.

This was the beginning of the growing fissure, which was to culminate at the Carlton Club meeting between Conservative Ministers and the Parliamentary rank and file.

Even so, the end was by no means inevitable. In May 1921 an event took place which probably determined the fate of the Coalition. Owing to ill health Bonar Law resigned his post as Chancellor of the Exchequer. His doctor had found that he was suffering from dangerously high blood pressure and ordered him to take a complete rest for several months. Thus ended one of the most successful partnerships in political history.

It would be difficult to imagine two more sharply contrasted characters than Lloyd George and Bonar Law. Lloyd George was exuberant, mercurial, imaginative and possessed of immense vitality. Bonar Law was reserved, melancholy and cautious but endowed with the gift of judgment. In 1912, after Balfour's resignation, he became Conservative Leader as a compromise candidate. The two leading rivals were Austen Chamberlain and Walter Long. Neither of them would give way to the other, and their supporters were equally inflexible. Eventually, therefore, the parties settled for Bonar Law. Lloyd George's comment was 'the fools have chosen their best man by accident'. In 1916 it was Bonar Law who played the leading part in bringing about the fall of Asquith and making possible the accession of Lloyd George.

In his biography *The Unknown Prime Minister*[1], Mr Robert (now Lord) Blake has fully described how close was the understanding between them. On one occasion Bonar Law described his work in the war as 'hanging on to the coat-tails of the Little Man (Lloyd George) and holding him back'. As Chancellor of the Exchequer from 1916 onwards Bonar Law occupied 11 Downing Street. Every morning Lloyd George walked along the corridors between the two houses. They would be closeted together for an hour or more. Lord Blake quotes the words of Dr Thomas Jones, who as a member of a Cabinet secretariat, had every opportunity to observe the relations between the two men :

> For over four years the one never took an important step without conferring with the other, and to compute the contribution of Bonar Law to the partnership, it would be necessary to know not only the policies and projects as the sanguine quality which he approved, but also those which he resisted, modified or defeated. That colleague has placed on record his sense of the value of Bonar Law's searching criticism and his real courage when together they were responsible for the momentous decisions of the European war.

This was not all. Bonar Law was a highly successful leader of the House. One of the causes of the eventual breakdown was the gulf between the Conservative leaders notably Austen Chamberlain and Birkenhead, and the rank and file in the House of Commons. It may be surmised that, if Bonar Law had remained, such a gulf would never have developed. It is, of course, just possible that he might have broken with Lloyd George before the end. But it is highly unlikely. Like the others he would have remained under the spell.

Bonar Law had gone. Yet Lloyd George still remained as the head of a brilliant team. Above all, it included Birkenhead and Winston Churchill. They were close friends. Their association in 1922 has been described by Amery :[2]

---

[1] *Eyre & Spottiswoode,* 1955.
[2] *My Political Life* : Hutchinson, 1953.

Of the personal relationships which affected the situation the dominating one was the close association between Churchill and Birkenhead. They had long been intimate friends, personally even when most strongly divided in public affairs. Carson's 'Galloper' Smith and the Minister were prepared, if need be, to sacrifice Carson's Ulstermen by force, were also messmates as officers of the Oxfordshire Hussars, both were young, had already gone far, and meant to go further. Both were, in the better sense of the word, political adventurers, fundamentally patriotic and public-spirited, not unwilling to throw themselves into any fray in which they might distinguish themselves and win promotion. Both had a rare gift of eloquence; in Birkenhead's case vividly fluent; in Churchill's case diligently studied and continually maturing. Birkenhead had the more brilliant mind, but Churchill's was the stronger character.

Almost throughout its career the Coalition Government, like other British Governments before and since, was hag-ridden by the problems of Ireland. The pattern was always the same. On the one side was the gunman supported by a large section of the population. On the other were the police and soldiers, sometimes provoked almost beyond endurance. Nineteenth-century Governments, including Liberal Governments, had been constrained to resort, however reluctantly, to coercion. Mr Gladstone had declared that, 'The resources of civilization are not yet exhausted', and had interned Parnell. He later entered into the Kilmainham Treaty. A similar problem arose from 1919 onwards. The report from the press might almost be repeated verbatim in recent months. Thus, on 3rd May 1920, the *Morning Post* reported:

> The week-end activities of Irish rebels include attacks with firearms on soldiers and police, attempts at deliberate murder and barrack-burning.

On 4th May the headline was 'The Surrender to Sinn Fein', and on the 11th they reported the murders of two sergeants and two constables killed by bullets fired by assassins in hiding. On the 19th they recorded the setting-up of a rebel 'court' in Dublin.

The Government recruited the Black and Tans, a special force so described because of their uniforms. As has happened on other occasions, they resorted to reprisals against the civilian population[1] regardless as to whether the victims had any responsibility for acts of violence. Mr Asquith, with unwonted indignation, denounced 'the hellish policy of reprisals'.

Yet a settlement was reached, and in December at Downing Street took place the meeting between the Coalition Ministers and the Irish

[1] e.g., against the Arabs in Palestine during the thirties.

Delegation, headed by Michael Collins and Arthur Griffith. By one of the ironies of history it would appear that the man who exercised the greatest influence with the Irish delegates was Lord Birkenhead – the former 'Galloper' Smith. Nevertheless this was a supreme example of Lloyd George's wizardry. Differences which were apparently insuperable were reconciled. The Treaty was signed and it appeared as if three hundred years of Anglo-Irish differences had been brought to an end.

Nevertheless the breach was widened between the Government and the Right Wing of the Conservative Party. The latter believed that the Treaty was a disgraceful surrender. Their attitude was expressed by the *Morning Post*. One of the most influential figures in Conservative politics was Sir Archibald Salvidge. He exercised enormous influence in Liverpool. He always held the strongest views on Ireland. Birkenhead, the Lord Chancellor, made a secret visit to Liverpool and met him at the Adelphi Hotel. Salvidge was persuaded. A few days later the hoardings and sandwich boards of Liverpool were plastered with a caption from the *Morning Post* – 'Salvidging Ulster'. The Conservative Party were with difficulty persuaded to accept the Treaty, and it was approved by substantial majorities in both Houses. Nevertheless the sense of betrayal remained and was fanned by later events. This was one of the contributory causes of the decision at the Carlton Club.

This then was the situation at the end of 1921. The Coalition was still predominant. Lloyd George remained the principal figure on the world scene. He had an outstanding team to support him. The Government had a considerable record of achievement. The Labour Party had not yet presented a credible alternative. The Liberal impulse, arising from Asquith's return at Paisley, seemed to have petered out. The principal issue throughout the year had been the Irish settlement. The Government had achieved, as it seemed, a spectacular triumph. Irish problems, however acute, had been shunted from Westminster to Dublin, and British electors, in so far as they were conscious of Ireland, breathed a sigh of relief. On the face of it the Coalition was riding high.

In these circumstances, Lloyd George toyed with the prospect of a General Election. Lord Beaverbrook has described a dinner party at Lord Birkenhead's house at the end of 1921. The guests were Lloyd George, Austen Chamberlain, Winston Churchill, T. G. Macnamara, Charles McCurdy, Sir Archibald Salvidge, Sir Llaming Worthington-Evans and Lord Beaverbrook. McCurdy was the Coalition Liberal Whip. He opened a discussion with a clear account of the reasons in favour of an immediate election. Lloyd George followed in the same sense. But Austen Chamberlain was opposed. Churchill was indecisive and Birkenhead expressed no opinion. The decision was postponed.

Lloyd George proceeded to Cannes, where there was an Allied conference. He was joined by Churchill, Sir Robert Horne, Worthington-Evans and Beaverbrook. The discussion was resumed at the Villa Valetta. Once again, opinions were divided. Churchill was uncertain. At this time he was almost fanatically anti-Bolshevik and he sought an assurance that in the next Parliament there would be an embargo against any traffic, political or economic, with the Russians. Lord Beaverbrook pursued his theme of imperial preference.

Nevertheless, it appeared that the Prime Minister had made up his mind. On 3rd January, the *Daily Chronicle*, which was the Lloyd George newspaper, announced that when the Prime Minister returned from Cannes he would advise the King to dissolve Parliament. On the following day the *Pall Mall Gazette* published a story that the Prime Minister's personal friends were preparing for a short and sharp campaign in which the great issues would be Ireland, the Washington Conference and national economy.

Now, however, there emerged upon the scene the figure of Sir George Younger. He was a brewer, a Scottish Unionist Member of Parliament and the Manager of the Conservative Party. He had one concern – to restore the powers of the House of Lords. A scheme had already been adumbrated. The Upper House was to be reduced in numbers but to be given an effective veto. In other words, the Parliament Act of 1914 which had marked the great Liberal victory over the Lords, was to be set aside. Until this was achieved, he was opposed to an election.

On 4th January, Younger wrote to the Prime Minister opposing a dissolution on the ground that there was no impending crisis. He warned that if an election were held, many Conservatives would not stand as Coalitionists but as independent Unionists. On the same day his views were made public. He gave an interview to the *Evening News*, intimating that if the General Election took place before the House of Lords were reformed, he and many of his friends would go to the country as Conservatives and not as Coalitionists. Then he sent all Conservative Associations a statement opposing an election. This was the beginning of the split between the Conservative leaders and the rank and file which, nine months later, was to destroy the Coalition.

At the end of January, there were two Liberal demonstrations, each held in the Queen's Hall. The Coalition Liberals held their meeting on Saturday, the 23rd, the Free Liberals on the following Monday. In each case the hall, which can take an audience of approximately three thousand was packed to capacity. At the Saturday meeting a resolution was moved congratulating the Government on its achievements. It was seconded by the Reverend Dr J. H. Shakespeare, D.D., who was at the time the outstanding leader of the Baptist community. He said that they frankly recognised that in the Irish settlement the Coalition Unionists had played the game; but that settlement had been brought about by one man alone – Lloyd George 'one of the most undauntable, gallant and wonderful figures in the history of the world'.

The Prime Minister embarked on a spirited defence of the Government's whole record. He emphasized in particular the Irish settlement. He could not, however, resist a dig at Asquith. Referring to one of Asquith's recent speeches, he said : 'Mr Asquith does not like us. It was a speech in parts very amusing – unconsciously [laughter]. As far as I can see the complaint is not that we are not doing the right things but that he would have done them three years ago. This is just like him. He was always prompt. He was always ahead of things. No wait and see about the matter [laughter]. Three years before anyone else thought of a thing he did it. The nation evidently could not keep up with his provident energy.'

The Free Liberals gathered in the same hall on Monday. It was for them a very special occasion. They had rejoiced enormously when Asquith had been returned at Paisley. 1916 had been avenged. They had expected the great Liberal Leader to reassert his supreme mastery, especially in the House of Commons. It had not happened. Except on Ireland, when he had denounced the Black and Tans, he had delivered no full-blooded attack on the Coalition. His attendance in Parliament had been perfunctory and the day to day (or night to night) leadership was still left to Sir Donald Maclean. So no one was certain how he would perform at this meeting.

The other principal speaker was Lord Grey. He was the Foreign Secretary who had taken Britain into the war. His reputation stood very high indeed. But he had been British Ambassador in Washington for the last two and a half years and therefore out of politics. This was his first speech since his return.

No-one was quite sure how the evening would go. The Liberal organisers had their misgivings. Perhaps Asquith would fail to attack. Grey had become an unknown quantity. So they laid on a third speaker – Lord Buckmaster. He was generally regarded as the outstanding Liberal orator of his day. If Asquith faltered and Grey had nothing of consequence to say, Buckmaster could be relied upon to redeem the occasion.

Lloyd George with his daughter Megan in November 1928

Philip Snowden, Chancellor of the Exchequer, on Labour's first Budget Day, 14th April 1930, standing on the steps of No. 11 with the despatch box

(*Left*) Ramsay MacDonald and his family in December 1907 and (*right*) Ramsay MacDonald leaving No. 10 to see the King on 23rd August 1931

Stanley Baldwin with Sir Austen Chamberlain leaving after the Conservative Party Meeting to discuss party policy at Caxton Hall, Westminster in June 1930

Herbert Samuel with Dr Benesh of Czechoslovakia and Norman Davis of the USA at the Geneva Disarmament Conference

In the event, the precaution proved unnecessary. The meeting was an immense success. Asquith re-asserted all his old mastery. In particular the audience cheered his reference to Lloyd George : 'I am too old and perhaps too disillusioned to look for anything like gratitude in politics, nor unhappily is it possible to teach some people good taste and good manners.'

Grey followed. He did so with dramatic effect. Not only did his speech mark his re-entry on the political scene. He was partially blind, and twice during his speech he paused and there was silence while he adjusted his spectacles and peered at his notes. This added greatly to the effect. He too made an all-out attack on the Government and the Prime Minister, especially in relation to foreign affairs. The Attorney General, Sir Gordon Hewart, had invoked the 18th-century parrot-cry 'Measures not Men'. Lord Grey commented :

'But the colleagues of the Attorney General have spoken quite differently. They spoke not so much of the measures as of the man – the one man, the only man, or as Mr Austen Chamberlain says, the same man. He says that it is such an advantage that in international matters we are always represented by the same man. The same man representing from time to time the same policy, and that policy a good policy, is good. The same man representing from time to time a bad policy is unfortunate. How unfortunate depends upon the nature of the policy. The same man from time to time representing a different policy is altogether bad.'

The Liberals were ecstatic. They had heard two superb speeches. There was no need for Lord Buckmaster to redeem the situation and, wisely, he confined himself to a few words of appreciation. Two days later in the *Nation* Massingham wrote as follows :

> The meeting was by all accounts wonderful. Not a six penny worth of expense was paid to any delegate or attendant; nevertheless men and women came hundreds of miles to see and hear; and their response to Mr Asquith and to Lord Grey recall something of the Gladstonian hero-worship; but Lord Grey's dramatic reappearance, the unusual power of his criticism and the response to it minds long given over to rather despairing years of politics have made him the 'Man of the Hour'.

The writer went on to refer to the possibility of a Grey Government. This indeed, was widely canvassed. On 29th January, the *Sunday Pictorial* published a feature article 'Lord Grey as Premier'. Mr Lovat Fraser wrote :

> There are a dozen men who could fill the office of Prime Minister

with competence and dignity and foremost among them is Viscount Grey of Fallodon whose reappearance in politics has made a deep impression.

In February there were three by-elections. Those were the days, before Gallup Polls, when by-elections were the only test of public opinion. On 20th February it was announced that Labour had won a sensational victory at Clayton with a turnover of 8,000 votes. At the General Election the Coalition majority had been 4,631. This was transformed into a Labour majority of 3,642.

On the following day the result was announced in North Camberwell. The Labour candidate, Mr C. G. Ammon who had been bottom of the poll in 1918, was now returned with a majority of over 1,000.

Finally there was the contest in the Bodmin Division of Cornwall. Eighty per cent of the electors went to the polls. At the General Election Sir Charles Hanson, a former Lord Mayor of London, had received 12,288 votes as against 8,705 cast for his Liberal opponent, Isaac Foot. The turnover, by the standards of those days, was sensational. The result was announced at Liskeard :

    Isaac Foot – Liberal   13,751
    Major-General Sir Frederick Pool (Coalition Unionist) 10,610

This was the beginning of the end. A leading article in *The Times* stated : 'The issue is : do the electors wish this discredited, vacillating and hesitating administration to remain in office?'

The tide of by-election reverses continued. In March there was a contest in Inverness. At the General Election the Coalition Liberal candidate had secured a majority of over 5,000 against the nominee of the Highland Land League. Now there was a fight between a Coalition Liberal and an Independent Liberal. The Coalitionist succeeded by the narrow margin of 316. The lesson was the same as at Clayton, North Camberwell and Bodmin.

The battle within the Conservative Party continued. No-one could doubt the growing restiveness of the rank and file. But the leaders – at this stage without exception – remained loyal to the Prime Minister. On 23rd February at the Junior Carlton Club, Lord Birkenhead stated what came to be known as the Cabin Boy speech :

'We are told that the time has come – and I will make no complaint if some of you agree with this view – to dissolve the Coalition and that the time has come when the Conservative Party should make an independent appeal to the electorate. I am going to allow myself the freedom of very great plainness of speech on this question. Just as I took no offence at all when some of my friends cheered the proposal that the Conservative Party should make an independent speech [sic] so equally they may exhibit no offence if I state my own view and the conduct which I propose to adhere to whoever else adheres to it. I take the view that that is a course of insanity, and so far as I know there is no responsible Unionist leader in the Government or out of it who takes a different view. In these circumstances I am not one of those who, when the tempest rages, and when the captain would naturally be on the bridge, would give any particular encouragement to the cabin boy who seizes the helm and I am more than ever of that opinion when the cabin boy has announced that he does not intend to make another voyage.'

This speech was not well received by the Conservative rank and file.

On 3rd March Austen Chamberlain made a speech at Oxford. He disclosed that the Prime Minister had offered to resign in favour of himself or some other Conservative leader. He then stated that he had consulted his colleagues and they had unanimously replied 'Mr Lloyd George'. They thought the national interest and even the interest of their own Party would not be served but would be injured by the Prime Minister's resignation.

On the following day at Loughborough Churchill declared :

'I submit that the Coalition is deserving of hearty support. It is a very good Government though I say it as shouldn't. I go further and say that it is the best Government I have ever seen.'

Finally, and most surprisingly, there was Baldwin. On 18th March he followed Lord Derby in a meeting at the Junior Carlton Club. He rallied to the defence of Lloyd George :

'I deprecate very much the indulgence in wholesale abuse and attributing to him everything which goes wrong . . . We were glad enough to join with him in 1918 . . . and there are a large number of Tories in the House of Commons today who would never have been there if they had not had the Lloyd George token in 1918.'

If ever they had to dissolve partnership with the Coalition Liberals Mr Baldwin hoped that they would 'part as gentlemen'. It is strange that this speech has never been referred to by Baldwin's biographers or, indeed, by any of the historians of the last days of the Coalition.

A few days earlier there had taken place the Montagu resignation. Ever since the Amritsar debate, the Conservative back-benchers had hated Montagu. According to an account in the *Manchester Guardian*, quoted by Dr Trevor Wilson, Montagu-baiting became a regular sport. Their 'bitterest and most cruel personal attacks' were accompanied by deep-throated and sustained outbursts of cheering from the Conservative back-benchers and the derisive shouts of 'Resign', 'Bring him out' and 'Shame on him'.

At the beginning of March the Government of India addressed a despatch to Montagu as Secretary of State. In the strongest terms they emphasized 'intensity of feeling in India regarding the necessity for a revision of the Sèvres Treaty' with particular reference to the freedom of the Straits, the future of Constantinople and the entitlement of the holy places. Without consulting any of his colleagues, and on his own responsibility, Montagu published the despatch and it duly appeared in the press. This was regarded as a gross breach of Cabinet responsibility. Montagu was required to resign. When Austen Chamberlain announced the resignation in the House of Commons on 19th March, the Conservative back-benchers were 'delirious with joy'. Now was the time, they said, to get rid of Fisher and Shortt (the Home Secretary). Montagu hit back in a speech at Cambridge two days later :

'An accusation of a breach of the doctrine of Cabinet responsibility from the Prime Minister, of all men in the world, is a laughable accusation. It is grotesque. What are the circumstances? The head of the Government at the present moment is a Prime Minister of great eccentric genius whose contribution to the well-being of his country and of the world have been so well advertised as to require no "*words*" from me. Whose achievements are so well known, but who has demanded the price which is within the power of every genius to demand – and that price has been the total, complete and absolute disappearance of Cabinet responsibility ever since he formed his Government.'

Lloyd George's main concern was with the pacification of Europe. Unemployment in Britain had risen to the two million mark. It was clear to him that, since Britain was primarily a trading nation, the stability of European markets was a matter of the greatest concern, and in particular he wished to bring Russia back into the comity of nations. It was with these ends in view that he attended the Conference at Cannes in January and Genoa in April. The result in each case was little short of disastrous.

It was at Cannes that he persuaded the French Prime Minister, M. Briand, and the Italian Prime Minister, Signor Bonomi, to play golf. Neither of them had ever touched a golf club before. An observer commented that nothing on the music-hall stage had ever equalled this performance. That evening Lloyd George and Briand had a long conversation. They reached complete accord, but they had reckoned without the French press. Next day the Paris newspapers contained satirical pictures and reports of M. Briand's performance. The man who could so behave was, they suggested, unfit to represent his country, and there was an angry debate in the Chamber of Deputies. Briand returned to Paris where he was forced to resign and was replaced by Raymond Poincaré. The new Prime Minister was a rigid French Nationalist who never agreed with Lloyd George.

All hopes were centred on the April Conference at Genoa. Lloyd George and Barthou, the French Foreign Minister, attended the Conference. Lloyd George wanted Germany and Russia admitted to the Conference and its committees on equal terms. He asked :

'Is Germany, a nation of 63 million people, and Russia, with 120 million people to be left standing on the doorstep until we call an end?' That is not equality, and such a thing as you suggest cannot be tolerated for one moment.'

Then, however, came shattering news. On Easter Sunday, 16th April, Rathenau for Germany and Chicherin for Russia signed in draft the Treaty of Rapallo whereby Germany recognised the Bolsheviks as the *de jure* Government of Russia. Germany renounced all claims against Russia, but subject to the proviso that Russia should compensate no other claimant. The Genoa Conference continued for some weeks longer, but little or nothing was or could be achieved. Lloyd George was bitterly attacked in the British press, especially by *The Times.*

The Editor of *The Times* was Wickham Steed, and he had been specially despatched to Genoa by Northcliffe. He was given information which was, in fact, untrue regarding a meeting between Lloyd George and Barthou at which Lloyd George was said to have declared that the entente was at an end. Barthou, at Lloyd George's request, read a letter denying that he had ever uttered such words. This may have been the reason why, when Lloyd George returned from Genoa to London, he received a tremendous welcome at Victoria Station comparable to that when he had returned from Versailles.

In the House of Commons only 30 Members, recruited from the extreme Right and the extreme Left, voted against him. Nevertheless the fact remained the Government had in effect nothing to show for all their efforts at Cannes and Genoa.

During the summer of 1922 the main topic of controversy was the sale of honours. This was nothing new. For many years the Liberal and Conservative Parties had augmented their funds from this very source. As early as 1905 the Conservative Honours List had been regarded with suspicion. There was therefore nothing new in the practice of the sale of honours, but under the Coalition the traffic was stepped up beyond all precedent. The top price for a peerage was £150,000. A barony might cost £80,000 and a baronetcy £50,000 and ordinary knighthoods £10,000 to £12,000.

It would appear that by these means Lloyd George accumulated a personal fund (although not, of course, for his private use) of over £3,000,000. The Lloyd George Fund has been frequently referred to by historians and was to become the subject of major controversy within the Liberal Party. There were, however, two funds. If anyone wished to secure an honour he could apply to either the Coalition Liberals or to the Coalition Unionists. Sir George Younger, the Unionist Chief Whip, complained: 'These damned rascals come to me demanding to be made knights and, when I refuse, go straight round to Lloyd George's Whips' Office and get what they want from him.' He always referred to this as 'poaching'.

There is still a considerable mystery about the Conservative Funds. The Treasurer of the Party was Lord Farquhar. Undoubtedly a great deal of money was paid into his account. What happened to it no-one knows. J. C. C. Davidson has recorded[1]:

> What made matters worse was that Lord Farquhar, who at that time was still acting as though he was Treasurer of the Party, had failed mentally and was playing fast and loose with funds which were sub-scribed to the Tory Party and which he was paying into his own bank-ing account.

In particular there was a gift from Lord Astor, who died in 1919. This apparently amounted to £200,000. Farquhar stated to Lord Edmund Talbot that he had given £40,000 to a charity in which the King was interested and divided the rest between Conservative and Coalition Liberal Funds. It appears that no payment was ever made to the Conservative Funds. In January 1923 Lord Farquhar refused to sign a cheque for £20,000 drawn on the Central Office account, for the payment of salaries and bonuses connected with the recent General Election. Apparently he took the view that the money had been given to the Coalition and did not belong to the Conservative Party. Bonar Law expressed the 'strong suspicion' that he had handed sums – perhaps large sums – to Lloyd George for his Party while acting as the Conservative Treasurer. Presumably the truth will never be discovered. On the 30th August 1923, Lord Farquhar died. His will contained a number of lavish bequests to various members of the Royal Family. But all to no

[1] *Memoirs of a Conservative*: Weidenfeld and Nicolson, 1969.

effect. There was no money left in his estate : he was virtually bank-rupt. Lord Beaverbrook has given the following account : [1]

> The Treasurer was dismissed from his office and called to his Fathers all in the space of six months. His fortune had vanished and also his prestige in the West End as a friend of the Royal Family, and in the City as a burning and shining light in finance. Shortly before this call to his Fathers, the new Earl was invited to dinner by Lord Birkenhead. There and then the bolting Tory Ministers, Balfour, Chamberlain and Horne, proposed to Farquhar that they should be regarded as the continuing Tory hierarchy and the Treasurer's funds should be put at their disposal. The plan failed and the truth was – there were no funds. Horace had spent the lot.

The storm broke with the publication of the Birthday Honours in June. In particular it centred on the peerage conferred on Sir Joseph Robinson. He was a South African of shady reputation. There had, how-ever, been no communication with the South African Government. Churchill, as Secretary of State for the Colonies, had not been consulted and was furious. The King shared his anger which he expressed to the Lord Chancellor. Lloyd George instructed Captain Guest, the Coalition Liberal Whip, to inform Sir Joseph that he must decline the honour. Guest and a colleague called on Robinson to convey this message. Robinson was deaf and supposed that they had come to congratulate him. He uncorked a magnum of champagne. Eventually the forbidding tidings were made clear to him and, with great reluctance, he agreed to the course proposed.

This was only one example. The King himself had protested against the Honours List and the Lord Chancellor, Lord Birkenhead, said to Lloyd George : 'I don't want to add to your troubles, but I cannot defend that list of peerages in the House of Lords'. It was only with the utmost reluctance that he consented to do so.

On 17th July there was a debate in both Houses. It was proposed and agreed that there should be a Select Committee to enquire into the honours system. Parliament, however, was less interested in the future than in the past. The revelations were startling. In the House of Lords the Duke of Northumberland quoted from a letter to 'two people living in different parts of England' in identical terms :

> Dear Sir, I am requested to set before you a social matter of a very confidential nature which it is thought may be of interest to you. Will you kindly let me know whether you can suggest a meeting within the

[1] *The Decline and Fall of Lloyd George* : Collins, 1963.

next few days in London or elsewhere? I cannot put more in a letter.
P. S. In case you might care to find out, I am well known to . . . of . . .

Here followed the name of a well-known baronet in the North of
England. The Duke went on to recount how one of the recipients of
this letter had interviewed the baronet who had informed him that it
had emanated from Downing Street that he had mentioned the
recipient's name as being worthy of an honour and he would have to
pay £40,000 for a baronetcy.

One of the gentlemen concerned had an interview with a tout whom
he recorded as saying :

I am authorised to offer you a knighthood or a baronetcy, not of the
Order of the British Empire – no nonsense of that kind – but the real
thing. A knighthood will cost you £12,000 and a baronetcy £35,000.
There was some difficulty in the past through people paying in advance
and failing to receive the honour. This has lately been overcome by
arranging for a deposit in joint names, but on this occasion there will be
no complication of that kind. You will be asked to meet someone in high
authority, probably in Downing Street, and after the introduction, but
not until three or four days before the list is announced, you will be
asked to pay £10,000 or £30,000 as the case may be . . . But you need
not pay the deposit until you are absolutely assured that the honour will
be given. There are only five knighthoods left for the June List – if you
decide upon a baronetcy you may have to wait for the Retirement
List . . . I assure you that all enquiries regarding yourself have been
made and satisfactory interviews received, so that you may be sure
there will be no difficulty. It is unfortunate that the Government must
have money but the Party now in power will have to fight Labour and
socialism which will be an expensive matter.

The Prime Minister agreed to the setting up of a Select Committee
to consider the present methods of submitting names of persons for
honours and to report their changes if any were necessary. He was,
however, opposed to an inquiry into the past. He recalled how similar
charges of trafficking in honours had been made against earlier Governments. Indeed, he described similar debates in 1894, 1908 and 1914. He
quoted a speech from one of these debates :
'The titles and declarations in vogue in this country are distinctions
lacking in dignity, prestige and royal worth, as the methods by which
they are obtained are corrupt and nauseous.'
He went on to state that in the last six years there had been excep-
tionally heavy honours lists in consequence of the war.
Mr Asquith followed. He spoke of the burdens which arose on a

Prime Minister. Of all the arduous duties there were none in his experience 'more thankless, more irksome and more inevitable than the
recommendation of honours to the Crown'. He went on to say :

'But I will say this – and I say it with the utmost emphasis and, I
think I may say, with the clearest conscience – but during the whole of
those years, when my lists of honours were often criticised as being
humdrum and commonplace, studded and even stuffed with medio-
crities, I do not remember a single occasion during the whole of that
time when the name of any person whom I recommended for distinction by the Crown was adversely commented upon on the ground of
unworthiness or of a bad record on the part of the recipient.'

Sir Frederick Banbury from the Conservative back-benches referred
to Lord Vestey who had been ennobled on the ground that he had
'devoted his life to the production and preservation of food supplied by
refrigeration . . . materially helped to cheapen the food supply of the
people, rendered immense services during the war to the country and
provided, gratuitously, a whole cold storage accommodation required
for war purposes at Boulogne and Dunkirk.' Sir Frederick went on to
mention 'in the case of Lord Vestey the curious fact that the great
service he rendered his country by moving his business out of the country,
and evading payment of income tax, super tax and excess profits duty
was not communicated'.

The most damaging speech came from Mr Ronald Macneill. He
referred in particular to the case of Lord Waring. Whether or not he
knew it, Lord Waring was sitting in the gallery. He recalled how, before
the war, Lord Waring was managing director of a large business in
London which went into bankruptcy. The shareholders had suffered a
substantial loss. Then the war came along and Lord Waring made for
himself a very considerable fortune. Why, Mr Macneill enquired, could
anyone imagine why this particular businessman, whose shareholders
had lost large sums of money through misfortune possibly or bad management, while he made a fortune for himself in the war in another
direction, was singled out for this very high honour ?

At this point Lord Waring sitting in the distinguished strangers
gallery interjected : 'That is a false statement.' Mr Macneill continued,
unperturbed. He went on to deal with the case of Sir Archibald Williamson, also recently ennobled. He was the head of the firm of Balfour
Williamson and Company who did business in South America. His
information was that during the war the laxity of this firm in relation
to trading with the enemy was notorious. A statement had been drawn
up in the Foreign Office containing different heads of accusation against

this firm. It had been communicated to the Consulate-General in Chile with the request that they should go through it and see whether they were able to confirm it or not. The statement came back from the Consulate-General confirming what was said and with one or two other items added. It quoted a letter from Sir Archibald Williamson to one of his houses in Chile saying that it was quite unnecessary for them to pay too much attention to the Government Regulations against trading with the enemy as he was in a position to see that they did not get into trouble. A further charge was that this firm was selling fuel oil to certain German nitrate factories in 1915 and 1916.

Mr Macneill speculated as to whether the Law Officers of the Crown had been consulted as to a prosecution. However that might be, he enquired whether it was not strange that this particular gentleman, of whom these facts were known to the Government, should have been singled out among all the honourable Members of the House to be rewarded for his services either to the country or to the Party of which he was a member.

The Select Committee was set up with the eventual result that the traffic in honours for money was brought to an end.

There was no vote in either House. Nevertheless the prestige of the Government was severely diminished. There had been no real answer to the allegations. This remains a strange chapter in political history which has never been fully explained. There can be no doubt that both the Coalition Liberal and Conservative Whips engaged in the sale of honours on an unprecedented scale. How far was this known to their respective leaders? In 1927, Lloyd George stated :

> Honours Lists during my Premiership . . . were prepared by the Chief Whips in the usual way. They were then submitted to the joint leaders of the Coalition, myself and Mr Bonar Law and afterwards Mr Austen Chamberlain, who succeeded him . . . For my part I have no information as to who amongst the persons put forward had or had not subscribed towards the Party funds.

He did not know, or perhaps he did not enquire too closely. Throughout his career he was concerned with ends rather than with means. At the time when the Honours List of 1922 was being prepared, he was almost entirely concerned with foreign affairs. On 23rd March, he had written to Lord Beaverbrook :

> I mean to go wherever the policy of the European pacification leads me. There is nothing else worth fighting for at the present moment.

Office is certainly not worth a struggle apart from what you can accomplish through it. It is the policy that matters and not the Premiership.

When the Birthday Honours List was published Lloyd George was at the abortive Conference at Genoa.

Here then was the situation at the beginning of the Parliamentary Recess. The Coalition Government had suffered one reverse after another. The by-elections at the beginning of the year had given a sombre indication. In the international sphere nothing had been achieved at Cannes and Genoa. Ireland was still not pacified. The Conservative rank and file were obviously disaffected. Yet there was a great division between them and their leaders. So far as Birkenhead, Austen Chamberlain, Balfour and Horne were concerned, they were still under the personal magnetism of Lloyd George, and indeed there was as yet no general revolt.

At the beginning of the year the demand for an election had been resisted by Sir George Younger. He was the keeper of the Unionist conscience. Yet, on the 29th September, he delivered a speech to the Scottish Unionist Association in which he had 'trembled to think what might happen if the Unionists had differences among themselves and if they quarrelled with the friends (i.e., Coalition Liberals) with whom they worked so long'. He trusted 'that they would keep on friendly terms with those with whom we have acted so long, and will form, in that case, a bulwark against the Socialist Party.'

Even so, with all these reverses no-one could be certain that the Coalition would not continue. Lloyd George was still unquestionably the outstanding figure in British politics. As was said at the time by one of his colleagues, 'His name was known in every cottage in the land.' Moreover, he commanded the complete allegiance of almost all his Conservative colleagues in the Cabinet. The only exceptions were the Foreign Secretary, Curzon, who was naturally affronted by Lloyd George's personal management of foreign affairs, and the unknown President of the Board of Trade, Stanley Baldwin, who scarcely ever opened his mouth in Cabinet.

Among the Junior Ministers, however, the feeling was very different. Throughout 1922 there was a rising tide of discontent. Lord Eustace Percy has described 'the curious flavour of disreputability' which haunted the Lloyd George administration. He goes on to say that 'by those whom it offended it was universally ascribed to Lloyd George's personal cookery'. He does not think that this was mainly attributable to the honours scandal, but rather 'that the Civil Service did not feel safe with him'. He refers to the verdict of one of Lloyd George's wartime colleagues who described Lloyd George as 'a very able little man, and in some ways a very wise little man, but he doesn't know how to behave'.

Early in August the discontents of the Conservative Junior Ministers came to a head. They asked to be allowed to meet the whole body of Conservative Cabinet Ministers. There is no complete record of this occasion, and we do not know precisely what grievances were dwelt on by the Junior Ministers. According to Austen Chamberlain they 're-peated their doubts and dislikes'. The principal spokesman for the Government was Lord Birkenhead. According to Amery he began by rating them for their impertinence in having asked for a meeting at all when they had already been informed of Cabinet Ministers' views. He went on 'in the most astonishing arrogant and offensive manner' to lecture them for their silliness and want of loyalty. The Junior Ministers left spluttering with indignation.

The final breach came over the situation in the Middle East. At the end of the war Turkey had been shorn of her empire. She had suffered overwhelming defeat. The most prominent Turkish leaders were exiled to Cyprus, where they developed cordial personal relations with their captors. This made way for the emergence of a hitherto unknown figure, Mustapha Kemal. He led one of the most astonishing national revivals in modern history, and today his picture may be seen in all parts of Turkey. Lloyd George was emotionally and passionately pro-Hellenic. There was no-one whom he more greatly admired than Venizelos.

Churchill has described how, on more than one occasion during these years, he invited Lloyd George to state the foundations of his policy. According to his recollection, Lloyd George replied[1] :

> The Greeks are the people of the future in the Eastern Mediterranean. They are prolific and full of energy. They represent Christian civilization against Turkish barbarism. Their fighting power is grotesquely under-rated by our Generals. A greater Greece will be an invaluable addition to the British Empire. The Greeks by tradition, inclination and interest are friendly to us; they are now a nation of 5 or 6 million and, in 50 years, if they can hold the territories which have been assigned to them, they will be a nation of 20 millions . . .
>
> The Greeks have a strong sense of gratitude, and if we are the staunch friends of Greece at the period of her national expansion, she will become one of the guarantees by which the main intercommunications of the British Empire can be preserved. One day the mouse may gnaw the cords that bind the lion.

[1] *The World Crisis: The Aftermath*: p. 399.

The dream of Greek expansion was soon dispelled. In August the Greek armies suffered overwhelming defeat at the hands of Mustapha Kemal and were literally driven into the sea at Smyrna. There was a small British force at Chanak guarding the zone which had been declared neutral in the Treaty of Sèvres. There appeared to be a grave danger that the victorious Turks would invade Europe. The Government decided to take a strong line and if necessary to call upon the Dominions for military support. The French differed and withdrew. The British Government persisted. On 10th October the Turks agreed to an armistice while the Treaty of Sèvres was re-negotiated.

Whatever the unwisdom of the encouragement which had earlier been given to the Greeks, the Government had acted with courage and resolution. They had countered the threat of a Kemalist invasion of Europe. On the face of it they had achieved a remarkable success. Yet it was this episode which brought about their fall. The explanation may perhaps be found in a letter which Bonar Law addressed to *The Times* on 6th October. It was reprinted in the *Daily Express* on the following day. He supported the Government in its 'decisive warning to the Turks'. If it had not been given they would, in his view, have attempted to enter Constantinople and cross into Thrace with horrors similar to those which had occurred in Anatolia. It was therefore undoubtedly right that the British Government should endeavour to prevent these misfortunes. It was not, however, right that the burden of taking action should fall on the British Empire alone. He ended :

> We cannot alone act as the policemen of the world. The financial and social condition of this country makes that impossible. It seems to me, therefore, that our duty is to say plainly to our French Allies that the position in Constantinople and the Straits is essentially a part of the Peace settlement as the arrangement with Germany, and that if they are not prepared to support us there we shall not be able to bear the burden alone, but shall have no alternative except to imitate the Government of the United States and to restrict our attention to safe-guarding the more immediate interests of the Empire.

This letter, as Lord Blake has stated, was the death knell of the Coalition. It was a declaration for isolationism. Undoubtedly it appealed to the current mood. The British public were tired of foreign adventures. They were not in the least concerned with the position in the Straits. The only question which now remained was whether Bonar Law would return to active politics. The story has often been told, notably by Beaverbrook, of his prolonged hesitation and how at the last

moment he was persuaded (chiefly by his sister) to attend the meeting
at the Carlton Club.

On 15th October the leading Coalition Ministers dined at Churchill's
house. They were contemplating an election under the Coalition banner.
The Chief Whip, Sir Leslie Wilson, was strongly of opinion that the
Government should wait until the Conservative Party Conference at
the end of the month before going to the country. Austen Chamberlain
demurred, and proposed instead to summon a meeting of all Conservative Members of Parliament at the Carlton Club. This was to be held
on 18th October. According to Lord Beaverbrook it was at Lloyd
George's own suggestion that it was postponed until the 19th. A by-
election was taking place at Newport in South Wales. An Independent
Conservative was opposing the official Coalition candidate. It was
generally expected that the split vote might let in the Labour candidate.
Again according to Beaverbrook, Lloyd George calculated that such a
result would have a salutary effect on the Conservative rank and file.
They would have a dramatic warning of the danger of splitting the anti-
Socialist forces.

The day drew near, and with it the emergence of Stanley Baldwin. He is
the supreme enigma of British history between the wars. His public
image, as presented over many years, was that of the antithesis of Lloyd
George. The Welshman had been devious and untrustworthy – so the
legend ran. Baldwin was the epitome of all the English virtues – by no
means clever (always a term of abuse) or imaginative, but wholly
straightforward. John Bull in excelsis! Here was a figure who would
inspire universal trust.

This was a complete misconception. Baldwin was by no means the
plain, blunt character of public imagination. He was a very considerable master of the English language and his speeches, especially on non-
political occasions, are studded with memorable phrases. For example :
'Dictatorship is like a great beech tree. Very splendid to look at, but
nothing grows under it.' He had this in common with Lloyd George –
they were both essentially patriotic. But their patriotism took wholly
different forms. Lloyd George, in his later years, was concerned with
Britain's role in the world. An outstanding example is to be found at the
end of the war in his tenacious and successful resistance to Wilson's
American doctrine of the freedom of the seas. Baldwin, throughout his
career, was profoundly bored with foreign affairs. Due to his earlier
experience in his family firm, he was far more interested in avoiding the
dangers of class war. This was illustrated in one of his most famous

speeches as Prime Minister when he resisted a Private Member's Bill for curbing the Trade Unions with the peroration 'Give peace in our time, O Lord'.

Until October 1922 he was an almost completely unknown figure. When in 1916 Bonar Law became Chancellor of the Exchequer, he was persuaded by J. C. C. Davidson, supported by the Conservative Chief Whip and the Chairman of the Party, to appoint Baldwin as his Parliamentary Private Secretary. According to Wickham Steed this was on the assumption that he was discreet enough to be 'safe' and 'stupid' enough not to intrigue. In 1917 it was proposed to make him Financial Secretary to the Treasury. Bonar Law had his doubts. He was not sure whether Baldwin 'carried enough guns for the job'. Eventually, however, he was persuaded (again by Davidson) to give Baldwin a trial.

In 1919 Baldwin wrote a letter to *The Times*. He referred to the national exhaustion and the gravity of the nation's finances. The wealthy classes had an opportunity of service which would never recur. They should therefore impose upon themselves a voluntary levy. He stated that he had been considering the matter for nearly two years and had estimated his own estate at a total of about £580,000. He had decided to realise 20% of that amount or, say, £150,000 of the new War Loan and present it to the Government for cancellation. The signature was 'F.S.T.'. The letters stood for Financial Secretary to the Treasury. Here is one of the enigmas of Baldwin's career. No doubt this was a magnificent gesture. But, in view of the signature, did he really suppose his identity would go undetected?

In March 1921 he entered the Cabinet as President of the Board of Trade. He made no outstanding contribution to the record of the Government. According to Lloyd George's recollection he hardly ever spoke during Cabinet meetings. In later days he told Lord Eustace Percy how he had sat there as a 'new boy', saying little, but watching what went on, and wondering whether the Government of England 'would ever be clean again'. According to Mr Rhodes James[1] he was highly discontented throughout 1922. Contemptuous references to 'the goat' became more frequent in his conversation and correspondence, and he was responsible for passing on to the *Morning Post* (in relation to the sale of honours) the allegedly Afghan proverb: 'He who lies in the bosom of the goat spends his remaining years plucking out the fleas.' Nevertheless the fact remains: he continued as a member of the Lloyd

[1] In J. C. Davidson: *Memoirs of a Conservative,* edited by Robert Rhodes James, p. 113, Weidenfeld & Nicolson, 1969.

George Cabinet and it is not recorded that he ever expressed a dissentient opinion.

From 9th September Mr and Mrs Baldwin were on holiday at Aix-les-Bains. He returned on 1st October during the height of the Chanak crisis. Mrs Baldwin followed him on 12th October and they met at Victoria. He described how, at a meeting of Unionist Ministers, it had been decided to have the General Election and go to the Country at once under the Lloyd George banner as Coalitionist. He had stated that he for one could not and would not do it; he must be free to stand as a Conservative and he could not serve under Lloyd George again. This would mean that he would drop out of politics altogether. Nevertheless he did not resign. He continued as a member of the Lloyd George Cabinet.

Finally there came the meeting at the Carlton Club. Until the last moment leading Conservative Ministers had clearly expected a favourable result. On the morning in question there was announced the result of the Newport by-election. It was sensational:

Reginald Clarry (Conservative)	13,515
W. J. Bowen (Labour)	11,425
W. Lyndon Moore (Liberal)	8,845

At the General Election the Coalition Liberal had had a majority of 3,846 over Labour. The lesson was unmistakable. *The Times* commented: 'The sensational result declared at 2 a.m. has completely confounded all the prophets. Even those who are closest to the Conservative candidate on Tuesday night were willing to argue that the Labour Party was certain to win. So confident were the Labour Party of victory themselves that I heard Mr Henderson state that he would not be satisfied unless Mr Bowen had a majority of 2,000.' The Coalition was no longer an electoral asset, it was a liability. No-one will ever know how the meeting would have gone if the electors of Newport had voted differently.

Baldwin made the decisive speech. He referred to a letter in *The Times* in which a Conservative peer had described the Prime Minister as 'a very live wire'. He preferred the phrase of the Lord Chancellor – 'a dynamic force', and proceeded as follows:

'A dynamic force is a very terrible thing; it may crush you, but it is not necessarily right.

'It is owing to that dynamic force, and to that remarkable personality, that the Liberal Party, to which he formerly belonged, has been smashed to pieces; and it is my firm conviction that, in time, the same thing will happen to our Party. I do not propose to elaborate, in an assembly like this, the dangers and the perils of that happening. We have already seen, during our association with him in the last four years, a section of our Party hopelessly alienated. I think that, if the present association is continued, and if this meeting agrees that it should be continued, you will see some more breaking up, and I believe the process must go on inevitably until the old Conservative Party is smashed to atoms and lost in ruins.

'I would like to give you just one illustration to show what I mean by the disintegrating influence of a dynamic force. Take Mr Chamberlain and myself. Mr Chamberlain's services to the State are infinitely greater than any that I have been able to render, but we are both men who are giving all we can give to the service of the State; we are both men who are, or who try to be, actuated by principle in our conduct; we are men who, I think, have exactly the same view of the political problems of the day; we are men who, I believe – certainly on my side – have esteem and, perhaps, I may add, affection for each other; but the result of this dynamic force is that we stand here today, he prepared to go into the wilderness if he should be compelled to forsake the Prime Minister, and I prepared to go into the wilderness if I should be compelled to stay with him. If that is the effect of that tremendous personality on two men occupying the position that we do, and related to each other politically in the way that Mr Chamberlain and I are, that process must go on throughout the Party. It was for that reason that I took the stand I did, and put forward the views that I did. I do not know what the majority here or in the country may think about it. I said at the time what I thought was right, and I stick all through to what I believe to be right.'

This was the decisive speech. The meeting voted overwhelmingly against the Coalition and on the same day Lloyd George resigned – never to return to office. Thereafter Baldwin was held up to the public gaze as a supreme example of patent honesty – the antithesis of the devious Lloyd George. It is strange that so few historians or biographers have pointed out the manifest contradiction. At the time when Baldwin made this speech he was still President of the Board of Trade and still a member of the Lloyd George Cabinet. He had never, so far as is known, raised any objection to the Government's policies or conveyed even the mildest protest to the Prime Minister himself. It is worth recording an entry in Lord Hankey's diary[1] for the 21st October. He was attending a Guildhall luncheon:

[1] *The Supreme Command*, 1914-1918: Allen & Unwin, 1961.

While we were awaiting the arrival of the Prince of Wales and I was standing among a group of Cabinet Ministers – Chamberlain, Worthington-Evans and others, Boscawen edged up to me and behaved in an offensively friendly manner. This annoyed me a good deal, because Boscawen, with Baldwin, was the 'Judas' of the Cabinet, who betrayed Chamberlain and Lloyd George at the Carlton Club, and his colleagues were distinctly giving him the cold-shoulder at the Guildhall.

The appellation is not undeserved. Baldwin may, as his biographers state, have been appalled at the 'moral disintegration' which had taken place under Lloyd George. Nevertheless he had continued to serve under his banner without any protest whatsoever until it became expedient to overthrow him.

The Baldwin Government took over. They were, in the words of Lord Birkenhead, 'second-rate brains'[1]. Thus, as Professor Mowat pointed out, the reign of mediocrity began. The pygmies took over

'Called to this task by Dullness,

'Jove and Fate.'

The style of government completely changed. It became wholly un-adventurous. Bonar Law won the General Election with the promise of 'Tranquillity' and Baldwin himself campaigned in 1929 on the slogan of 'Safety First'. Baldwin was governed by one paramount consideration – Lloyd George must never be allowed in office again.

---

[1] Lord Robert Cecil: 'Second-rate brains and second-rate character'.

CHAPTER IV

1931

PARLIAMENT ADJOURNED for the Summer Recess on 31st July 1931. Normally it does not re-assemble until late October. On this occasion, however, everyone in politics foresaw an early recall. The report of the May Committee, advocating swingeing cuts in expenditure and especially in unemployment benefit, was published later the same day. But its main contents were already generally known. Throughout July, there had been talk of a National Government. Only such a Government, it was said, would be strong enough to carry the report into effect.

Labour had been uneasily in office since May 1929. At the General Election they had obtained 288 seats. The Conservatives, with a slightly higher popular vote, numbered 260. The Liberal total was only 59 and was immediately reduced to 58 by the defection of Sir William Jowitt who accepted the office of Attorney General in the Labour Government. They had obtained no less than $5\frac{1}{4}$ million votes as compared with about $8\frac{1}{2}$ millions for each of their opponents and were therefore grossly under-represented. Nevertheless, they held the fate of the Government in their hands. If they all voted together in the same lobby with the Conservatives, they could bring about its downfall. In fact this never happened. They had frequent party meetings presided over by Lloyd George or, in his absence, by Sir Herbert Samuel. Decisions appeared to have been reached. It made no difference. When the division bells rang, some Liberal Members would vote for the Government and some against. There were others who abstained.

But disunity was not confined to the Liberals. Indeed each of the three parties was in a state of extreme disarray. Of course the Government still had its assets. First and greatest was the traditional loyalty of the Trades Unions and of the organised industrial workers throughout the whole country. The other consisted in the personalities of the Prime Minister, the Chancellor of the Exchequer and the Foreign Secretary.

Ramsay MacDonald's reputation has suffered because of his long decline. In the last years of his Premiership (1934–1935) he was a pathetic figure. His powers were obviously failing and his faults of indecision and extreme ambiguity became more apparent every time he stood at the despatch box. The consequence has been that his earlier performance has been in large measure forgotten or under-rated. Some of his colleagues were always critical. But among the Labour rank and file his prestige had been immense. Wherever he went great crowds assembled to hear him. There had been nothing quite comparable in British politics since the days of Gladstone and the Midlothian Campaign.

His physical appearance was immensely impressive. He had a handsome leonine head and a deep melodious voice. Every generality was made to seem profound. To take a single example, in 1927 he addressed a meeting of undergraduates in the Oxford Union Hall. At that time, the University Labour and Liberal Clubs were both extremely active. Each appealed for the support of the politically minded elements in the University. Ramsay MacDonald had a magnificent theme. He quoted the lines of Browning about 'The broken arc' and 'The perfect round'. Liberalism, he said, was 'the broken arc', and Socialism 'the perfect round'. This form of literary allusion was perfectly suited to an undergraduate audience.

MacDonald particularly shone on the great public occasion. He presided in the most admirable manner over the London Naval Conference in 1930 and the first Indian Round Table Conference when it assembled in the Royal Gallery. In the autumn of 1929, he visited the United States and delivered a series of speeches. When they were afterwards published, they were described by *The Manchester Guardian* as 'Of exceptional merit both for form and manner, and, being nearly all extemporary, were really a wonderful tour de force. The attack, vigour and manly diplomacy could scarcely be overpraised.'

By October 1930 the Government were in serious trouble. They were clearly failing to deal with the nation's economic malaise. Unemployment was steadily mounting and had passed the two million figure. The Labour Party's Annual Conference met at Llandudno. There were fierce attacks led by Mosley and Maxton. Nevertheless, the result was a personal triumph for Ramsey MacDonald. Mr McNeill Weir has described the occasion :[1]

The audience awaited his appearance with nervous expectancy. They were excited, thrilled with the thought that the Prime Minister was

[1] *The Tragedy of Ramsay MacDonald* : Secker & Warburg, 1938.

coming to speak to them. That fact gave them recognition and their Movement a national significance. It was for this tremendous occasion that many of them had come to Llandudno from far and near. Now the great moment had arrived. At the psychological instant, he stood before them. His reception was sensational. The great host rose to its feet as one man and shouted a tumultuous welcome.

After the impulsive cheering had ended and the audience had again settled down, it was seen that the face of the Prime Minister was drawn and haggard. It was the face of one stricken with a mortal blow, and the great crowd looked anxiously at the tragic figure. His first words, spoken with deep emotion, gripped the hearts of his audience. 'I am sure,' he said, 'that you will not misunderstand me if I confess to you straight away that, had I listened to my feelings alone, I should not have been here this morning; but we die and men remain, and whatever one's feelings may be, my duty has brought me here'. He continued : 'Yesterday you passed, in language of tender feeling and appropriate appreciation, a resolution regarding what happened on Sunday'. This was a reference to the loss of Lord Thomson and other public servants in an airship disaster :

'I see here men to whom death is an ever-present companion whilst they earn their daily bread – my old friends, the miners. On Sunday, it was not so much the earning of daily bread that made those men face death; it was that magnificent, inherent quality of humanity – the quality of not only acquiring and living and possessing, not only the quality of holding to what they know, but the equality of pioneering, of extending power and personality into the unknown. It is that great quality, my friends, that had driven our forebears over seas never hitherto ploughed by keel of ship, over lands never hitherto marked by the path of human feet, and, at last, we are in the air, and we shall conquer the air as we have conquered the desert and conquered the sea. The Air Service, by the death of Lord Thomson, lost a great and conspicuous servant. Those of us who are human in our hearts and have got all the weaknesses of human hearts – love for fellows, love for beauty, love for lightsomeness – have lost a companion like unto ourselves, whose place will never be filled.'

He paused; there was a murmur of sympathy, and he feelingly added :

'May I, Miss Lawrence, for a moment turn this gathering from a Party gathering into a national one, and take the opportunity of this platform to thank France, the Government of France, and the people of France, for their great helpfulness, for their understanding courtesy, for their wonderful and friendly consideration, and, finally, for the honour they are showing our dead today? France knows how to stand by the side of the mourner.'

Philip Snowden was the complete antithesis to MacDonald. He was a master of lucid and incisive speech. He invariably knew his own mind. In August 1929, he greatly added to his popularity by his conduct at the Hague Reparations Conference. There he appeared in the role of the iron Chancellor, determined to obtain fair treatment for his country. He was a great apostle of orthodox finance. Above all, he was a fanatical free trader.

Thirdly, there was Arthur Henderson at the Foreign Office. He was one of the principal builders of the Labour Party. As Foreign Secretary, he came to be regarded as the great champion of disarmament and the League of Nations. By the end of the 1920s, there was a great public reaction against every form of military exercise. The horrors of the trenches and the seemingly useless slaughter culminating in Passchendaele became the favourite themes of writers and playwrights. It was a mood of pacifism which lasted until the middle 1930s. Its immediate result in British politics was merely to increase the prestige of 'Uncle Arthur'. He was, after all, the Chairman of the Disarmament Conference.

These three leaders still commanded the allegiance of the Labour masses. Nevertheless, a mood of profound discontent prevailed on the Labour back benches. Every month the unemployment figures mounted. The dole queues were a familiar sight in every industrial centre. The unemployed lived on the margin of subsistence. Moreover, unemployment was a far more tragic phenomenon than it is today. A shipyard worker in Jarrow or a jute worker in Dundee was not merely confronted with a few weeks of idleness; he faced the prospect of remaining unemployed for months or even for years. But the Government seemed wholly incapable of solving the problem.

One of the most powerful speeches delivered in the House of Commons in those years came from Oswald Mosley after his resignation. He derided the pitiful efforts of Ministers. Mosley overplayed his hand. He committed the cardinal error of moving a vote of censure at a Party meeting of the Parliamentary Labour Party. This, of course, was heavily defeated. Later he destroyed his own career by seceding from Labour altogether and seeking to create his New Party. But the profound discontent which he expressed was widely echoed both inside and outside the House of Commons.

The Conservatives, albeit for different reasons, were scarcely less unhappy. Mr Baldwin's position as leader was insecure. He had twice led the Party to defeat – in 1923 and in 1929. The slogan of 'Safety First' in the 1929 election had wholly failed to catch the mood of the electorate. Indeed, the general impression of his last administration had been of indolence and torpor. Colonel Moore-Brabazon expressed a widespread feeling when in 1928 he declared from the Conservative Back Benches 'The snores of the Government resound through the country'.

He was probably saved by the attacks of the Press Lords. In 1930 Lord Beaverbrook mounted his 'Empire Crusade' in favour of protection and imperial preference. At a by-election in the safe Conservative seat of South Paddington, an Empire Crusader, sponsored by Lord Beaverbrook, was victorious over the official Conservative candidate. Baldwin reacted more strongly than at any time in his career. He attacked the newspaper proprietors as those 'who wished to exercise power without responsibility – the prerogative of the harlot throughout the ages'. The rival forces confronted each other at another by-election in St Georges, Westminster. On this occasion the official candidate, Mr Duff Cooper, had a majority of 5,710 over the independent Conservative candidate sponsored by the Press Lords. Even so, it was a formidable revolt.

Furthermore, the Conservatives were divided over India. The Round Table Conference on Indian Constitutional Reform met in the Royal Gallery in 1930. What was clearly contemplated was the advance towards responsible Government in India. The Right Wing of the Conservative Party were outraged. They found their spokesman in Winston Churchill. This is one of the strangest episodes in Churchill's career. He had served in India as a subaltern in 1897 and had never returned to that country. At no time did he understand Indian nationalist aspirations. There had been a series of widely publicised meetings in New Delhi between the Viceroy, Lord Irwin (later Lord Halifax), and Mahatma Ghandi. Churchill in a public speech referred to :

'The nauseating and humiliating spectacle of this one-time Inner Temple lawyer, now seditious fakir, striding half naked up the steps of the Viceroy's Palace, there to negotiate and to parley on equal terms with the representative of the King-Emperor.'

There is no doubt that these sentiments made a wide appeal to the Conservative rank and file. In the circumstances of those days, it may have been fortunate for Baldwin that the malcontents were led by this particular leader. In the early 1930s Churchill was still widely mistrusted by members of all Parties. He had twice changed his allegiance and this was not lightly forgiven. It was still true, as was said of him by the Tory leaders in 1916, that 'There is no man in the country who has more admirers and fewer followers'.

Thee Liberal dilemma grew ever more agonizing. Under the inspiration of Lloyd George and the guidance of Keynes, they had conducted the most intelligent and imaginative election campaign of modern times. They proposed to solve the problems of industrial stagnation and mass unemployment by a programme of great public works. It was distinctly similar to Franklin Roosevelt's New Deal in the United States during the 1930s. Looking back, everyone must regret that it failed. In the result, it attracted an extra 2,000,000 votes to the former Liberal total. But the British electoral system of single-Member constituencies is heavily weighted against third Parties. Only 58 Liberal Members were returned.

The 58 could never feel secure. Their general standard of ability was almost certainly higher than in either of the other Parties. Moreover, they were, for the most part, dedicated to public life. But outside the Celtic fringe they had no secure electoral base. They could not expect to repeat the whirlwind campaign of 1929 and, as the by-elections increasingly showed, an immediate General Election would be disastrous. In personal terms this would be a more serious matter than in either of the other Parties. A young aspiring Conservative or Labour politician need not have despaired if he lost his seat; there was always a good chance that he would be returned at a by-election or be selected for some safe constituency. No such prospect existed in the Liberal Party; a Member who was defeated at the polls might well anticipate permanent eclipse. The Liberals, therefore, had every reason to maintain the Labour Government in office sooner than risk a General Election.

There was, however, another and more important consideration. The Conservatives, urged on by the Press Lords, were once more committed to introduce protection. To Liberals free trade was the ark of the covenant. Every Liberal had been brought up to regard the repeal of the Corn Laws as one of the great milestones in British history. In 1906 they had achieved a record electoral landslide mainly on the issue of free trade versus protection. In 1923 they had resisted Baldwin's tariff proposals and had raised their numbers in the House of Commons to over 150. The folly of tariffs and the sheer iniquity of 'Food Taxes' (i.e., duties on imported food stuff) had been a major theme of Liberal speeches of many generations. Before the First World War, Liberal children had been taught to sing :

> Tariff Reform is on the run,
> On the run, on the run,
> Tariff Reform in on the run
> And so is the Referendum ...
>
> Tariff Reform means work for all
> Work for all, work all,
> Tariff Reform means work for all
> Chopping up sticks in the workhouse.

But now the protectionist enemy was once more at the gate – more formidable than at any time since 1846. Liberal views on free trade were shared by many Labour Ministers and especially by the Chancellor of the Exchequer, Philip Snowden. So here again, was a compelling reason for maintaining Labour in office.

At the beginning of the Parliament, the Liberal leaders were by no means uncritical of the Government. This became apparent when, in December 1929 the Government introduced a Bill to provide for the future of the coal industry. This in particular provided for production quotas for each pit; a system wholly offensive to Liberal ideas of free enterprise. The Bill was attacked on its second reading both by Herbert Samuel and by Lloyd George, and the Party decision was to vote against it. But when the division was called the Government survived by a majority of 8. Two Liberals voted in favour of the Bill and twelve abstained or were absent unpaired. From this moment it was apparent that the Liberal leaders could not rely on their flock to overthrow the Government. The alternative was to seek an accommodation : and this they proceeded to do. The basis was to be electoral reform. Ever since 1918 the Liberals have suffered from a perpetual grievance. Owing to the electoral system they are forever under-represented. The Labour Government were not prepared to introduce proportional representation as the Liberals desired. But they brought in a Bill providing for the alternative vote in single-Member constituencies. This passed the House of Commons and had reached the House of Lords before the dissolution came in September 1931. In effect, the Liberals were continuing to maintain the Government in office in return for electoral reform.

But they were by no means unanimous. Even more than their larger rivals the Liberals were a party of conflicting personalities. Lloyd George was still at the height of his powers. His vitality, his wit and his extra-ordinary gift of pictorial speech had in no way abated. Indeed the speeches which he delivered inside and outside Parliament, between 1929 and 1931, were some of the most brilliant of his whole career. But his outstanding quality (as has already been observed in the second chapter of this book) was single-mindedness. He never lost himself, as do many politicians, in the day-to-day conduct of affairs. There was always one supreme objective. In 1916, it had been to win the war. Now it was to attack deflation and unemployment by great schemes of national development. He had not abandoned his election programme. Indeed he continued to urge it upon the Government and if, as very nearly happened, there had been a Labour/Liberal coalition in the summer of 1931, he would have sought to carry it into effect.

The Deputy Leader was Herbert Samuel. He was an urbane cultivated Jew and no-one can doubt his intellectual qualities. His prestige was remarkably high. He had administered the Palestine Mandate with a considerable measure of apparent success. He had presided over the Royal Commission on the Mines. It was his formula which had led to the settlement of the General Strike. In the two years preceding the election he had delivered a series of outstanding public speeches. But he was the complete opposite of Lloyd George. He had none of Lloyd George's panache or instinctive grasp of the essential issues. Indeed, he did nothing by instinct; everything was rationalised. From this contrast of temperaments it followed that, although for a time they worked closely together, they were never much in sympathy. This became increasingly apparent in succeeding years. A remark of Lloyd George's obtained wide circulation in political circles : 'When they circumcised Herbert Samuel they threw away the wrong bit !'

There were two remaining figures with established reputations – Sir John Simon and Walter Runciman. Simon was a strange and little understood figure. He was an immensely successful lawyer and he brought to politics the qualities which make for success at the Bar. He was physically strong; he could work all night; he could master the most complicated brief in an incredibly short space of time; and he had the gift of apparently lucid analysis. Every problem, no matter how complex, could be made to appear almost unbelievably simple. This is the art of the advocate. But it is not always a successful technique in politics.

He had, moreover, one characteristic which was, to say the least, unfortunate. He was, not by choice, but by temperament, an essentially lonely figure. He was incapable of easy communication with his fellow human beings.[1] This was not by his own wish. On the contrary, his attempts at cameraderie were something of a by-word. It was frequently

---

[1] J. C. C. Davidson wrote in 1923 in a letter to Lord Stamfordham: '. . . nor has Sir John Simon in any way altered the reputation for coldness and inhumanity which he has earned on all sides.'

repeated of him in the Temple that one day he would pass you by without a glance. Next day he would seize you warmly by the arm and call you by the wrong christian name. It is said that during the 1930s he besought his colleagues to address him as Jack. Only Mr J. H. Thomas could bring himself to comply.

A Liberal Member of Parliament who had known him for years summed him up. He said : 'Every night John Simon kneels by his bedside and prays "Oh Lord make me a good fellow".' It was the one prayer which was never granted. He appeared remote and Olympian. He was in fact an extremely sensitive man. During the first war he had suffered a traumatic experience. In 1916, he and other Liberal Ministers had threatened to resign their offices if conscription were introduced. The others, including Walter Runciman, were induced to withdraw their resignations. Simon alone persisted and led a small body of Members into the Lobby against compulsory service. He then returned for a time to his practice in the Temple.

The English Bar is a unique profession. London barristers work, lunch, dine and congregate together in the four Inns of Court. There can be no parallel to the degree of physical proximity in which they live. For the most part this is a pleasant and welcome association. It can, however, be the reverse. At this time, feeling about the conduct of the war was running extremely high. Simon was left in no doubt that the action was intensively unpopular, not only with the general public, but among his own profession. After a few months he accepted a commission in the Army.

These matters cannot be proved. But it may well have been, this experience which affected the whole of his later career. Very few martyrs are prepared to encounter the faggots a second time. Now he had to face another reverse. He had been Chairman of the Indian Royal Comcission. For two years he had sacrificed his profession and devoted himself entirely to the problems of India. He and his fellow Commissioners had travelled throughout the sub-Continent. They had listened to a variety of witnesses and they had produced a monumental report. Any man might have regarded this as the principal achievement of his whole career. Then the cruel stroke fell. The Labour Government decided to summon the Indian Constitutional Conference. It met in the Royal Gallery in November 1930 to consider future advances towards responsible government. The Simon Report was almost completely ignored. Its recommendations were treated as being already out of date. Although all three British political Parties were represented at the Conference, Simon himself was not offered a seat at the table.

Walter Runciman was until 1931 the epitome of Right-Wing Liberalism. He was the spiritual heir of the Victorian industrialists who had brought about the repeal of the Corn Laws but bitterly opposed the social reforms of Lord Shaftesbury. He was himself a millionaire and chairman of a shipping line founded by his father. The Liberal slogan in Gladstonian days had been 'Peace, Retrenchment and Reform'. Runciman was never prominent as a reformer but he strongly believed in retrenchment. It was the profound conviction of himself and his friends that most State expenditure was wasteful and unnecessary and that the national budget could and should be substantially pruned.

All his life he had been a dedicated free trader. He was also a leading advocate of temperance. A Liberal colleague once remarked, 'Runciman's politics are extremely simple. He is a ship owner and therefore he supports free trade. He is the director of several insurance companies and believes in temperance because he wants the working man, instead of spending his wages on beer, to save them up and put them into an insurance policy.'

He profoundly distrusted Lloyd George, with whom he had nothing in common. The social reforms of pre-war days and the Keynesian programme of 1929 made no appeal to him whatsoever. Since the General Election he had rarely attended the House of Commons and concentrated almost wholly upon his business interests.

Among Liberal back benchers there were two who were to play a considerable part during the summer months. One was Ernest Brown. The other was Leslie Hore-Belisha. Ernest Brown was, in the full sense of the term, a professional politician. During the war he had joined the Army as a private soldier and had been promoted to the rank of lieutenant. He was later described on innumerable posters as 'Lieutenant Ernest Brown'. After demobilisation he became a paid speaker for the Liberal Party. He would spend the whole working week addressing Liberal meetings up and down the country. On Sundays he was a Baptist lay preacher. This was during the age of the public meetings when audiences, favourable or hostile, still crowded into halls and schoolrooms to listen to political orators. Interruptions were frequent and persistent, hecklers thick on the ground. At turbulent gatherings Brown was in his element. He had every argument at his finger-tips; he knew the answer to every question and he had one other considerable advantage. In those days, when loudspeakers were still a rarity and orators had to make themselves heard above the din without any mechanical aid, he had the loudest and most resonant voice in public life. As a writer in the *Daily Express* once put it : 'He bawled his way through England'.

Hore-Belisha is today chiefly remembered by reason of his sudden eclipse in January 1940. This was when Chamberlain compelled him to resign his post as Secretary of State for War. It was a downfall from which he never recovered. Until that moment, however, his political career was a spectacular success. He was the first undergraduate to be elected President of the Oxford Union after the war. He joined the Liberal Party. At the 1922 General Election the rift between the followers of Lloyd George and Asquith had not yet been closed. North Cornwall, a predominantly Liberal stronghold, was represented by a Lloyd George Liberal. Hore-Belisha was sent down to the West Country to oppose him. At the last moment, however, this move was abandoned and the young man was left without a constituency to fight. There was only one vacancy – Devonport. It was regarded as an almost impregnable Tory stronghold. The only industry was the dockyard, and dockyard workers were traditionally Conservative. A Labour candidate was already in the field and it was thought to be almost inevitable that the Liberal would come a bad third.

Hore-Belisha was in no way deterred. At the outset of his campaign he insisted, to the dismay of his more staid supporters, on hiring a stagecoach. Seated on the box, he drove through the streets of Devonport. As the election neared its climax the retiring Conservative Member, Sir Clement Kinloch-Cook, was reported as having referred to him as 'a little chit of a fellow'. Hore-Belisha seized on the phrase and delivered a speech which rang through the West Country :

'I am proud to be called "a little chit of a fellow", because I am rather older than Napoleon was when he led to victory the greatest armies that the world has ever seen; because I am older than Alexander was when he conquered the then known world, because I am rather older than Hannibal, probably the greatest general the world has ever seen.'

After citing scientists, poets like Keats and Shelley, politicians, including Pitt, who was Prime Minister at the age of twenty-three, he finished with these words :

'There was one more little chit of a fellow that we must never forget; one of the greatest generals in English history. When the heights of Abraham had been stormed they went up to the old general and he had "the wind up". They went to a younger general and he said : "I would not care to undertake the job". They went to Wolfe, a young chit of a fellow. He said "I'll do it or I'll die !" He did it and he died. There were three million "little chits of fellows" who protected my opponent and his home in the war. If you want a monument to the achievement of the older politicians, you may find it across the Channel. It is three hundred miles long and half a mile deep and it is studded with the tombstones of "little chits of fellows" who stood between Sir Clement Kinloch-Cook and utter destruction.'

It was in vain for Sir Clement to deny that he had ever used the phrase. When the polls declared, his majority was reduced to a mere 1700. Fourteen months later, in December 1923, there was another General Election. The Liberals swept almost the whole of Devon and Cornwall. Hore-Belisha was elected with a majority of over a thousand. There followed in October 1924, a General Election of a very different character. This was the Red Letter Election which swept the Conservatives back into power. With one single exception, the West Country Liberal Members went down to defeat. The exception was Devonport. By what seemed an electoral miracle, Hore-Belisha saved his seat by 500 votes.

This unique achievement was in no sense a triumph for Liberal principles. It was achieved entirely by an appeal to local patriotism. Hore-Belisha presented himself as the champion of his constituents and as one who understood all their problems. An electorate consisting mainly of dockyard workers and service pensioners was particularly susceptible to this form of appeal. The slogan which appeared on every hoarding was 'Devonport first, Devonport last and Devonport all the time'. Ten years earlier, after a full public inquiry, Devonport had been amalgamated into the Borough with the neighbouring towns of Plymouth and Stonehouse. Hore-Belisha declaimed to his enthusiastic listeners 'We want the Charter back in Devonport'.

It was parochial in the extreme. Nevertheless it succeeded and during the ensuing Parliament Hore-Belisha was the only Liberal spokesman for the traditionally Liberal West Country. He did not then play any very noticeable part. But after 1929, he became prominent as the constant tormentor of Labour Ministers. He showed increasing hostility towards the Government and in May 1931, led a significant revolt against Lloyd George's leadership.

The Annual Liberal Conference, attended by some 2000 Delegates, assembled at Buxton. A Resolution was tabled in the names (among others) of Hore-Belisha and Ernest Brown. It proclaimed the independence of the Party. No-one doubted what it meant. The Conference was being invited to condemn Lloyd George's policy of supporting the Labour Government. An amendment was duly tabled indicating satisfaction with the leadership.

On the day in question the debate was fixed for the afternoon. First of all, however, Lloyd George addressed the Conference in the morning. He was in his most brilliant form. Quoting a phrase of Lord Oxford he said : 'There are some who say look neither to the right nor to the left but keep straight on'.

A delegate in the body of the hall said 'Hear, hear . . .'

Lloyd George fastened upon him : 'Ah, my friend, before the war there was a great ship which set out on its maiden voyage across the Atlantic. A message came over the ether ". . . there are icebergs on the course you are pursuing". But the Captain looked neither to the right nor to the left; he went straight on. Let me say here and now I am opposed to *Titanic* seamanship in politics and as an old mariner I would not drive the ship on to the icy floes that have drifted into our seas from the frozen wastes of the Tory past. If the National Liberal Federation in its wisdom this afternoon decides to take another course [voices – hear, hear] I would advise my friends to put on their life belts and plant their deckchairs as near as possible to the boats; unless, of course, any of them have already made arrangements to be picked up.' [Cheers and laughter and 'rub it in'.]

This was Lloyd George at his most effective and it swept the Conference. The only false note was in his final peroration when he spoke of the Liberal ship 'presenting its bill of lading at the Great White Throne'.

When Hore-Belisha rose in the afternoon he was already defeated. Nevertheless, he delivered a defiant speech ending with the words 'If you pass this amendment you have destroyed the Liberal Party'. The amendment was overwhelmingly carried. There was later an echo of this debate in the House of Commons. On the 20th May, Sir John Simon referred to Lloyd George's peroration with icy scorn. He pointed out that a bill of lading was a document given not by a ship but to a ship, and was scathing about 'this mixture of bad law and the Book of Revelations'. The rejoinder came in a later debate on the 20th July. Lloyd George spoke from his place on the Opposition Front Bench below the gangway. Simon was sitting three places away from him. Lloyd George, pointing at the floor, said : 'Better men than he have changed their party and crossed that floor of the House of Commons. But none has done it leaving such a slimy trail of hypocrisy behind him.'

Throughout 1930 and 1931, the unemployment figures continued to mount. They passed the 2,000,000 mark. In June 1930, Ramsay Mac-Donald invited the Conservative and Liberal leaders to a three-party Conference. The Conservatives declined; the Liberals accepted. Thereafter there was a series of meetings lasting over six months between MacDonald, Snowden, Vernon Hartshorn (Lord Privy Seal) and Lloyd George who was accompanied by Lord Lothian and Mr Seebohm Rowntree. The Liberals continued to urge their programme of national development. In February, Samuel moved a resolution in the House of Commons calling on the Government to implement the Labour/Liberal proposals for dealing with unemployment. It was carried without a division. But it was in this debate that Lloyd George urged the Chancellor not to be influenced by the 'money Barons of the City of London'[1].

It was at this time that George Lansbury wrote to Lloyd George begging him to join the Labour Party. Lloyd George replied that by so doing he would antagonise millions of Liberal supporters. But he emphasised the common purpose.

June 1931 was a month of international crisis. The Credit Anstaldt, the national Bank of Austria, was in danger of bankruptcy and was only saved by an immediate loan from the Bank of England. France and the United States were constrained to agree to suspend for a year payment of all reparations and war debts. In this atmosphere of mounting anxiety Ramsay MacDonald and Lloyd George grew momentarily closer together. They met in the last week of July and agreed for the first time on a Labour/Liberal coalition. On his return from the meeting Lloyd George dictated to Frances Stevenson the following memorandum:

> Generally speaking, Labour would like an alliance. They would be willing to drop certain of their present Ministers . . . Ramsay would be Prime Minister. Lloyd George would be Leader [of the House] at the Foreign Office or the Treasury. Ramsay thinks he can adjourn early in August and resume late in the autumn, and then continue till the next Budget. No fear of immediate Election. It might be contemplated that the Army, Air and Navy join up under one Ministry. . . .

If this agreement had been carried out the whole course of British politics might well have been changed. The electoral breach between Liberalism and Labour had begun in 1918. Until that time they had been virtual allies. In the constituencies three-cornered fights were a rarity. There was a tacit agreement between the Party machines about the division of seats. Labour voters had in general supported Liberal candidates and vice-versa. The Labour decision at the end of the war to fight in complete independence had destroyed this common front — to the great advantage of the Conservatives. In 1922 and again in 1924,

[1] This was a favourite phrase of Lloyd George. On one occasion Churchill retorted, 'Yes, but who made them barons?'

Stanley Baldwin and Neville Chamberlain arriving at Downing Street for the Economic Conference on 13th August 1931

The first Cabinet Meeting of the National Government in 1931, taken at No. 10
From bottom to top: Ramsay MacDonald, J H Thomas, Lord Reading, Stanley Baldwin,
Philip Snowden, Lord Sankey, Sir Philip Cunliffe-Lister, Sir Samuel Hoare, Mr Neville
Chamberlain and Sir Herbert Samuel

Ramsay MacDonald giving his statement after a meeting with constituents at Seaham
Harbour, Durham, on 3rd October 1931

Tory Governments were returned on minority vote but with a substantial majority in the House of Commons. This was not the only consequence. The Liberals still commanded the allegiance of many able men who could greatly have strengthened the Labour Governments of 1924 and 1929. Belonging to a third party, they were debarred from ministerial careers.

Suddenly it appeared that this state of affairs might come to an end. After the rapprochment agreed upon between MacDonald and Lloyd George had become effective, the Left-Wing Parties would once more have become electoral allies. The history of the 1930s might have been completely different. Lloyd George would have been the most powerful figure in the Cabinet and it is impossible to suppose that he would have agreed to the deflationary policies adopted by the National Government in the succeeding weeks. Indeed, there might well have been no National Government.

This is one of the great 'might have beens' of our political history. It never materialised. On 1st August, Lloyd George was taken seriously ill. He was suffering from a prostate gland and had to undergo a serious operation. This took place at his London home. A day or two later he was taken to his country house at Churt. There he continued for a time to direct the affairs of the Liberal Party. Samuel and other Liberal leaders made frequent visits to his bedside. But for the time being he was incapable of holding office.

It is here only necessary to recite in briefest outline the events of the previous three months. On the Continent of Europe there had been a series of financial crises. On 11th May Austria's largest bank, the Credit Anstaldt of Vienna, in effect declared itself bankrupt. Its liabilities were guaranteed by the Austrian National Bank to which in June the Bank of England made an advance of 4.3 million pounds. Germany was the next victim. Here political developments led almost to economic consequences. The Nazis had achieved a sensational advance in the elections of September 1930. For the first time they appeared as a force seriously to be reckoned with. In June 1931, there were communist riots in the Ruhr.

These developments inevitably affected the money-market. In the first week of June the Reichsbank lost 150 million marks in gold and bills of exchange. The figure in the second week was 540 millions. In the two days 19th–20th June, the total was 150 millions. The president of the Reichsbank was constrained to approach the Governor of the Bank of England (Montagu Norman) for a credit from the Bank of England, the Federal Reserve or the Bank of International Settlements. The Federal Reserve made French participation a condition of their own.

At this stage President Hoover intervened. He proposed a one-year moratorium of all inter-governmental war debts and reparations. This was not finally accepted until 6th July. The delay was due in the main to French intransigence. The French Government were determined to frustrate the proposal announced during the previous March for an Austro-German customs union. In this they succeeded. It was a disastrous victory since it played directly into the hands of the Nazis. In July, there was a flight from the mark and all Banks closed their doors for two days. There were similar events in Rumania and Hungary.

Looking back, it appears inevitable that Britain should have been seriously affected. In the House of Commons on 30th July, Neville Chamberlain drew attention to the gravity of the position. For the Government Snowden admitted that it was extremely serious and hinted at the need for drastic economies. In these circumstances the publication of the May Report could not have occurred at a more unfortunate moment. Its findings came as an immense shock to everyone outside the inner circles of politics. The majority report estimated a deficit by April 1932 of 120 million pounds. They recommended new taxation amounting to 24 millions and economies to the extent of 96 millions. This latter sum was to be found in part by reductions of all public salaries including Judges, Ministers, Members of Parliament, Civil Servants, Teachers, and the pay of the Armed Services. But the principal saving was to be made by reducing expenditure on the unemployed by 66½ millions including a 20% reduction in weekly benefits.

It was this recommendation and the controversy which it engendered which brought about the fall of the Labour Government. The events during the month of August and the parts played by individual politicians and bankers had been canvassed by many historians. Probably the most authoritative account is contained in Mr Reginald Basset's *1931: Year of Crisis.* It is supplemented by Mr McNeill Weir's *The Tragedy of Ramsay MacDonald.* Mr McNeill Weir was MacDonald's Parliamentary Private Secretary. He was also a dedicated member of the Labour Party and this, naturally enough, colours his whole narrative.

On 11th August, MacDonald and Snowden met the representatives of the Bank of England. Montagu Norman was away. The spokesmen for the Bank were the Deputy Governor, Sir Ernest Harvey, and Mr E. R. Peacock, a Director. They told the Ministers :

(1) that we were on the edge of the precipice and, unless the situation changed radically, we should be over it directly, (2) that the cause of the trouble was financial but political, and lay in the complete want of confidence in H.M.G. existing among foreigners, (3) that the remedy was in the hands of the Government alone.

MacDonald agreed that these conclusions should be revealed to the leaders of the other Parties. Accordingly, the Deputy Governor met first Chamberlain and later Samuel on the following day. Thereafter, there were meetings between MacDonald and Snowden and the Conservative and Liberal leaders. The Cabinet Committee agreed to submit to the full Cabinet a list of economies amounting to £78½ million. The question of a 10% cut in unemployment benefit and of a revenue tariff was excluded from the report.

On 19th August, the Cabinet met and sat from 11 in the morning until 10.25 at night with brief intervals for lunch and dinner. They agreed on economies of £56½ million.

On 21st August, there was a three-Party conference at which the Prime Minister met the Conservative and Liberal leaders. He told them that the Cabinet had modified the economy Committee's plan and had struck roughly one-third off the proposals. When Sir Samuel Hoare protested, the Prime Minister asked: 'Well, are you prepared to join the Board of Directors?' Hoare replied that if this was seriously meant, it would demand serious consideration.

Throughout these days the Labour Cabinet had found themselves in an agonising dilemma. They were ill-equipped to face it. Most of them had had considerable experience of working-class life and the problems of the shop-floor. But they were almost entirely ignorant of the world of banking and finance. It was difficult, if not impossible, for them to dispute the advice which the Government had received from the bankers. This was uniformly to the effect that, failing drastic economies including a reduction in unemployment benefit, the country would be faced with immeasurable disaster. But the remedy proposed was appalling. Labour was the party of the poor and the under-privileged. Labour Members of Parliament understood far better than their Conservative opposite numbers the tragedy of unemployment. A 10% cut meant reducing the weekly benefit for a man and wife from 36/- to 27/- and for a single man from 17/- to 15/6d.

The phrase was being widely used in the Press 'Equality of Sacrifice'. As Labour Ministers pointed out, there was no equality of sacrifice here. A 10% cut in an unemployed household entailed infinitely greater hardship than a 10% cut in the salary of a Cabinet Minister.

Until the last stages, this was the attitude of the whole Government. As recently as 11th June, the Prime Minister had promised the Parliamentary Labour Party that there would be no reduction in benefit : 'No attempt to shorten the period of benefit and no increase in contributions.'

The crisis point was reached on 23rd August. The Cabinet reassembled at 8.45 p.m. Sir Ernest Harvey, the Deputy Governor of the Bank, arrived at Downing Street with a telegram from the American Bankers, Messrs J. P. Morgan & Co. They expressed the view that there was little prospect of the American public being willing to take up a public loan unless and until Parliament had already passed the necessary economy legislation. Although it was not stated in terms it was clear that such legislation would include a cut in unemployment benefit. The telegram was read to the Cabinet. According to Mr Harold Nicolson, loud protests were heard by those waiting in the next room and Harvey thought 'that pandemonium had broken loose'. MacDonald appealed to his colleagues to accept the proposals including a 10% cut in unemployment benefit. There is some dispute as to the exact number of those who refused. Basset is probably right when he says that a majority of the Cabinet favoured acceptance but that 9 Ministers (out of 21) were inexorably opposed. In these circumstances it was clear that the Government could not continue, and MacDonald was authorised so to report to the King. According to Snowden, he was further authorised to advise His Majesty to hold a conference next morning with Mr Baldwin and Sir Herbert Samuel. It is not clear what was expected to happen at such a meeting.

The Prime Minister left the Cabinet at 10.10 p.m. He arrived at the Palace at 10.35 p.m. What actually happened is a matter of some dispute, but according to the record of Sir Clive Wigram, the King's Secretary, the King impressed on MacDonald that he was the only man to lead the country through this crisis and hoped he would re-consider the situation. According to Wigram, MacDonald 'tottered into the King's room a broken man, scared and unbalanced. Half an hour later he strutted out beaming with self-satisfaction.'

Next morning the King held a conference at Buckingham Palace. MacDonald, Baldwin and Samuel were present. They agreed on the formation of a National Government. MacDonald returned to Downing Street and informed his colleagues. He emphasised that it was to be 'a Government of individuals whose task would be confined to dealing with the financial emergency'. They dispersed. But MacDonald asked Snowden, Thomas and Lord Sankey to remain behind and asked them to join him in the new Government. He assured them the new administration would not exist for a longer period than to dispose of the emergency and that when that was achieved the political Parties would resume their respective positions. It was not to be a coalition Government but a National Government for one purpose only. As soon as the financial crisis had been settled there should be a General Election and at that General Election there would be no merging of political Parties and no 'Coupon' or other Party arrangements. It was afterwards alleged that MacDonald had schemed for the downfall of the Labour Government. He himself strenuously denied it. In his opening speech at the ensuing General Election he said on 12th October :

'I strove until almost the last sand in the glass had gone through to keep the Labour Government in office. That was my policy. My policy was not to go out but to remain in. I failed. Then the National Government had to be hurriedly constructed because there was no time to lose.'

This was not quite accurate. It is clear that, at the end of July, MacDonald had agreed with Lloyd George on the formation of a Labour/Liberal coalition. There was also a discussion with Lord Stonehaven reported in the Life of Chamberlain. But the evidence does not support the conclusion that MacDonald plotted the downfall of the Labour Government and the ensuing destruction of Labour at the polls. Rightly or wrongly, he genuinely believed that the economy measures were essential. But he did not undergo a complete transformation. This is shown by his attitude when he met the junior Ministers in the Labour Government on 25th August. In effect, he advised them not to follow him. He pointed out that they were young men, that they had their lives before them and their future careers to consider. They should therefore dissociate themselves from him and the National Government and join what would now become the Labour Opposition. He could hardly have made such a statement if he had expected the National Government to last for more than a few weeks.

The new Cabinet consisted of 10 members, 4 drawn from the Labour Party, 4 from the Conservatives and 2 from the Liberals. Other appointments announced on 25th August consisted of 4 Conservatives and 3 Liberals. Throughout these days Parliament was in recess. But the Parliamentary Labour Party was summoned to a meeting at 2 p.m. on Friday, 28th August. The meeting was also attended by the National Executive of the Labour Party and the General Council of the Trades Union Congress. Neither MacDonald nor Snowden attended. McNeill Weir has recorded[1] how he went to Downing Street earlier in the week.

[1] *The Tragedy of Ramsay MacDonald.*

MacDonald informed him that he was going to Lossiemouth on the afternoon train :

> The announcement that he was going back to Lossiemouth so soon surprised me. I said so. 'Ah, yes,' he said wearily, but still without turning, 'I must get away. I've had an awful time. I'm very tired. I need a rest.' 'Then you are not going to the meeting of the Parliamentary Labour Party and National Executive tomorrow?' 'No,' he replied very deliberately, 'I am not going to any Labour Party meeting on Friday.'

MacDonald afterwards explained that the invitation to the meeting had not reached him until he had made arrangements to leave for Lossiemouth. Nevertheless, this is one of the strangest episodes in the whole story. He was still the leader of the Party. Up to this moment his position had been unchallenged. His prestige was still immense. One can only speculate as to what would have happened if he had attended and addressed the meeting. It is perhaps too much to suppose that the Parliamentary Labour Party would have accepted the economy proposals or supported the National Government. Almost certainly, however, the Party would have been far more evenly divided. As it was, support of the Government was left to the Lord Chancellor, Lord Sankey and Mr Malcolm MacDonald. The meeting came down overwhelmingly against the Government.

Almost immediately an acute difference arose within the ranks of the Government. Opinion in the Conservative Party swung rapidly in favour of a General Election. On 21st September, the Conservative 1922 Committee declared unanimously for an early election on the basis of a national appeal by the National Government. But they also declared that there should be an immediate imposition of an emergency tariff. Here the problem arose. On what programme was such an election to be fought? Overwhelmingly the Conservatives were in favour of protection. The majority of Liberals still clung to their free trade convictions. If the Prime Minister acceded to Conservative wishes, he must inevitably face the resignations of Snowden and the Liberals and the Government would lose its 'national' character. He himself would become the prisoner of the Tories.

There followed a serious division in the Liberal ranks. It was due not to ideological but to personal reasons. After the formation of the original Cabinet it had been necessary to appoint the junior Ministers. Seven of them including two Whips were Liberals, nominated by Sir Herbert Samuel. These nominations had been agreed at Churt between Samuel and Lloyd George. At any rate Samuel raised the possibility of appointing certain of the dissidents including Hore-Belisha and Ernest Brown who had revolted against the leadership at Buxton. Lloyd George would have none of it. Such appointments, he declared, would be 'a premium on disloyalty'. The new Liberal junior Ministers were therefore drawn entirely from those who had supported the leadership throughout. In his memoirs[1] Samuel makes this comment :

> But when it came to making appointments in the Ministry, Lloyd George, not being willing to let bygones be bygones, raised strong objection to one or two of my suggestions for junior posts. As he was the leader and I acting only as his deputy, I could not insist; those exclusions gave rise to difficulties afterwards.

This is a masterpiece of understatement. The news was received with the utmost chagrin and anger by the dissidents. Ernest Brown met one of the new junior Ministers in the hallway of the National Liberal Club.[2]

They were both accompanied by their wives. In a voice that almost shattered the rafters, he burst out : 'It's mean, Isaac, it's mean. He can forgive his enemies. He can't forgive his old friends. He knows very well it matters more to me than to any of the others. I'm the only professional politician of the lot.'

Hore-Belisha did not waste his time in vociferous complaint. He drafted a memorandum for submission to the Prime Minister. This was to be signed by Liberal Members. The signatories assured MacDonald of their unequivocal support. The memorandum read :

> We, the majority members of the Liberal Party, desire to assure you of our support in any measures you consider necessary to take in the interests of the finances and trade of the country.

The purpose was obvious – to cut the ground from under the feet of the Liberal leaders. If Samuel and his colleagues refused to accept Conservative demands for an immediate election and for a programme including tariffs, no matter. There were other Liberals who would be amenable. Even if Samuel and his friends resigned the national façade could still be preserved. For several days Hore-Belisha canvassed support. The success of the manoeuvre seemed assured when he obtained the signatures of both Simon and Runciman. There were some twenty others including several dedicated free traders. There was, however, one notable withdrawal. On 21st September, Norman Birkett wrote to

[1] *Memoirs* : Cresset Press, 1945.
[2] I myself was present.

Hore-Belisha a letter which fully illustrates the dilemma of the Liberal Members :

My dear Leslie,

I find that the document you were good enough to ask me to sign has been given a publicity and a construction which I did not contemplate.

The conception in my mind was a general support of the Prime Minister in his efforts to deal with the Nation's interests at this time of undeniable crisis.

But I now find that it is being interpreted as a general declaration in favour of tariffs, and as a stimulus to a General Election to be fought on the question of tariffs.

The views which have been expressed on the meaning of the document are such that it is impossible to allow my name to remain there : for it was never my intention by a stroke of the pen to subscribe to a policy of tariffs, or to link myself with any movement for a General Election.

I deeply regret this situation which has arisen, and I am quite sure you are not responsible for it : but I cannot allow any misunderstanding to persist which places me in the position of appearing to promise my support to something which is quite opposed to what I thought was the position.

I shall continue to support the National Government, and will be guided at all times in the future by the national interest (and this is no idle word !) : but the construction which is being placed upon the document is one which is contrary to my intention, and I should be glad if you could withdraw my name to avoid future misunderstandings.

Yours ever,
NORMAN BIRKETT.[1]

Nevertheless the memorialists continued on their way.

As late as 20th October, the Prime Minister was still resisting an appeal to the country. He wrote to Samuel :

Obviously there is not even a theoretical justification for an election now.

But Conservative pressure mounted. Samuel records in his memoirs[2]:

Within a week of sending me that definite expression of his opposition, MacDonald unconditionally surrendered.

The question now arose as to whether Samuel and his colleagues should join in the appeal to the country or whether they should resign.

[1] *The Life of Lord Birkett of Ulveston*, Hertford Hyde, Hamish Hamilton, 1964.
[2] *Memoirs* : Cresset Press, 1945.

If the former, should there be a joint election manifesto and if so, what was to be said about tariffs?

On 5th October, Sir John Simon was reported in the Press:

> I cannot help feeling that the game of formula-hunting has gone on long enough. The reality of the national crisis is not in dispute, and in such circumstances the best course is for the country to put its confidence in the Prime Minister, which I feel sure it is quite willing to do. That is the course I mean to follow. I have the best of reasons for knowing that this is also the view of many other Liberal Members of Parliament and we are forming an organisation at once for the purpose of carrying it into effect.

This was the beginning of the Liberal Nationals. It was regarded at the time as another Liberal split. It was far more than that. It was a permanent secession. Like the Liberal Unionists 47 years earlier, the Liberal Nationals became absorbed in the Conservative Party. In their case, however, the absorption was far more rapid and far more complete. The Liberal Unionists in their early years had retained some of their old notions, especially in the realm of social reform. It was probably due to the influence of Joseph Chamberlain that the Conservative Government in 1894 passed the first Workmen's Compensation Act. No such influence, so far as anyone could discern, was exercised by their successors during the 1930s. With the single exception of Mr Clement Davies, who gradually dissociated himself from the Government during the later 1930s, they became the obedient servants of their Tory masters. In return they received their quota of offices and honours.

In these circumstances, the search for an election formula continued. Eventually it was agreed that each Party should issue its own manifesto and that the Prime Minister should publish his own message to the nation in terms to be approved by Baldwin and Samuel. Having achieved this uneasy compromise the Government appealed for 'a doctor's mandate'. This meant that, if they won the election they were to be free to adopt whatever measures they thought necessary. In the ensuing election campaign there were many differences of emphasis. Conservative candidates did not conceal their protectionist leanings. The orthodox Liberals had distinct reservations and most of them declared unequivocally their opposition to 'food taxes' (i.e., duties on imported foodstuffs). No such reservations were made by Liberal National and National Labour candidates. In effect, they pledged themselves to unqualified compliance with Government policies whatever they might be.

These distinctions made little impression upon the electors. They were concerned with the economic stability and the fate of the pound. The Labour Party denounced what was described as 'a bankers ramp'. Their lost leaders were denounced, in Mr Attlee's phrase, of having been guilty of 'the greatest betrayal in the political history of this country'. MacDonald, in the words of Mr Edwin Scrymgeour, was 'the First Lord of the Treachery'. In these circumstances the obvious conflict on tariffs between different wings of the Government seemed momentarily of small importance.

This was the first General Election in which sound broadcasting played a really important part. It was generally agreed that the greatest impact of all was Snowden's broadcast on 17th October. He described the circumstances leading to the formation of the National Government. He said :

'I would warn the electors against being influenced by other considerations than the one issue. That one issue on which you should vote is, as I have stated elsewhere, whether we should have a strong and stable Government in this time of national crisis, or whether we shall hand over the destinies of the nation to men whose conduct in a grave emergency has shown them to be unfitted to be trusted with responsibility. I regret that other issues are being raised in this Election. The position is too serious to have the national unity threatened by divisions on a subject which is no essential part of the work in front of the National Government.'

He went on to describe himself as a stern and unbending free trader. But he warned his hearers that the Labour Party was not a free trade Party.

The election was unique in British history. It was fought not on a programme but on a formula. This was set out in MacDonald's personal appeal to the nation :

'The Government must therefore be free to consider every proposal likely to help, such as tariffs, expansion of exports and contraction of imports, commercial treaties and mutual economic arrangements with the Dominions.'

This was the 'doctor's mandate'. Every Government candidate gave his own interpretation. The issue of free trade versus protection was canvassed in varying degrees. Mr Ramsay Muir, Chairman of the National Liberal Federation, sent a letter to all associations and candidates repudiating the suggestion that sitting Members should not be opposed by Liberal supporters of the National Government. He proclaimed the Party's unwavering faith in free trade :

We must not abstain from fighting protectionist sitting members merely because they support the Government.

The Conservatives on their side were not unwilling to oppose Liberal sitting Members. It is often recalled that Baldwin, in a public speech, deprecated the action of the Darwen Conservatives in opposing Bannerman. He said :

'I do not think that to oppose a leader of the party that forms part of the National Government is quite what I should call playing the game.'

He did not throw his mantle over other Liberal Ministers. Mr Amery travelled to North Cornwall to speak against Sir Donald Maclean, who was then the sitting Liberal Member. Milner Gray was a junior Minister in the Government. Alan Lennox-Boyd was adopted to oppose him. He availed himself of the Liberal National secession. A communication was sent to their newly-established headquarters asking if Mr Milner Gray had their support. The answer was duly received that the organisation 'had no knowledge' of Mr Milner Gray's candidature. What effect this exchange had upon the electorate it is impossible to determine. But Lennox-Boyd was returned by a substantial majority and remained Member for Mid-Bedfordshire until his retirement to the House of Lords in 1959. Nevertheless it is probably true to say that in the great majority of constituencies the tariff issue was played down. Food taxes were still believed to be unpopular.

When the result was declared it appeared that the electors had voted overwhelmingly for 'National' candidates, regardless of their political views. In Sparkbrook the arch-protectionist, Mr Amery, increased his majority from 2,992 to 15,979. In the Colne Valley, Philip Snowden's old seat, the Liberal candidate, Mr E. L. Mallalieu, received Snowden's personal blessing and achieved a sensational victory. In his maiden speech in the House of Commons he described himself as 'one of those Colne Valley or Ickornshavian free traders'. (Snowden had become Lord Snowden of Ickornshaw).

The conclusion is unavoidable. The electors voted overwhelmingly for the idea of national unity. There can be no doubt that even among the unemployed themselves, the section of the community who suffered most from the economy programme, a substantial number of votes went to Government candidates. Even so, no-one foresaw the outcome. That the Government would win was never really in doubt. No-one would have been surprised if they had achieved a majority of 100/150.

But the actual result exceeded their wildest hopes. These were the figures :

Conservative	471
Liberal National	35
Liberal	33
National Labour	13
National	2
Independent	2
Labour	46
I.L.P.	6
Lloyd George Liberals	4

Even these figures scarcely convey the magnitude of the Government's triumph and the Labour disaster. Everywhere except in the slums of Glasgow and the mining valleys of South Wales the wave was irresistible. Even in Durham, which was thought to be impregnable, Ramsay MacDonald was returned with a 5,000 majority, and only two constituencies held out. The Labour leadership was swept away – Henderson, Greenwood, Morrison, Dalton – all were defeated. This had a profound effect on the future of the Party. Among former Labour ministers only Lansbury, Cripps and Attlee were returned. Attlee saved his seat at Limehouse by 400 votes. In 1934 he succeeded Lansbury as the leader of the Party. Thereafter he became Deputy Prime Minister under Churchill in 1940 and Prime Minister in the Labour Government of 1945. It is in no way derogatory of his career to say that this would scarcely have happened had it not been for the disappearance of the other popular contenders for the leadership in the holocaust of 1931.

The Cabinet was enlarged from ten to twenty. On this occasion the Liberal Nationals were brought in. Sir John Simon became Foreign Secretary and Runciman President of the Board of Trade. Hore-Belisha and Ernest Brown received their due rewards as Under-Secretaries. At the same time Sir Herbert Samuel and his colleagues continued for a short period in the Government. Naturally enough the Conservatives took the majority of offices.

The list of Under-Secretaries was significant, not so much for its inclusions as for its omissions. Two in particular were passed over – one was Harold Macmillan and the other was Robert Boothby. Both had obvious claims. But neither was a pillar of Party orthodoxy. Moreover, Boothby had been Parliamentary Private Secretary to Churchill from 1924 to 1929 when Churchill was Chancellor of the Exchequer. The association continued – and Churchill was regarded with the utmost disfavour by the Tory leaders in 1931. The exclusion of these two continued throughout the thirties, and neither achieved office until the fall of the Chamberlain Government. This was not purely a personal matter, as will be shown later in this chapter. The insistence on party orthodoxy was the main characteristic of Parliamentary life during the thirties.

Almost immediately the division in the Government over fiscal policy began to appear. The Debate on the Address largely turned on free trade and protection. It was particularly marked by the conversion, if conversion it can be called, of Churchill, who had been throughout his life a convinced free-trader. He had broken with the Tories in 1904, largely on the fiscal question. During his time as Chancellor of the Exchequer he had remained, to the indignation of most of his Party's back-benchers, an inveterate opponent of import duties in any shape or form. Even during the 1931 election he had played down the tariff issue. Now, however, he had reached the end of the road so far as fiscal controversy was concerned. The debate turned on whether the National Government had a mandate for the immediate imposition of import duties. Mr Churchill said:

'Every Member of this House knows what his declarations were to his constituents and what his answers to questions were. He knows what he put in his election address; he knows what his relations with his constituents became and were during the course of the Election and what constitutes good faith between him and his constituents. Every Member therefore in any submission to the House is a judge of the mandate which he has individually received and the sum of the individual mandates constitutes the effective mandate of the House of Commons.'

Within a matter of weeks the issue was settled. The Conservatives in the Cabinet, led by Neville Chamberlain, were determined on tariffs. The National Liberals, of course, acquiesced. Ramsay MacDonald was not prepared to persist in opposing. This left Sir Herbert Samuel and his Liberal colleagues, together with Lord Snowden. They might have been prepared to accept import duties purely as an emergency measure. But it became clearer every day that what was intended was the complete abandonment of free trade. They offered their resignations.

The Government were in a considerable dilemma. They had been elected on a national appeal as representing all three parties in the State. Within a few weeks the façade was beginning to crack. The departure of the Liberals and Lord Snowden so soon after the election would have affected the life of the Government and definitely impaired its credibility. What was to be done? In these circumstances resort was had to an astonishing device – 'the Agreement to Differ'. The dissidents were to remain in the Government, but they and their followers were to be free to speak and vote against the Import Duties Bill. It was an arrangement unheard of since the eighteenth century. The doctrine of joint ministerial responsibility had been accepted for over a hundred years. It was axiomatic that, whatever their private reservations might be, ministers must accept and defend the collective decisions of the Government, otherwise they must resign. This essential principle was jettisoned for the first though not the last time in modern parliamentary history.

The second reading of the Import Duties Bill took place on 4th February 1932. It was moved by Neville Chamberlain. For him it was an intensely dramatic occasion. His father had been the prophet of tariff reform and had been routed in 1906. Naturally enough his peroration was the most emotional of his life. The Conservatives rose to give him a standing ovation. His older brother, Austen Chamberlain, came down from his back bench seat to the Treasury Bench to wring him by the hand. Attlee followed. Then Amery, the arch-priest of protection gave the Bill a modified blessing, though saying that it did not go nearly far enough. There followed the unique spectacle of the Home Secretary (Sir Herbert Samuel) rising on the Treasury Bench to oppose the Bill moved by the Chancellor of the Exchequer. This was one of Samuel's most effective speeches. It is described by Baldwin's biographers as 'a vehement attack that stupefied the House'. It was received with fury on the Conservative back benches. They were reluctantly prepared to accept the 'Agreement to Differ' and listen to a formal speech from the Home Secretary. What they found intolerable was that he should make an extremely good speech. They went into the lobby in a condition of seething indignation.

But Samuel did not escape attack from a different quarter. One of the speakers in the debate was Megan Lloyd George. At times she bore an almost uncanny resemblance to her father. As in his case, she could use words like a whiplash. On this occasion she excoriated Samuel and his colleagues who had remained in the National Government after Lloyd George had withdrawn his support. She described Samuel's addressing the corpse of free trade in the language of Mark Antony over the body of Caesar :

'Oh pardon me thou bleeding piece of earth
    That I am meek and gentle with these butchers !'

Baldwin, who wound up the debate, referred to her speech and described Samuel as saying,

'Heaven deliver me from this Welsh fairy.'

There was not a dissimilar scene on the third reading. Time was limited. A single day had been allotted for the completion of the report stage and the third reading. It had been arranged that there should be only three third-reading speeches. Isaac Foot, the Liberal Minister for Mines was to speak from the Front Bench for the dissident Liberals. He was to be followed by Sir Stafford Cripps for the Labour Opposition. Finally Mr Chamberlain was to wind up.

The report stage dragged on through the afternoon and evening. The Liberal members suspected that the Conservatives were deliberately playing out time in order, if possible, to avoid anything but a formal third reading. In the event an hour was left. Isaac Foot was told that he must confine his speech to six minutes. In this brief space he had to express the free trade convictions of a lifetime. That he succeeded in doing so, was shown by the response he obtained. When he sat down the Conservative back-benchers, led by Lord Winterton with both fists above his head, rose as one man, shouting, 'Resign ! Resign !' Chamberlain described the speech as 'the last despairing cry of one who knows that he has seen the end of free trade'.

The Liberals remained in the Government until the following autumn. Then there took place the Ottawa Conference. The intention of the Government was to create an Imperial *Zollverein*. The bonds of Empire were to be drawn closer by commercial ties. Britain was to continue to grant free entry for all produce from the Dominions and Colonies while imposing tariffs against the rest of the world. The Dominions, on their side, were to encourage British exports at the expense of the rest of the world. To arch-protectionist Conservatives like Neville Chamberlain and Leo Amery this must have seemed like the realisation of a life-long dream − the final accomplishment of Joseph Chamberlain's vision in 1903.

The event was wholly different. A few years earlier Empire Free Trade might have become a reality. By 1932 the Governments of Canada, Australia and New Zealand had already embarked on courses of extreme protection. In particular this was true of Canada. The Prime Minister, Mr Richard Bennett, had already in 1926 repudiated the notion of Empire Free Trade. As Chairman of the host country he presided at the opening of the Conference. He has been described as 'being possessed of the manners of a Chicago policeman and the temperament of a Hollywood film star'. He had been elected on a programme of 'Canada First' with the support of Canadian manufacturing interests.

A similar attitude was adopted by Australia, and to a lesser extent by South Africa and New Zealand. All these countries were prepared to accord Britain preference. This, however, was of little value if the duties were still too high to enable British exporters to compete with domestic industry on anything like equal terms. The Conference very nearly broke down. The final stage is described in Baldwin's biography[1] by Middlemas and Barnes :

> Neither the Meat Agreement based on 18 months' premium, nor that with Canada was made until the last possible minute, and then only after a prolonged and desperate struggle. They were due to be initialled on Friday evening, and signed the next morning, Saturday 20th August. First there was trouble with Bennett, and when at 1.30 a.m. on the Saturday morning it was finally resolved, Bruce stormed in to say he was not going to sign with Australia. He had been misled, betrayed in fact . . .

Eventually agreement was reached. Geoffrey Dawson, the Editor of *The Times*, who had been present throughout the Conference wrote to the Editor of the *Winnipeg Free Press* :

> No-one can regard it (the outcome of the Conference) as altogether satisfactory; but I am quite impenitent in my feeling that it was well worth while – if only for its influence as a process of education.

In effect, the Ottawa Agreements were a thoroughly one-sided bargain. The Dominions were guaranteed continued free entry into the British market. Britain was to increase or create tariffs on foreign imports, including wheat. Most striking of all, the British Government undertook to retain for the next five years the 10% duty on foreign goods. In return the Dominion Governments agreed to increase their preferences in favour of British imports. For the most part, however, this was afterwards achieved not by reducing the duty on British goods, already in some cases prohibitive, but by increasing further the tariffs on imports.

This was too much for Lord Snowden and the Liberals. In particular they objected to the undertaking to maintain tariffs against foreign goods for five years. This, they believed, was tying the hands of Parliament. Moreover, they maintained their traditional objection to duties on meat and wheat. The eleven Liberal Ministers resigned in a body. They paid a final visit to the Prime Minister, who undoubtedly regretted their departure. It left him more than ever the prisoner of the Tories. Before they left he made one wholly revealing observation : 'The last general election was a disaster.'

[1] *Baldwin: A Biography*, Weidenfeld & Nicolson, 1969.

The economic crisis of 1931, and the formation of a National Government with an overwhelming Conservative bias, had profoundly important results in every sphere of the national life. The first was immediately apparent in the realm of unemployment. With Neville Chamberlain at the Exchequer, Keynesian ideas had no chance of acceptance. The most extreme Treasury orthodoxy prevailed. There could be no question, as Chamberlain put it, of 'splashing money about'. The world causes which had led to the universal depression must be left to adjust themselves and there was little or nothing which the Government could do within the national economy to accelerate the process.

At the same time unemployment pay became the main target of the economy programme. Not only were the rates of benefit cut by 10%, contractual benefits were limited to six months. Thereafter, the unemployed men could only draw transitional benefit and this was subject to the household means test.

It would be difficult to exaggerate the misery and resentment which this aroused. The test was operated by the Local Public Assistance Committees, who applied their Poor Law standards. This was nothing new, but hitherto it had been confined to a class of paupers who were not only the least fortunate, but the least articulate members of the community. This class included the old age pensioners who had families with whom they could live, the permanently infirm and those who, if not actually unemployable, were hardly likely to be accepted by any employer. The Poor Law kept them alive on the lowest possible margin of subsistence, either inside or outside the work houses.

Now the household means test was applied to a wholly different category. Those affected did not belong to a pauper class. They were, for the greater part, respectable working men who were accustomed to work, with their traditional crafts and skills, and to maintain their own households. Now they were the victims of the economic blizzard. For the first time in their lives they were reduced to pauper status, and subjected to all the rigours of the means test. The practice varied from one district to another according to the predilections of the Local Public Assistance Committees. These differed considerably.

Nevertheless, standards were for the most part extremely harsh. Every resource must be taken into account – savings, however small, disability pensions and children's earnings – all were subjected to minute investigation. It was the children's earnings which led to the greatest heart burning. A boy or girl after leaving school might engage in some blind-alley occupation and bring home a few shillings a week. These trivial sums were carefully assessed down to the last sixpence. The head of the household might find himself literally penniless. He would literally have no money to spend on the simplest personal necessities or pleasures except in so far as it was contributed by his dependants. A widespread grievance was that of a newly grown-up son or daughter who might be saving to get married. No allowance was made for this situation. He (or she) must maintain the unemployed parent. Frequently this resulted in the breaking up of the household.

There were furious reactions throughout the country and especially, of course, in the areas of high unemployment. One example may be given. The Convenor of the Public Assistance Committee in Dundee wrote to the author as follows :

> My considered judgment as Convenor of Public Assistance in a great industrial Constituency is as follows : The reduction of the dole from 26s. for two to 23.3d is a tragedy. From a basic subsistence level thousands of our countrymen are now at their wits end to keep the home going and are definitely in the poverty stream. With 26s. the home could be kept going barely. There is not a half-penny over for clothing, boots, replenishments etc., with 23.3d. The means test has been effective in cutting out masses who have not been requiring extra money and who are battening on the State, and the savings over the country must be enormous, but in a case of decent workers, idle through no fault of their own, it is a scandal that recipients of Poor Law relief, are sometimes in a better position than they.

Here then was the prospect for the unemployed industrial worker. While still drawing standard benefit, he must live on an amount quite inadequate for his basic needs. When the benefit expired, he was subjected to the humiliations of the means test.

Anyone who queries the fundamental difference of outlook between British political parties should study the debates in Parliament between 1931 and 134. There was a continuous volume of protest against the treatment of the unemployed and the operation of the household means test. But it came almost entirely in the Labour Party, the four Members of the I.L.P., the Liberals who followed Samuel and Lloyd George and one or two dissident Conservatives.

It aroused no echo from the ranks of loyal Government supporters. 1934 was the year of the hunger marches. From Dundee, Glasgow, the North-East Coast and South Wales they marched to London to demonstrate against the conditions under which they were condemned to live and the proposed creation of the Unemployment Assistance Board, immune from democratic control. It was proposed that their spokesman should be heard at the Bar of the House of Commons. Sir Herbert Samuel's support of the proposal was received with consternation and fury on the Government benches.

Nothing more clearly illustrates the attitude of the Government and its critics than the debate on unemployment which had taken place in the House of Commons on 12th February 1933. The principal speech from the Treasury bench was delivered by the Chancellor of the Exchequer, Mr Neville Chamberlain. Having dismissed the Lloyd George proposals for national development on the ground that the Government should not 'splash money about' in the hope of absorbing the unemployed, he continued as follows :

'But I do not think that any thoughtful Member of this House now believes that the maladjustments which have brought about the world-wide unemployment are likely to be corrected so rapidly and completely that we can look forward with any confidence to the reduction of unemployment to a comparatively small figure, even, shall I say, in the next 10 years.'

This dismal pronouncement produced an unexpected reaction. Winston Churchill was in his seat below the gangway. The plight of the unemployed was not one of his familiar themes and very rarely did he embark upon an extempore speech. Nearly all his parliamentary orations were prepared with immense care and were recited from memory. On this occasion, however, he remarked to a neighbour, 'This is more than I can stand.' When Chamberlain sat down Churchill at once rose to his feet :

'I must say I think something should be done to express the feeling of disappointment, and even of hopelessness, which must have arisen in many hearts.' He proceeded upon his precise and well-marshalled orderly discourse :

'Ten years ! Is that the last word of His Majesty's Government ? There is this frightful, moral agony of unemployment. Take the case of three million unemployed. You are not merely dealing with the weaker brethren, with men who hardly ever kept a job, but you are dealing with a couple of million men who have hardly ever been out of work in the whole of their lives. Take these men. I see the figure of the breadwinner, the father of the family, sitting in his chair in his cottage. Ten years, his wife has perhaps got a job – perhaps she has got his job – and his daughter may have got a job. His son, a young boy, may have some blind-alley occupation. The father of the family whose honour and faith are pledged to carry the dependants on his shoulders, sits there in his chair, a burden upon the house, helpless in the midst of those whom he had vowed himself to defend, his very right to exist challenged in the land for which perhaps he had been ready to sacrifice his life not many years ago. It is no good going to that man and saying 'keep pegging away'. What has he to keep pegging away at?'

On this, as on other occasions, Mr Churchill invoked no response from the Treasury bench. It is true that during the middle 1930s there was some degree of economic recovery and unemployment fell beneath the two million mark. Pressure of public opinion constrained the Government to bring in a measure giving some assistance to a few designated 'special areas'. The outlook of the Government in economic affairs remained unchanged until the outbreak of war. This was part of the legacy of 1931.

The second result was in the realm of foreign affairs. To some extent all three political parties must share the blame for the early 1930s. The need to re-arm became more apparent every year. The mood of the nation, however, was still profoundly pacifist. For a time all three Parties behaved accordingly. In 1934, both Oppositions voted against a modest increase in the Service Estimates. In the 1935 General Election, Baldwin gave his notorious undertaking that there would be 'no great armaments'.

This may partially explain, though it cannot excuse, the Government's record regarding the Italian invasion of Abyssinia. When Mac-Donald and Simon met Mussolini at Stresa in April 1935, they were fully aware of Mussolini's intentions. But no questions were asked and the subject of Abyssinia was never raised. Mussolini, who had already received some kind of assurance from Laval, must have been left with the impression of British indifference. Then followed the events of the autumn. It was clear that the invasion was imminent. Sir Samuel Hoare, who had succeded Simon at the Foreign Office, declared at Geneva:

'The League stands, and my country stands with it, for the collective maintenance of the Covenant in its entirety, and particularly for steady and collective resistance to all acts of unprovoked aggression. The attitude of the British nation in the last few weeks has clearly demonstrated the fact that this is no variable and unreliable sentiment but a principle of international conduct to which they and their Government hold with firm enduring and universal persistence.'

Public response in the United Kingdom was immediate. There was here a singular illogicality. Although the prevailing mood was intensely pacifist as already stated, the League of Nations inspired great sentimental attachment. To millions of people it seemed to embody the desire for peace. Sir Samuel Hoare's speech was almost universally acclaimed except on the Right-Wing of the Conservative Party.

The Government seized the opportunity to hold a General Election. They would probably have won in any event. But their apparent stand over Abyssinia placed the issue beyond any doubt. On the principal issue of the day the Labour and Liberal Parties were effectively disarmed. So on 14th November the Conservatives triumphed at the polls. They could not, of course, repeat the landslide of 1931. Nevertheless they achieved a total of 387 seats with 33 Liberal Nationals and 8 National Labour allies. Labour had 154 Members and the Liberals, including Lloyd George and his three followers, 21.

There were rumours of a backstairs intrigue. These were generally disbelieved. On 22nd November, Mr Wickham Steed wrote in a letter to *The Times* : 'Most Englishmen are persuaded that neither the Prime Minister nor the Foreign Secretary would lend himself to any attempt that was less than honourable. They are not so sure of the French Government . . .' And five days later Sir Arthur Salter contributed a long letter emphasising the importance of oil sanctions. On 3rd December, *The Times*'s leading article proclaimed : 'British policy towards the Abyssinian War has suffered no hesitations or diversions since it first took shape, and it goes resolutely forward.'

All this was sheer illusion. On the day before he delivered his speech at Geneva, Sir Samuel Hoare had arrived at a secret agreement with M. Laval ruling out military sanctions, any measure of Naval blockade and the closure of the Suez Canal. And in Paris on 8th December, he agreed to the Hoare/Laval plan. Abyssinia was to give up two-thirds of her territory. Some was to be ceded to Italy outright. A larger area was to be declared 'a zone of economic expansion and settlement reserved to Italy'. In return Abyssinia was to receive a corridor to the sea.

There was a furious public reaction. *The Times* published its famous leading article on 'A Corridor For Camels'. Baldwin was compelled to sacrifice Hoare and declared that the proposals in the Hoare/Laval plan were 'absolutely and completely dead'.

Nevertheless, the result was the same as if they had been ratified. On 10th June 1936 Neville Chamberlain made a speech to the 1900 Club in which, without any previous consultation with the Foreign Office or even the new Foreign Secretary, he described the continuance of sanctions as 'the very midsummer of madness'. On 18th June, the Government announced that sanctions would be abandoned. Mussolini had won and the League was finally discredited. It was a lesson that was not lost upon Hitler.

The Government survived a furious debate in which they were scathingly denounced by Lloyd George in one of the most powerful speeches of his whole career :

'I have never before heard a British Minister . . . go down to the House of Commons and say that Britain was beaten, Britain and her Empire beaten and that we must abandon an enterprise we had taken in hand.'

He ended with a quotation from Chamberlain :

'The Rt Hon Gentleman said at the last general election : "The choice before us is whether we shall make a last effort at Geneva for peace and security or whether by a cowardly surrender we shall break all the promises we have made and hold ourselves up to the shame of our children and our children's children". Tonight we have had the cowardly surrender and there [pointing to the Treasury Bench] are the cowards.'

Seldom, if ever, in Parliamentary history can a newly-elected Administration have presented so abject a spectacle; yet their Parliamentary majority was scarcely affected – a highly significant phenomenon. Among Conservative Members, only Mr Harold Macmillan voted against them. For a time he renounced the Party Whip.

This was the beginning of the policy of appeasement. The relative position of the Parties was reversed. Thenceforward it was the Conservatives and their allies who appealed to pacifist sentiment. If any Liberal or Socialist announced the surrender to Mussolini he was 'a war-monger'.[1] The capitulation of 1936 was the logical prelude to the Munich Agreement two years later.

This was the most serious consequence of 1931. It may, of course, be said that it did not inevitably follow. In theory a 'National' Government with an overwhelming majority in the House of Commons and massive support in the constituencies should have been in a stronger position to conduct a determined foreign policy than an Administration supported only by a single Party. Such a theory, however, would have taken no account of the Government's inherent and personal weaknesses. After five years it was 'National' only in name. The Liberal National and National Labour parties had long ceased (even if they had ever done so) to make any distinctive contribution. They were no more than the camp followers of the Conservative Party, and the Conservative rank and file, whether in Parliament or outside, were by no means enthusiastically united in support of sanctions and the League.

Admittedly there were only a few voices (notably that of Mr Amery)

[1] In 1937 my father Isaac Foot, who had lost his seat at Bodmin in 1935, stood for a by-election at St Ives. He denounced the Government's surrender over Abyssinia. The cry immediately was raised 'A vote for Foot, is a vote for war.' He was defeated by 200 votes.

which had been raised in outright opposition from the start. But this was not an issue which made any profound appeal to the great mass of Conservative opinion. It is significant that in the final debate referred to above, Mr Harold Macmillan was alone. Otherwise, not a single voice was raised from among Government supporters in outright opposition. Many of them undoubtedly regarded the surrender to Mussolini with silent relief.

There were also the personalities involved. Sir Samuel Hoare never appears to have realised the apparent significance of his own speech at Geneva. It is said that as he left the Assembly, he was considerably surprised by the warm congratulations of his own civil servants. But however this may be, he was never the most powerful figure in the Government. The effective triumvirate consisted of Baldwin, Simon and Chamberlain.

Baldwin's character has already been discussed. (See chapter 3). Undoubtedly he was his Party's greatest electoral asset. When the election results of 1935 were discussed in the Lobbies of Westminster, it was generally reckoned that his image had been worth at least a million votes for the Conservatives. After the beginning of the war he became intensely unpopular as one of those mainly responsible for British unpreparedness. We know now that he was a fairly consistent advocate of speedier rearmament and endeavoured to overcome Chamberlain's resistance at the Treasury. And yet, at the height of the election campaign he had declared : 'Do not fear or misunderstand when you have heard me say that we are looking to our defences . . . I give you my word that there will be no great armaments.'

The position of Sir John Simon is easier to understand. He had inherited that part of Victorian Liberal tradition which was profoundly isolationist and distrusted all foreign entanglements. As Foreign Secretary he had always discountenanced any suggestion that the League of Nations should concern itself with the Japanese invasion of Manchuria. His persistent isolationism was starkly revealed in 1939, after the German Army had entered Prague, and Czechoslovakia had ceased to be an independent State. The whole policy of Munich lay in ruins. Yet even so, speaking in the House of Commons, Simon continued to resist the idea of effective action against an aggressor. It would, he said, involve our foreign policy being decided by 'a whole lot of foreign countries'.

Chamberlain's volte-face is the most striking of all. He was, it now appears, the only Member of the Cabinet seriously to contemplate the imposition of oil sanctions – the one measure short of force which might have proved effective. In the course of the campaign, he had used the language cited by Lloyd George in the debate. And yet it was he who sounded the retreat when he declared that the continuance of sanctions would be 'the very midsummer of madness'. And it was he who, eighteen months later, raised his glass in Rome to 'The King of Italy and the Emperor of Ethiopia'.

These are the characters who were responsible for the policy which led on to Munich. There was, however, a further consequence of the events of 1931. It consisted in the intensification of Party discipline. The Whips had exercised sporadic authority since the middle of the 19th century. Their role is constantly mentioned in Trollope's political novels. Thus we find Phineas Finn :

> 'If it comes to be a question of soul-saving, Mr Bunce, I shan't save my place at the expense of my conscience.'
> 'Not if you knows it, you mean. But the worst of it is that a man gets so thick into the mud that he don't know whether he's dirty or clean. You'll have to wote as you're told, and of course you'll think it's right enough. Ain't you been among Parliament gents long enough to know that that's the way it goes?'

And in 1884 Gilbert had written the Sentry's song in *Iolanthe* :

> When in that House MPs divide
> If they've a brain and cerebellum or two
> They have to leave that brain outside
> And vote just as their leaders tell 'em to.

But their authority was limited. They were often set on defiance by individuals or groups of Members. It was a Liberal revolt on the subject of cordite which brought about the fall of the Rosebery Government in 1895. There were always Members on both sides – such as Leonard Courtney, the Member for Bodmin – who prided themselves on their comparative independence. Throughout the controversy on Irish Home Rule during the years immediately preceding the war in 1914, there were two West Country Liberal Members who consistently supported the exclusion of Ulster. No-one attempted to subject them to Party discipline, either at Westminster or in their constituencies. But after 1931 the climate changed. The Labour Party embarked on a long chapter of attempted regimentation. This began before the election. For many years all Labour candidates for Parliament had been required to sign a pledge that they would not vote for any Motion, Amendment or Prayer contrary to the decision of the Party meeting. It was recognised that on certain matters, 'for example, religion and temperance',

Members might have good grounds for conscientious scruples and in such cases they might abstain from voting.

At the 1931 Conference, the leaders demanded that these rules should be strictly observed. Arthur Henderson asserted that he would accept individual abstentions based on conscience, but not cross votes. Many Members of Parliament, notably Josiah Wedgwood and F. W. Jowett, objected. Jowett declared : 'If the policy of relieving Members of responsibility for their vote should finally be accepted by the Labour Party . . . the whole purpose of the system of representative Government will have been challenged.'

One immediate result was the split between the Labour Party and the I.L.P. which formally disaffiliated in 1932. But the Labour Party itself continued to insist on rigid conformity. This was largely the result of the defection of MacDonald and his colleagues. There was a distrust of leadership. Authority must be vested in the Party machine, and active dissent, whether in Parliament or outside, must be sternly repressed. It was this attitude which led to the actual expulsion from the Labour Party in 1939 of Sir Stafford Cripps, Aneurin Bevan and George Strauss. They had advocated a Popular Front, which would have included both Liberals and Communists, to oppose the Chamberlain Government. They were expelled by the National Executive and the expulsions formally endorsed by the Annual Conference.

The Standing Orders have been the *damnosa hereditas* of the Labour Party ever since. They were suspended from 1945–1952 and then reimposed. It inevitably happens, especially in a Party of the Left, that such Draconian rules are broken. The Whip is withdrawn from the offending Members or they may even be threatened with expulsion from the Party. During the 1950s, Aneurin Bevan was again in danger of being expelled, and in 1961, five Labour Members were excluded from the Parliamentary Labour Party because they had revolted over the Service Estimates. It was, however, to be observed that none of them faced difficulties in his constituency. They were all readopted and all duly returned at the next General Election.

On the Conservative side, the effect of 1931 was, albeit for different reasons, much the same. Discipline was established which was almost military in character. The indulgence of earlier years entirely disappeared. This was mainly due to the nature of the Government's election appeal. They had not fought on a programme of specific measures but had asked for a 'doctor's mandate'. In other words, they were to be free to take any measures they pleased and could expect the uncritical loyalty of their supporters. Any recalcitrant Member who exercised his own judgment was guilty of a breach of faith with the electors, and of course, he forfeited any prospect of ministerial promotion. Hence the exclusion, already mentioned, of Mr Harold Macmillan and Mr Robert Boothby.

Unlike the Labour Party, the Conservatives had never handicapped themselves by a written code of behaviour. Their methods of enforcing discipline are less obvious though probably more effective. It has been said that the Labour Party specialises in public executions, the Conservatives in private assassination. The dissident Conservative does not have the Whip withdrawn. But he may have to face social ostracism, and the fountain of honour will not play upon him or any of his principal constituency supporters. Indeed, he may find himself disowned by his association.

This might well have happened to Mr Churchill. The Conservatives at Epping showed no apparent concern when he opposed the advance towards self-government in India. Many of them no doubt agreed with him. The situation was, however, quite different when he became the principal critic of the Chamberlain Government on foreign affairs and defence. Leading members of the constituency organisation publicly declared themselves against him. There was a move to adopt an official Conservative candidate. If there had been a General Election immediately after Chamberlain's return from Munich (which for the moment seemed a distinct possibility) he might well have lost his seat. He had been promised the support of the Liberals who had polled 10,000 votes in the previous election. But the glades of Epping were overwhelmingly Conservative and he might have suffered the fifth, and by far the most serious, defeat of his Parliamentary career.

From 1931 until 1940, the outstanding feature of Parliamentary life was the almost unvarying docility of Government supporters. The surrender over Abyssinia left them apparently unmoved. There were, of course, important resignations. Anthony Eden and his Parliamentary Secretary, Lord Cranborne, resigned in 1937 rather than countenance a further concession to Mussolini. Duff Cooper, a solitary figure, left the Government after Munich. It is almost inconceivable that their discontents were not widely shared on the Conservative Benches. But never did they receive in the division Lobbies any significant measure of support. In November 1938, a few weeks after Munich, the Liberals moved an amendment to the Address calling for the immediate creation of a Ministry of Supply to speed up re-armament. Mr Churchill made one of his most impassioned speeches :

'We have drifted on and we have drifted down and the question tonight is sharply, brutally even, whether we shall go on drifting or make a renewed attempt to rise abreast of the level of events. I put it as bluntly as I possibly can. If only 50 Members of the Conservative Party went into the Lobby tonight to vote for this amendment it would not affect the life of the Government but it would make them act. It would make a forward movement of real power, of real energy. We should get our Ministry of Supply no doubt, but much more than that we should get a feeling of renewed strength and a prestige outside this country which would be of real service and value . . . This is not a party question. It is not to do with party. It is entirely an issue which affects the broad safety of the nation.'

The appeal was made in vain. Only two Conservative Members voted with Churchill and the Liberals. In retrospect this is hard to understand, let alone justify. It can only be explained by the prevailing acceptance of rigid Party discipline which was the principal legacy of 1931.

Here, then, were the three consequences of the 1931 crisis. The first was the acceptance of inflexible Treasury orthodoxy with its consequence of stagnation and unemployment. The second was the policy of appeasement, first of Mussolini and later of Hitler, which resulted in the Second World War, and the third was the almost complete subordination of Members of Parliament to the Party machines.

CHAPTER V

1940

'The Ayes to the right, 281.
The Noes to the left, 200.
So the Ayes have it.
The House now stands adjourned.'

THE DATE WAS 8th May 1940. In the words of the customary formula
Mr Speaker FitzRoy declared the result of the most dramatic – and
incomparably the most important – decision in seven hundred years of
Parliamentary history.

Even the Great Division of 1831, when the Reform Bill was carried
by a single vote, appears insignificant by comparison. This was the only
occasion when not only the fate of a Government but the issue of defeat
or victory in a world war was decided in the lobbies of the House of
Commons.

When the figures were read out by the Government Chief Whip it
seemed like a Parliamentary miracle. On the Tuesday afternoon, when
the Norway debate began, it was not even certain that the Opposition
would divide the House.

Very few people will now defend the record of the Baldwin–Chamberlain Governments. They wholly miscalculated the danger from the Axis
powers. At one stage they were prone to exaggerate the danger of aerial
bombardment. Yet they let the Royal Air Force be greatly out-numbered
by the Luftwaffe. In foreign policy they were victims of their own illusions. During the early months of the war, that is before the Norwegian
invasion, they showed themselves infinitely complacent. Why was it that
Parliament, and to a large extent the country, supported them for so
long? In part it was due to the causes discussed in the last chapter.
Party discipline was stronger than ever before, and the mood of a great
number of electors was still thoroughly pacifist. But in part it was due
to an event which no-one at Westminster could have foreseen.

The General Election took place in October 1935, and the Conservatives had a reduced, though comfortable, majority. On 12th November there took place a Debate on the Address. Churchill attacked the Government for having failed to keep their pledge that in air power this country should no longer be inferior to any country within striking distance of our shores. He continued :

'The Government cannot make up their minds, or they cannot get the Prime Minister to make up his mind. So they go on, in strange paradox, decided only to be undecided, resolute to be irresolute, adamant for thrift, solid for fluidity, all-powerful to be impotent. So we go on, pouring more months and years away – precious – perhaps vital years for the greatness of Britain – for the locusts to eat.'

Baldwin replied :

'I put before the whole House my own views with appalling frankness. From 1933 I and my friends were all very worried about what was happening in Europe. You will remember at that time the Disarmament Conference was sitting in Geneva. You will remember at that time there was probably a stronger pacifist feeling running through the country than at any time since the War. I am speaking of 1933 and 1934. You will remember the election at Fulham in the autumn of 1933 when a seat which the National Government held was lost by about 7,000 votes on no issue but the pacifist. You will remember, perhaps, the National Government candidate who made a most guarded reference to defence was mobbed for it.

That was the feeling in the country in 1933. My position as a leader of a great party was not altogether a comfortable one. I asked myself what chance was there – with that feeling that was given expression to in Fulham so common throughout the country – what chance was there within the next year or two of that feeling being so changed that the country would give a mandate for rearmament. Supposing I had gone to the country and said that Germany was rearming and we must rearm, does anybody think that this pacific democracy would have rallied to that cry at that moment? I cannot think of anything that would have made the loss of the election from my point of view more certain.'

This was one of the most extraordinary speeches ever delivered in the House of Commons. As Baldwin's biographers, Middlemas and Barnes, have written, 'It could purely be read as a piece of naked opportunism'. This indeed was how it was understood. The biographers go on to say, 'At the time it aroused little interest in the House of Commons.' This is not the author's recollection. Members on all sides were appalled.

Baldwin's reputation plunged, both in the House and in the country.

Even the disciplined loyalty of the Parliamentary rank and file might have been insufficient to sustain him. Four days later the Abdication crisis broke. Already, of course, the Prime Minister was aware of the prospect. In the previous month Mrs Simpson had obtained a decree nisi at Ipswich. The English Press with difficulty had remained silent about Mrs Simpson and the heir apparent to the Throne. Not so the American Press. When meeting Baldwin on 16th November the King said: 'I want you to be the first to know, that I have made up my mind and nothing will alter it – I have looked at it from all sides – and I mean to abdicate to marry Mrs Simpson.'

There is no need here to trace the course of events ending in the actual abdication on a night in that November. It would, however, be difficult to exaggerate their effect on the political scene. Public feeling was overwhelmingly opposed to Mrs Simpson becoming Queen. Members of Parliament returning from their constituencies in all parts of the country reported the same reaction. Regardless of Party, there was almost universal admiration for the way in which the matter had been handled by the Prime Minister. So his speech of 'appalling frankness' was generally forgotten or brushed aside. At the same time Churchill, who had endeavoured to support the King, was discredited. So the Government went on its way with renewed authority.

Throughout these years there was a close understanding between Churchill and the Liberal leader, Sir Archibald Sinclair. It was an association which went back for many years. When, in 1915, Churchill had resigned office and gone to the front, Sinclair had been a major in his battalion. Since 1922 Sinclair had sat in Parliament as Liberal Member for Caithness and Sutherland. He had always taken a very special interest in the Royal Air Force, and indeed his maiden speech on 21st March 1923 was on the need for equality in the air with any other European power.

In the General Election of 1935 Sir Herbert Samuel was defeated at Darwen. Eighteen Liberal Members were left, including Lloyd George, his son Gwilym, his daughter Megan and a relative by marriage, Goronwy Owen. In the previous Parliament they had occupied a position of detachment. Now they associated once more with their fellow-Liberals. Lloyd George, of course, occupied a position on the Opposition front bench; the other three sat on the Liberal bench – the second bench below the gangway.

Lloyd George attended the first Party meeting after the General Election, and proposed the election of Sinclair as leader. Sinclair accepted, but on one condition – that emphasis should in future be laid on national defence. As the smaller Opposition Party the Liberals had limited opportunities of choosing subjects for debate. They could select 3½ Supply Days in the year and could move an Amendment to the Address. These opportunities were fully used. In particular the Liberals drew attention to the need for parity in the air. Moreover they demanded a Ministry of Supply. This was a matter which they raised in Parliament in November 1938, on the occasion to which reference was made in the last chapter, when Mr Churchill appealed in vain for the support of fifty Conservative Members.

It was at this time that Churchill was threatened with an official Conservative opponent in the Epping Division. If there had been an election immediately after Munich he might well have lost his seat. The Liberal candidate at the previous election, Mr Granville Sharpe, had polled 2,000 votes. He and the President of the Epping Liberal Association waited on Churchill. They assured him that, in the event of an early election, there would be no Liberal opposition and that they would do their utmost to induce Liberal voters to give him their support. This may have had something to do with the tribute which Churchill paid in the debate of 3rd April, 1939:

'I must say I think it is a fine hour in the life of the Liberal Party, because from the moment that they realised that rearmament was necessary they seemed to seek to bring forward together the material and moral strength of this country, and I believe at this moment they represent what is the heart and soul of the British nation'.

It is unfortunate that none of this appeared in the first volume of Churchill's memoirs of the Second World War, *The Gathering Storm*[1]. On the contrary, Mr Churchill referred to 'The utter devotion of the Liberals to sentiment apart from reality.'

The explanation may lie in the fact that this book was written just after the war, when Churchill was greatly chagrined that the Liberals refused to support him in the 1945 election.

The Labour Party played a somewhat different role. In part this was due to the character of their membership. In those days the Party in the House of Commons largely consisted of retired Trade Union officials. No doubt these old gentlemen provided an element of stability. But they took very little part in debate. Moreover they were more antipathetic to arms expenditure than the Liberals. Therefore the Labour Party continued for a time to oppose the Service Estimates. The inconsistency was frequently pointed out. The Labour Party denounced the aggression of the Axis Dictators. They wished to see the League of

[1] Cassell, 1948.

Nations act as international policemen. But, it was said, they refused to give the policeman his truncheon.

This attitude was somewhat modified in 1938 and 1939. The change was due to the influence of Hugh Dalton. Here was a remarkable character. He was a man of boundless vitality. He had served in the Army in Northern Italy in the first war. He had been Under-Secretary for Foreign Affairs under Arthur Henderson in the second Labour Government. He had travelled widely. He had marked predilections. His favourite country was Poland, and one of his personal friends was General Sikorski. On the other hand he loathed the Germans. This was not just an intellectual distaste, it was sheer antipathy. When, in 1940, on the formation of the Churchill Coalition, he became Minister of Economic Warfare, his satisfaction knew no bounds. He was blockading Germany.

On the other hand, Dalton was a leading exponent of Labour's political isolationism. During these years there was a series of attempts to draw together all the opponents of the Government's policies. In part, the inspiration came from the Spanish Civil War. In December 1936 there was held an 'Arms and The Covenant' meeting at the Albert Hall. The prime mover was Churchill, the Chairman was Walter Citrine, the Secretary of the Trade Union Council. The audience included members of all Parties. This was followed by the Unity Campaign, which was initiated at a meeting at the Free Trade Hall, Manchester, on 24th January 1937. It represented an agreement between the Socialist League, led by Sir Stafford Cripps, the I.L.P. and the Communist Party. A Unity manifesto was published, calling for 'Unity in the Struggle against Fascism, Reaction and War and against the National Government'. It advocated the return of a Labour Government as 'the next step in the advance to working class power'. Undoubtedly this had a wide public appeal. But the official Labour Party would have none of it. On 27th January the National Executive condemned collaboration with Communism in a document entitled 'Party Loyalty'. They expelled the Socialist League from the Party. Their document declared that the need was for 'A real and not a sham unity. The real United Front is that of the Socialist, Trade Union and Co-operative movements'. The Socialist League dissolved itself in March, but left individual members free to support the Unity Campaign. The Executive replied by threatening to expel Labour Party members who did so.

The movement for combined opposition was revived in 1938. On this occasion it made a wider appeal. No longer did it call merely for

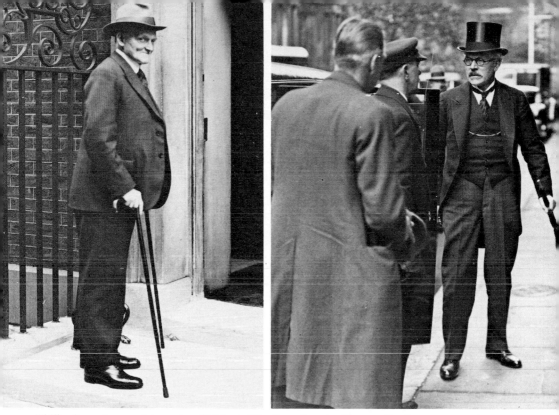

Philip Snowden arriving at a Cabinet Meeting after the Ottawa Conference on 27th August 1932, and (*Right*) Cabinet meeting on 30th September 1932. Ramsay MacDonald at Downing Street

The Ottawa delegates on the *Empress of Britain* on their way to Canada, 14th July 1932. L to R (seated) J H Thomas, Stanley Baldwin, Neville Chamberlain. (Standing) Sir Philip Cunliffe-Lister, Lord Hailsham, Walter Runciman and Sir John Gilmour

The British War Cabinet in November 1939. L to R (standing) Sir Kingsley Wood (Secretary of State for Air), Winston Churchill (first Lord of the Admiralty), Leslie Hore-Belisha (Secretary of State for War), Lord Hankey (Minister without Portfolio). L to R (seated) Viscount Halifax (Secretary of State for Foreign Affairs) Sir John Simon (Chancellor of the Exchequer) Neville Chamberlain (Prime Minister) Sir Samuel Hoare (Lord Privy Seal) and Lord Chatfield (Minister for the Co-ordination of Defence)

Leslie Hore-Belisha, Secretary of State for War, addressing militiamen at Guildford on 15th July 1939. The first draft of 34,000 militiamen started training that weekend.

working class solidarity. It was aimed at bringing together not only Labour and Communists, but also the Liberals and others who opposed the Government's policy. It appeared to be having a considerable success. In the autumn of 1938 there was a by-election at Bristol. Vernon Bartlett stood as an Independent with combined Liberal and Labour support. He achieved a signal victory over the official Conservative. But here again the official Labour Party would not have it. Constituency associations which supported the movement were threatened with disaffiliation. In January 1939 Cripps, who was himself a member of the National Executive, circulated a memorandum advocating a Popular Front Campaign supporting 'a popular policy of peace by collective action'. It was rejected by the National Executive. Cripps then circulated it to local Labour Parties and other organisations. Together with Aneurin Bevan and G. R. Strauss he was expelled from the Labour Party by the National Executive. His expulsion was moved by Dalton.

Cripps appealed to the Party Conference. As an exceptional indulgence he was permitted to address them. His speech was not a success, though in any case it would have made no difference. The debate marked the first appearance in public life of young Mr George Brown, representing the St Albans Divisional Labour Party. He was called to second the resolution put forward by the Executive. The occasion was described in *The Times*:

> In a maiden speech Mr Brown mingled impassioned indignation with reproach. Coming from one of the backward Labour areas he called plague on all party tension and appealed to the delegates to put an end to dissension.

This was received with immense enthusiasm. Cripps, Bevan and Strauss were escorted from the hall.

Again it is necessary to observe the date. It was 20th May 1939. This was after the German march on Prague. The policy of appeasement lay in ruins. War was only three months away. The Labour Party, and certainly Mr Dalton himself, were fully aware of the dangers ahead. Even so the tenets of Party orthodoxy remained.

Reference has already been made to Churchill's unofficial alliance with the Liberals across the floor of the House. On the Conservative side he could rely on Brendan Bracken, Robert Boothby, and his son-in-law, Duncan Sandys. However, a new grouping appeared in February 1938. This was when the Foreign Secretary, Mr Anthony Eden and the Under-Secretary, Lord Cranborne, resigned from the Government.

The principal cause, as is now well known, was Chamberlain's reply to Roosevelt. The American President had suggested to the Prime Minister a conference of the leading powers to consider ways of returning to more peaceful international relationships. It was a move of the utmost significance. If followed up it might have resulted in the end of American isolationism and it is at least conceivable that World War II might have been averted. But when the message arrived Eden was on holiday in the South of France. Chamberlain poured cold water on the plan. He suggested that it be postponed, stressed his own hopes for a friendlier atmosphere and his intention to give *de jure* recognition to the Italian occupation of Abyssinia. The Opposition was ignored because, as Churchill has said, 'This narrow, obstinate man turned away the proffered hand stretched out across the Atlantic'.

Eden, when he returned, was naturally furious. He managed to procure a somewhat more conciliatory message to be dispatched to Washington : but the damage had been done and the President never reverted to his hope. This was unknown at the time to the general public who thought that the cause for the resignations was Chamberlain's appeasement of Mussolini. The Franco Government was being maintained in large part by Italian volunteers. There had been a token gentleman's agreement in 1937. This contemplated the withdrawal of volunteers and the cessation of Italian broadcast propaganda against Britain.

In February Mussolini made a new offer for negotiations. Chamberlain was entirely in agreement. Eden was against. There was an interview on 18th February between Chamberlain, Eden and the Italian Ambassador Signor Grandi. Chamberlain aligned himself completely with Grandi. Two days later it was announced that Eden and Cranborne had resigned. Their resignation speeches were delivered to a packed House. Indubitably Cranborne was the more effective of the two, especially when he denounced 'surrender to blackmail'.

At this time Eden's prestige in the country stood very high. At any given moment there is only a limited number of politicians whose existence is realised by the general public. The man in the street (if he can be said to exist) is probably familiar with the names of the Prime Minister, the Leader of the Opposition, a few political veterans and one or two colourful figures. He would, as a rule, have great difficulty in recalling more than a dozen names.

During the 1920s and early 1930s this list would have been almost exclusively composed of established figures who had been on the scene before the war, or at least the early twenties. They would have included

Lloyd George, Churchill and Baldwin and possibly the two Chamberlains. Eden was the first young man during the thirties to obtain this degree of recognition. He was an attractive figure. His Homburg hat soon became famous. More important, he undoubtedly made a special appeal to the idealism of the thirties – that idealism which found its expression in the peace ballot and the support of the League of Nations Union.

This widespread feeling was not adequately reflected in the House of Commons. But a group of young Conservatives attached themselves to Eden. They were joined by Harold Nicolson, who has recorded a meeting of 9th November 1938. There were present Amery, Lord Cranborne (later Lord Salisbury), Sidney Herbert, Ronald Cartland, Sir Edwin Spears, Derrick Gunston, Emrys Evans, Anthony Crossley, Hubert Duggan. Harold Nicolson writes[1]:

> It was a relief to me to be with people who shared my views so completely and yet did not give the impression (as Winston does) of being more bitter than determined and more out for a fight than for reform.

Nevertheless, on 24th November Nicolson wrote:

> We still do not really constitute a group and Anthony still hesitates to come out against the Government.

It was this hesitation which characterised the group and its leader up to the beginning of the war. They were thoroughly unhappy and critical of the Government. Nevertheless they would not go into outright opposition, and they would not make common cause with Churchill and the Liberals.

Here, then, was the political grouping in the years preceding the war. Across the floor was the Churchill–Liberal alliance. The Liberals entirely accepted Sinclair's leadership. On the Opposition benches there was the Labour Party, which was just becoming increasingly realistic, but to a great extent, deprived of effectiveness by its own brand of particularist orthodoxy and the divisions which resulted. On the Government side there was the Eden group, critical but ineffective.

No-one who was present will forget the scene in the House of Commons on 28th September. Chamberlain was recounting the gloomy story of his meetings with Hitler at Berchtesgaden and Godesberg. Then his Parliamentary Private Secretary, Lord Dunglass, (later Sir Alec Douglas-Home), was seen proceeding along the second bench with

[1] *Diaries and Letters,* edited by Nigel Nicolson, Collins, 1966-8.

a document in his hand. He passed it to Simon, who laid it before the Prime Minister.

Chamberlain said, 'That is not all. I have something further to say to the House yet. I have now been informed by Herr Hitler that he invites me to meet him at Munich tomorrow morning. I need not say what my answer will be.'

There was mass hysteria on the Government benches. With only one or two exceptions Members leapt to their feet. They cheered; they waved their order papers; some of them wept with relief. But this demonstration was almost entirely confined to the Government side. A legend has grown up that the whole House rose in one united demonstration. This is untrue. Labour and Liberal Members (with one single exception) grimly kept their seats.

Chamberlain returned bringing 'peace with honour' and the document signed by Herr Hitler and himself. This declared that the Munich Agreement 'was symbolic of the desire of our two peoples never to go to war with one another again'. Apparently Chamberlain had not at first intended to reveal it to the cheering crowd which greeted him on his return to London. But as he looked out at the scene of wild enthusiasm in Downing Street he yielded to the obvious temptation and read it out.

Undoubtedly the Munich Agreement was in the first place immensely popular. There was a wave of relief, especially among the women voters. *The Times* declared : 'No conqueror returning from victory on the battlefield had come adorned with nobler laurels.' But the mood of euphoria soon passed away. The debate in the House of Commons was critical in the extreme. Churchill said :

'I will begin by saying what everybody would like to ignore or forget but which must nevertheless be stated, namely that we have sustained a total and unmitigated defeat and that France has suffered even more than we have.'

And then, in November, came further news from Germany. The German Ambassador in Paris was assassinated by a Jewish boy. The reaction was a wave of persecution against the German Jewish community. As this became known to the British public there was a very sharp reaction.

Nothing, however, could shake the complacency of the leading Ministers and more especially of Chamberlain himself. On 3rd October he had a conversation with Lord Swinton, who until the previous year had been Secretary of State for Air and largely responsible for the development of the fighter programme. Chamberlain sought his support in the House of Lords.

Swinton said, 'I will support you, Prime Minister, provided that you are clear that you have been buying time for rearmament.'

Chamberlain produced a paper which had been signed by Hitler and said, 'But don't you see, I have brought back peace.'

This complacency continued. On 10th March 1939 Chamberlain informed the lobby correspondents in the House of Commons that 'Europe was settling down to a period of tranquillity'. On the same day Sir Samuel Hoare attacked the 'jitterbugs' who were predicting war. He said he envisaged a new age in which the three dictators, Hitler, Mussolini and Franco and the British and French Governments would work together in endeavouring to ensure peace, to raise the standard of living to a height never before possible. This attitude was exemplified in the notorious *Punch* cartoon with the caption 'The Ides of March'. It showed a nightmare of war disappearing through the window and John Bull waking from his night's rest. This precisely represented the attitude of Chamberlain and his leading colleagues.

On the same day that the cartoon appeared the German armies marched on Prague. Czechoslovakia as an independent State ceased to exist. It was replaced by the German Protectorate of Bohemia and Moravia. The Gestapo moved in. Chamberlain's immediate reaction was strangely muted.

He told the House of Commons: 'It's natural that I should bitterly regret what has now occurred. Do not let us on that account be deflected from our course. Let us remember the desire of all the peoples of the world still remain centred on hopes of peace.' But two days later he delivered a far more emphatic speech in Birmingham. After declaring his sympathy for the 'proud, brave people who have suddenly been subjected to this invasion, whose liberties are curtailed, whose national independence is gone,' he went on to say, 'Is this in fact a step in the direction of an attempt to dominate the world by force?' If so, Britain would resist it to the utmost of her power.

The first step in such resistance was the Polish Guarantee. On 31st March Chamberlain declared to the House of Commons that in the event of any action which clearly threatened Polish independence and which the Polish Government accordingly considered it vital to resist with their national forces, His Majesty's Government would feel themselves bound at once to lend the Polish Government all support in their power. In the ensuing debate a few days later it was left to Lloyd George to point out that any such support could not be effective without the co-operation of the Soviet Union.

But in spite of these traumatic events, the outlook of Ministers (with the exception of Halifax) remained fundamentally unchanged. This had been made clear in the debate on 15th March. In what was perhaps the most effective speech of his career. Eden retorted :

'This, the greatest democracy in Europe to make a national effort without parallel in its history'. He proceeded 'I beg Hon. Members to give heed. It would not be a mere party political matter. It is our duty forthwith to examine, as we must examine, the new military and strategic positions that confront us in Europe, to consult all those nations who are like-minded with us, wherever they may be and of whatever colour, to discuss with those nations what our policy should be and where we will make our stand, and, having determined that, make with them at once a military plan to give effect to our decision.'

Simon replied in behalf of the Government :

'It is a really necessary principle of British foreign policy, whatever the complexion of the Hitler Government, that while we have our definite commitments and while we have principles on which we ought to agree, it is essential that we should not enter into an extensive in-definite commitment, with the result that the control of our own foreign policy will depend not on this country, on this Parliament, on the elec-tors, but upon a whole lot of foreign countries.'

This was the authentic voice of the isolationists. In matters of foreign policy Simon was at least consistent – perhaps unconsciously so. He was the spiritual heir of Bright, and the Liberal pacifists of the nine-tenth century who had hated war and disliked all foreign entangle-ments. It is true that the Polish Guarantee a fortnight later represented a departure from this doctrine. But the importance of Simon's declara-ion lay in the fact that he was one of the triumvirate – Chamberlain, Simon and Hoare – who were in effective control of the Government. A great deal has been written about the abortive negotiations with the Soviet Union and the dilatory manner in which they were approached by the British Government. In a sense this is a reflection of their funda-mental outlook. They were constrained to give guarantees to Poland and later to Rumania. They could not avoid negotiations with the Soviet Union. This, however, might involve commitments from which they instinctively recoiled. It may be that this is the psychological explanation for the dilatory and half-hearted manner in which the negotiations were carried on. Chamberlain had three times flown to meet Hitler. No Minister was despatched to Moscow. First Mr William Strang, a Foreign

Office official, was sent, followed by a Service Mission. They did not fly. In each case they proceeded by a leisurely sea voyage across the North Sea and the Baltic.

The attitude of the Eden group towards the Government as a whole and the Prime Minister in particular seemed to vary. Thus, in the debate on 3rd April 1939 Harold Nicolson said :

'I wish merely to add my pebble to that great bastion of support which the Prime Minister must now feel he has behind him. I think it is only fair and fitting that those who have criticised the Munich Agreement should admit that on one point at least we made a miscalculation. We grossly underestimated the effect which the Prime Minister's visit would have on the German population. I see now that the impression derived by the German people from the presence in their midst of that resolute pacifist, that determined civilian, is an impression which has sunk so deep and so wide into the German conscience that no propaganda, or artifice on the part of Dr Goebbels, no injection of fear and envy, of hatred or of malice in the exhausted veins of the German people will remove from their minds and their memories the consciousness that that statesman visited there for one purpose only, namely the avoidance of war. I think we must admit, those of us who criticised Munich at the time, that although the Agreement left us later with so many disillusions and such grave disappointment, that personal impression remains. It would be the Prime Minister's great justification in history; and today it remains one of our greatest assets. Let us exploit that asset.'

The only full-blooded attack from among this group on the Prime Minister came from Ronald Cartland. When on 2nd August the House rose for the summer recess, it was proposed to adjourn until 3rd October, with the proviso that the Speaker might recall the House on the advice of the Prime Minister. From the Labour benches Arthur Greenwood moved an amendment that the House should return on 21st August. Chamberlain resisted and treated the matter in effect as a vote of confidence in himself. Ronald Cartland, the young Member for Kings Norton, sprang to his feet and declared :

'We are in a situation that within a month we may be going to fight and we may be going to die'. (Hon. Members, 'Oh !') 'It is all very well for Hon. Members to say 'Oh'. There are dozens of young men today training in camp and giving up their holidays and the least we can do here, if we are not going to meet together from time to time and keep Parliament in session is to show that we have in that place a democratic institution. I cannot imagine why the Prime Minister could not have made a great gesture in the interests of national unity. This is much more important, as my Right Hon. Friend the Member for Sparkbrook said, to get the whole country behind him rather than make jeering, pettifogging speeches which divide the nation. How can the Prime Minister ask for real confidence for himself as Prime Minister, and as leader of the country rather than the leader of a party? I frankly say that I despair when I listen to speeches like that to which I have listened this afternoon.'

Not surprisingly it gave great offence to the Members sitting round him. Sir Patrick Hannon was the Member for another Birmingham constituency and a well-known figure in the Conservative establishment. Speaking with furious indignation he said :

'We have heard this afternoon a very remarkable speech from the Member for Kings Norton (Cartland). As I was partly responsible for getting him his present seat I apologise to you, Mr Deputy Speaker, and to the House, for the poisonous quality of the speech he delivered this afternoon.'

He ended by expressing on behalf of his colleagues present 'our profound devotion to the Prime Minister and our complete confidence in the policy he is pursuing.' Moreover there was no doubt that most Members endorsed the sentiments expressed by Sir Patrick Hannon. He spoke for the great mass of Government supporters. Nothing, it seemed, could induce them on any issue whatsoever to vote against the Prime Minister.

This was the strangest phenomenon of political life in 1939. Chamberlain was not a magnetic, nor even a comparatively attractive figure. He made no appeal to the imagination. He did not appear, like Baldwin, as the embodiment of insular good humour and common sense. He had suffered an enormous reverse. His belief in Hitler's good faith was shown to be a complete delusion. The phrase 'Peace with Honour' had been shown to be a hollow illusion. So had the policy of appeasement. Yet despite this he still possessed the genuine loyalty of the great majority of Conservative Members.

On 2nd September the House appeared to be on the verge of an explosion. It was a Saturday evening. The German Army had invaded Poland forty-eight hours before. Everyone expected that Britain would fulfil her guarantees by declaring war on Germany. At the request of the French, Chamberlain was delaying the declaration. But he could not say so, and it appeared for the moment as if the British Government would go back on their pledge. The House was appalled. This was the occasion when, as Greenwood rose to follow the Prime Minister, Amery shouted across the floor 'Speak for England'. And when a few minutes later the House rose Greenwood sought out the Prime Minister in his room. 'Unless we are at war by tomorrow night neither you nor I can hold this House of Commons.'

Whether or not this was a true assessment no-one will ever know. The next day Britain declared war. Parliament met on the Sunday for the first time in three hundred years. There was a sense of anti-climax and the House of Commons gave almost formal assent to a series of Emergency measures. The Government was reconstructed. Churchill and Eden returned to office. It did not appear as if there could be any serious threat to the ascendancy of Chamberlain and his colleagues. Yet less than eight months later they were overthrown.

Of course the immediate cause of this was the Norway disaster. This, however, was only the climax of a continuing process. During the next eight months a series of events resulted in the continuous erosion of confidence. Members of Parliament, however strong their party loyalty was, could not fail to be aware of the manifest errors of the Administration and the growing dissatisfaction in the country.

This dissatisfaction began with the reconstruction of the Government. When a war begins the creation of new Departments becomes inevitable. This creates the opportuniy to bring in younger men. Chamberlain did not seize it. His Government was already a government of old men and more old men were called in. Colonel Hankey became Lord President of the Council at the age of 62. In view of his unique experience as Secretary of the Cabinet it was perhaps understandable. The next post to be filled was that of Minister of Shipping – obviously an appointment of the highest importance. To the general amazement the Prime Minister appointed Sir John Gilmour. Sir John was 64 years old. In earlier years he had been a highly inarticulate Home Secretary. He had retired to the back benches in 1936 and had become one of the respected father figures of the House of Commons. Everyone had naturally supposed that his Ministerial career was at an end. Now, however, he was entrusted with a key war-time post. There was universal astonishment. Miss Ellen Wilkinson asked what qualifications the new Minister possessed for his appointment. Chamberlain snapped back 'Character and experience'.

It was also necessary to create a Ministry of Information and to appoint a Minister. In war-time this is the most controversial of all Departments. It is, in effect, a Ministry of Propaganda. It has to decide what news should be released and what form it should take. It is besieged every day by journalists whose demands for news must somehow be met. It must wage a continuous battle with the Service Departments and the Foreign Office, whose invariable line is in favour of concealment. Everything depends on the personality of the Minister – his experience of the Press and his flair for public relations. Chamberlain appointed Lord Macmillan, who was 67 years old. He was a distinguished Scottish judge who in fact for many years had sat at the Court of Sessions and later in the House of Lords. In 1937 he had published a delightful volume of collected addresses which included such subjects as 'Law Making', 'Law and Religion', 'The Ethics of Advocacy' and 'The Professional Man'. They had been delivered to various learned societies such as the Edinburgh Philosophical Institution and the Royal Medico-Psychological Association. No-one could doubt his intellectual prowess. But also no-one could discern anything in his career which qualified him to be a war-time Minister of Information.

In wartime there is inevitably a large increase in public expenditure. No doubt this has to be watched. Nevertheless the attempt to observe a rigid code of Treasury control took several forms which could hardly be defended.

Here are two examples : On Sunday, 3rd September, after the declaration of war had been announced, the House of Commons proceeded to pass, with very little dissent, a series of wartime measures. One of them provided for the grant of pensions to those whose sons were killed in the war. It was, however, further provided that anyone who drew such a pension would become ineligible for the statutory old age pension. It was at once pointed out from the Liberal benches that there had been no such prohibition in the First World War. The Minister in charge of the Bill was constrained to agree to an amendment, with the result that those who lost their sons would be eligible for both pensions. Of course it could be said that the matter was put right at the first Parliamentary opportunity. But why had the Treasury officials ever supposed that the proposals could be justified or that it would be tolerated by Parliament? And why had the Minister agreed?

On 18th October there was a debate on Dependants' Allowances and Disability Pensions. Only a single back bench speaker supported the Government. Otherwise there was a universal chorus of criticism. The proposed allotments for servicemen's wives and families were universally regarded as inadequate. It was 17/– for a wife, 5/– for the first child, 3/– for the second, 2/– for the third and 1/– per week for each further child. Of course these allowances had to be increased.

Secondly, there was the Royal Warrant on Disability Pensions. It contained the following provision :

A disability shall not be certified to be attributable to military service during the war unless there is definite evidence of the wound, injury or disease in contemporary official records, or, where such records are not available, there is other definite collateral evidence, and in either case the evidence is good and sufficient and leaves no doubt in the mind of the certifying medical authority that the disability was in fact attributable to war service.

It was abundantly clear that in any dispute over eligibility for a war pension everything was to be weighted against the claimant. If there was the slightest doubt that his illness or injury was due to war service that doubt would be resolved against him. It is difficult to understand the mentality of those who framed such a provision. Of course it could not stand up to Parliamentary criticism. Following the debate on 18th October the Royal Warrant was withdrawn and redrafted in very different terms. Here again the question suggests itself : how could anyone in the department concerned or any competent Minister suppose that such an instrument would be allowed to remain unamended?

On 31st October there was a further debate which did nothing to restore the credit of the Government. The subject was the Defence Regulations. One of the unhappy memories of the First World War was of DORA (the Defence of the Realm Act) and the restrictions imposed thereunder. Now the Government assumed similar powers. They could arrest and detain persons without trial under Regulation 18(b). They could impose a curfew. They could suppress newspapers. They could prosecute anyone who engaged in allegedly subversive propaganda. No-one suggested that emergency powers should not be conceded in time of war. These regulations, however, were even more draconian than those in the First World War. They contained provisions which could have made impossible any form of criticism of the Government or its agents. One example will suffice :

No person shall endeavour to cause disaffection among any persons engaged (whether in the United Kingdom or elsewhere) in His Majesty's service.

The word 'disaffection' was not defined. This was typical of the extreme imprecision with which the Regulations were drafted.

It was further laid down that 'No person shall endeavour, whether orally or otherwise, to influence public opinion (whether in the United

Kingdom or elsewhere) in a manner likely to be prejudicial to the defence of the Realm or the efficient prosecution of the war.' Thereafter public opinion was defined as including 'the opinion of any section of the public'. It was obvious that these provisions, if strictly applied, might inhibit any form of free expression. What aroused even greater concern were the powers of detention under Regulation 18(b). The detainee might indeed go before an Advisory Committee. But there was no provision that he would even know the cause of his detention or the case that he had to meet.

There was a considerable furore. The nation was engaged in a war for freedom. On every hoarding Government posters appeared : 'Your freedom is in peril. Defend it with all your might.' It was, to say the least, a strange anomaly that the Government should take powers to suppress every form of free expression.

From the Liberal benches, with Labour support, a Prayer was moved to annul the Regulations. The Home Secretary was Sir John Anderson. He was a distinguished Civil Servant whom Chamberlain had drafted into his Cabinet. But like many other newcomers he was never at home in the House of Commons. His defence of the Regulations wholly failed to convince the House. The debate drew near its close. There were Conservative Members who disliked the Regulations hardly less than the Liberals and Socialists. It is said that a number of them went to Sir Samuel Hoare, who was to wind up the debate. They made it clear that if there were a division they would not vote for the Government. This put Ministers in a considerable dilemma. If the Prayer were carried and the Regulations annulled, all the internees under Regulation 18(b) must be released the next day. And indeed every other action taken in pursuance of the Regulations must be brought to an end.

The Government could only give way. Sir Samuel Hoare rose in his place. He recognised the feeling on both sides of the House and he proposed an all-Party conference in which the Regulations should be completely reframed. This was accepted by Sir Archibald Sinclair on behalf of the Liberals. Within the next few weeks the all-Party conference met in a committee room and the Regulations were completely redrafted.

It is unnecessary here to discuss in detail the changes that were made. It was provided that the Home Secretary could only detain a suspect under Regulation 18(b) with reasonable cause. This led to the famous case in the House of Lords of *Liversidge v. Anderson*. It was further provided that those who were detained should be informed of the grounds of their imprisonment so that they would know the case they had to meet before the Advisory Committee. Then it was laid down that where the Home Secretary did not accept the Committee's advice he was to inform the House of Commons in a monthly report.

The offence of seeking to influence public opinion in a manner likely to prejudice the defence of the Realm or the efficient prosecution of the was was qualified by the words 'by any false statements, false document or false report'. Moreover, it was to be a defence to any prosecution for the defendant to prove that he had reasonable cause to believe that the statement, document or report in question was true. There were a series of further amendments, all of which remained in force throughout the war. This was a considerable triumph for the libertarians in the House of Commons and showed that, even in wartime, Parliamentary criticism could be fully effective. Nevertheless, the fact remained that the Government had sustained another major reverse. Undoubtedly the new version, drawn up by the all-Party conference, was a great improvement on the old. But the question was, why it should have been necessary? No-one who studied the matter could help observing the sheer incompetence with which the original Regulations had been drafted.

There were other grounds of complaint. The early days of the war were marked by an extreme degree of administrative muddle. This was a matter on which Members of Parliament were left in no possible doubt. Their postbags were evidence enough. Every Member received anguished letters from soldiers' wives whose separation allowance had not been paid, or from other victims of bureaucratic unpreparedness. The newly established systems of control produced results which were sometimes in the realm of fantasy. For example, it was discovered that a consignment of fish landed at Fleetwood was shunted about the railways for five weeks, and eventually, in a state of advanced decomposition, arrived at Aberdeen.

These discontents did not at first find expression on the floor of the House of Commons. Members were reluctant openly to attack the performance of the Government lest by so doing they should give encouragement to the enemy. To meet this situation a Committee was formed which met every week in an upstairs committee room. The Chairman was Clement Davies and the Secretary Eleanor Rathbone. Here critics of the Government, including among others Lloyd George and Duff Cooper, freely expressed their misgivings.

Nevertheless the growing volume of criticism in the country had no perceptible effect on the Government. Ministers displayed an astonishing degree of complacency. I myself encountered a member of the

Cabinet in Gayfere Street at this time. Everyone had been abjured to carry his gas-mask and I had accordingly complied. Not so the Minister. When I asked the reason he laughed and said, 'There is no need. We shall have the German Generals suing for peace by Christmas.'

He was not the only Minister to live in a world of illusion. On 17th January 1940 there took place the first debate on Economic Warfare since hostilities began. Everyone was aware, and not least the Germans, that during the First World War the blockade had been an immensely powerful and possibly decisive weapon. So plans had been made to bring it once more into effect. The Ministry of Economic Warfare came into existence as soon as the war began, and during the next five years played a role of considerable importance. Its functions went far beyond the administration of contraband control. Among other duties it had to assess the economic situation of the enemy. In the January debate the Minister, Mr Ronald Cross, delivered a speech of almost unbelievable optimism.

He said: 'At the end of four and a half months of war we find Germany in something like the same economic straits as she was after two years of the last war.'

He went on to say: 'Let me give the House these two contrasts – a neutral sent a cake to a German family this year. A warm letter of thanks came back in which the German said his family wondered if they would ever see another. On the other hand sufficient crayfish are being imported by aeroplane from the Danubian countries to supply a standing delicacy on the tables of the party leaders.'

He stated that shortages in Germany were already apparent in petrol, copper, iron, cotton, wool, oils and fats and in many other commodities. A warning note came from Mr Harold Macmillan who pointed out that Germany had been preparing for war for five years and had vast resources of many of the necessary materials for war.

Nothing, however, could shake the complacency of the front bench. Only a short time before, in a filmed interview, the Secretary of State for War, Mr Hore-Belisha, after a visit to the troops in France, had declared: 'The soldier has never been so well fed, so well clothed or so well equipped, and we are comfortably winning the war.' This mood continued until April 1940 when, just five days before the German invasion of Norway, Mr Chamberlain declared, 'Hitler has missed the bus.' Five days later he was met with the retort, 'Yes, but he's caught the boat.'

Ministers remained complacent. Nevertheless, throughout these early months of the war there was increasing discontent on the back benches.

In January the Prime Minister dismissed Hore-Belisha as Secretary of State for War. His reasons have never been fully explained. It is clear that there was growing incompatibility between the War Minister and the heads of the Army. Hore-Belisha had made himself a popular figure among the soldiers and it was widely believed that his dismissal was a surrender to the military hierarchy.

How far this is true will never be known. Chamberlain had informed Hore-Belisha that he was being dispensed with because of a 'prejudice' against him among the Army Chiefs, both in France and at the War Office. He would never specify the nature of the prejudice.

Public sympathy was undoubtedly with the discarded Minister. Hore-Belisha might have become a most formidable critic. He might, indeed, have been restored to office when the Chamberlain Government fell. But now a skeleton appeared from his past. In 1928 he had made a disastrous excursion into the City. He had no experience of business. Nevertheless he was a Member of Parliament. He had become Chairman or Director in five new companies. They had all ended in disaster. One example may be given. In October 1928 there was formed The City and Provincial Trust. It was to act as an issuing house; the Secretaries, Registrars or Transfer Agents for public companies, and as a trust and finance company. The prospectus, signed among others by Hore-Belisha, included the following passage :

> The Directors are in a position of influencing business under all three of the above headings, and from the offers now before them they have no hesitation in saying that the Company will be able to select from a considerable volume of profitable business. They are therefore of the opinion that the Company should earn very substantial profits on the capital employed, and as the expenses of this issue are more than covered by the existing Reserve Fund and the premiums receivable on the shares, the whole of this net profit will be immediately available to dividends and reserve.

The authorised capital was £100,000 in 5/– shares issued at 5/9d. The Company was wound up in November 1929. The shareholders got 2½d for every 5/9d subscribed. There were four other companies whose history was scarcely less unfortunate, although in two cases they were not wound up until a year or two after Hore-Belisha resigned from the Board. But there could be no doubt that his career in the City was an unmitigated disaster and he himself incurred a substantial loss. All this was forgotten, so far as it had ever been generally known, by 1940. But now, on 12th January, *Truth* published an article with the heading

'Belisha No Loss'. It set out in detail the history of the companies in which he had been concerned – the dates of their incorporation, the amount in each case and the authorised capital, the date of Mr Hore-Belisha's resignation from the Board and the date of winding-up. The impact was considerable. One question was asked at Westminster. Will he bring proceedings for libel? He never did. It is stated by Mr R. J. Minney in *The Private Papers of Hore-Belisha*[1] that he at once took the advice of eminent counsel, including Sir John Simon and Sir William Jowitt, and that the advice that he was given throughout this time was that it would not be in the national interest for him to take action against *Truth* with all the publicity it would involve. He said later : 'I confess that in the light of subsequent events, had I been guided alone by my own personal feeling, I would have taken action.' It should be added that fourteen years later *Truth* published what, in effect, was a complete apology. It referred to 'two articles containing unfair and baseless attacks upon him motivated by racial prejudice'. The present owner and editor repudiated the policy which could promote 'such examples of racial discrimination to disfigure its pages'. It was impossible, they said, to apologise for the actions of a previous editor, but they hoped that a rejection of his policies at this time might make it clear, as far as may be possible, that part of *Truth*'s past is now buried and forgotten.

But in January 1940 the damage had been done. The allegations in *Truth* remained uncontradicted and unexplained. Hore-Belisha's career never recovered.

Far more important, however, was the Debate on 17th March on Finland. On 30th November the Soviet Union had made their unprovoked attack on the Finns. The reaction in Britain was almost unanimous. Here was a case of naked aggression, no less reprehensible than the German invasion of Austria, Czechoslovakia and Poland. The sympathies of the Labour and Liberal Parties went out to the victims. The Conservatives were naturally antipathetic to Soviet Russia. Almost everyone was, therefore, agreed in condemning the Soviet aggressors, although there was a considerable difference as to how far Britain could or should assist the Finns. At one stage it was quite clear that the Government proposed sending an Expeditionary Force, though this was made impossible by the persistent neutrality of Norway and Sweden.

The war pursued its course. For many weeks the Finns held out in the face of overwhelming odds. At times it seemed as if they would achieve a miracle of resistance. The courage and tenacity of their soldiers

[1] Collins, 1960.

commanded world-wide admiration. But eventually, in March, they surrendered to the inevitable.

The Finnish war was debated in the House of Commons on 19th March. Six days earlier the Prime Minister had declared 'the Finnish Government had made repeated requests for materials and every one had been answered'. Anyone hearing this reply would have assumed, and been intended to assume, that the requests had been met. This was almost wholly misleading.

In the debate on 19th March Mr Harold Macmillan made what was probably the most effective speech of his career. He had been to Finland and observed at first hand the operations of the Finnish Army. He had also been supplied by the Finns with complete information. He informed the House that the British Government had only been able to send 25 howitzers out of 150 which had been asked for; and only 30 field guns out of 160; and that these consignments had not been despatched until a month after the request. As regards aircraft, 148 had been released to the Finns on paper, but only 101 had been despatched. Four had left England in December, 44 in January, 27 in February. The balance had been despatched in March, when they had ceased to be relevant. Faced with these disclosures Chamberlain was compelled to modify his earlier statement and to state that 'Every request was considered so far as it was possible'. But the damage to the Government's reputation in the House of Commons was irreparable. The downfall of the Chamberlain Government began in the Finnish Debate.

By this time the authority of the Government had largely disappeared. The question of an alternative was beginning to be discussed. One evening in April, a group of seven or eight Members met in the smoking room. They were drawn from all Parties. The question was discussed as to who should form a new War Cabinet. Each member of the group wrote down five names. When their suggestions were compared it was found that there was virtual unanimity. The five were Churchill, Halifax, Attlee, Bevin and Sinclair. The striking feature of this list was the inclusion of Bevin, who at that time was not even a Member of the House of Commons.

Even so, it seemed unlikely in the highest degree that the Government would in the near future be forcibly overthrown. The vocal critics on their own benches were still only a handful. There was nothing to indicate that any considerable section of Government supporters would depart from their ingrained habit of maintaining the Government in office whatever their private misgivings might be. Moreover, the Government majority of more than 200 appeared quite impregnable.

The German forces invaded Denmark on 9th April and on the same day were landed at five ports in Norway. The British Navy counter-attacked. They did not attempt, as had been originally intended, to seize Trondheim, but troops were landed at Namsos and Andalsnes. They could not, however, meet the attacks of the Luftwaffe and were evacuated after two weeks. A force seized Narvik, but had to be withdrawn a few days later. All this came as a tremendous shock to British public opinion and inevitably there was a debate in the House of Commons. It took place on 7th and 8th May 1940, and was unquestionably the most important debate in Parliamentary history. It resulted in the fall of the Government and, in the event, in an Allied victory. Nothing, however, could alter the formal proceedings of the House of Commons. The Official Report of 7th May begins with the following entry :

> Motion made and Question Proposed : That a sum, not exceeding £319,655 be granted to His Majesty, to complete the sum necessary to defray the charge which will come in course of payment during the year ending on the 31st March, 1941, for the salaries and expenses of the House of Commons, including the amount in aid of the Kitchen Committee. (Note, £155,000 has been voted on account).

> Motion made and Question Proposed : That the Chairman do report Progress, and ask leave to sit again [Captain Margesson], put and agreed to. Committee report progress to sit again tomorrow.

Then the Prime Minister rose to initiate a debate on the conduct of the war. No-one listening to his speech would have supposed that Britain had suffered a major defeat. He accepted that 'we have suffered a certain loss of prestige and a certain colour has been given to the false legend of German invincibility on land'. He dealt with the suggestion of a small War Cabinet following the Lloyd George pattern in the First World War. This he dismissed. Nevertheless he announced that Winston Churchill had become Chairman of the Military Co-ordinating Committee of the Cabinet and said, 'My Right Hon Friend very readily accepted the position.' He went on to say that thereafter Winston Churchill had been entrusted by the Cabinet 'with the guidance and direction of the Chiefs of Staff Committee.'

The Government were severely attacked by the two Opposition leaders, Mr Attlee and Sir Archibald Sinclair. Both of them had served in the First World War. Each of them criticised the sheer incompetence with which the Norwegian operation had been conducted. Speaking of men who had come back from Norway, Sir Archibald Sinclair said :

'These men gave me several examples of deficiency of equipment, but there are two which I ought to tell the House, of the muddle, waste and confusion that ought really to be the subject of enquiry. At one place two empty aircraft guns were landed. They had an unsuitable type of mounting. They were unprovided with height lines, they had no means of testing sights, no train, no fuse key to set fuses, no range tables and no trajectories to set to sights. The House will not be surprised to hear that these men told me that the guns were utterly useless.'

There followed speeches from Sir Henry Page Croft and Colonel Wedgwood. So far the debate had followed its normal pattern. It was clearly a bad day for the Government. Yet no-one thought that they would fall. Then there arose from the Conservative back benches Admiral of the Fleet Sir Roger Keyes. He had been the hero of the Zeebrugge expedition in the First World War. On this occasion he came to the House of Commons in his full uniform. He explained that he had done so for the first time because he wished to speak for officers and men of the fighting sea-going Navy who were very unhappy. He suggested that if a few ships had entered the Trondheim Fjord the whole result would have been different. 'It was surely worth almost any risk to win so great a prize.' He ended with a quotation from Nelson : 'I am of the opinion that the boldest measures are the safest'.

Sir Roger Keyes resumed his seat at 7.30. At 8.3 p.m. Mr Amery rose and addressed the House. This was the most exciting moment of his career. He had been an Under-Secretary in the Lloyd George Coalition of 1922 and (as recorded in an earlier chapter) one of those who had been in incipient revolt ever since. He had then been a Minister in the Conservative Government. He had not, however, been in office since 1931. He was on the extreme Right of the Conservative Party. In the days of Ottawa he had been the arch-Protectionist. When the Italians invaded Abyssinia his was almost the only voice raised in support of Mussolini. He combined both physical and mental energy in a remarkable degree and, although of very small stature, he was a leading mountaineer. Now he made the speech of his life. Remorselessly he exposed the sheer incompetence of the Norwegian Campaign. He denounced the Government :

'In recent years the normal weakness of our political life has been accentuated by a coalition composed upon no clear political principles. It was in fact begotten of a false alarm of the result of going off the Gold Standard. It is a coalition which has been living ever since in a twilight atmosphere, between Protection and Free Trade and between unprepared collective security and unprepared isolation.'

He went on to say that 'we must get into the Government men who could match our enemies in fighting standard, in strength, in resolution and in thirst for victory.' Then, with immense effect, he turned to the Front Bench and repeated what Cromwell had said to the Long Parliament :

'You have stood too long here for any good you have been doing, depart, I say, and let us have done with you. In the name of God, go.'

The effect of these two speeches from Sir Roger Keyes and Mr Amery was immense. At the beginning of the debate no-one had been quite certain whether there would even be a division. Now the possibility had come, and a few on the Government side had begun to consider the possibility of an adverse Conservative vote. Even so no-one foresaw the events of the next day.

The House reassembled on Wednesday afternoon. In private business it dealt with such important matters as the Brighton Marine Palace and Pier Bill and the Cardiff Corporation (Trolley Vehicles) Provisional Order Bill. Two well-known Members, Mr George Lansbury and Lt O'Connor had died, and suitable tributes were paid. Then the debate was resumed. Mr Herbert Morrison spoke for the Opposition. He attacked the triumvirate, Chamberlain, Simon and Hoare. He made it clear that the Opposition intended to force a vote and that every Member had a responsibility to record his particular judgment. Then Chamberlain made his fatal error. He said :

'It may well be that it is a duty to criticise the Government. I do not seek to evade criticism, but I say this, to my friends in the House, and I have friends in the House, no Government can prosecute a war effectively unless it has public and Parliamentary support. I accept the challenge, I welcome it indeed. At last we shall see who is with us and who is against us, and I call on my friends to support us in the Lobby tonight.'

This was perhaps the most ill-judged speech ever delivered in the House of Commons. Britain had suffered a major defeat. In any view this was a moment of supreme crisis. The reaction of the Prime Minister was to put on the Whips. He had completely failed to realise that the normal proceedings of the House had no relevance at this moment.

The speech produced a reaction which he could hardly have foreseen. At this moment Lloyd George was not in the Chamber. He was in fact undecided as to whether he would take part in the debate. His daughter Megan was sitting on the Liberal bench[1]. She rose and dashed out of

---

[1] I was sitting beside her. I remember saying, 'Your father must speak now.' But she did not need telling.

the House. Five minutes later Lloyd George came in.　●

For many years there had been a mutual antipathy between Lloyd
George and Chamberlain. Lloyd George had been persuaded to appoint
Neville Chamberlain as Director of National Service, during the First
World War. In later years he would describe their first meeting. He was
leaving for a conference in Paris, and Neville Chamberlain was introduced to him at Waterloo Station. Lloyd George was accustomed to
say : 'I was appalled.' [Lloyd George was something of a phrenologist].
'He had the smallest head of any man I had ever seen. Never trust a
man with a small head.'

Apart, however, from phrenological differences the two men were
wholly contrasting types. Lloyd George was discerning and imaginative
He was sometimes capable of major errors, as when he was deceived by
Hitler in 1936. His illusions did not last. Chamberlain was a man of
obvious integrity. If he had been Prime Minister in Victorian times he
might have been reasonably successful. He was, however, a bigoted and
isolated man who wholly failed to understand the problems with which
he was confronted. His early training had been in business and not in
politics. This was his drawback and it draws a moral. Business men in
politics are almost invariably disastrous. They seek to apply wholly unsuitable techniques. But however this may be, the final confrontation
between Lloyd George and Neville Chamberlain took place on the
afternoon of 8th May 1940.

Lloyd George rose at 5.37. As was his habit he began almost inaudibly,
so that Members shouted 'Speak up'. This is the technique of a Welsh
preacher. Everyone is straining to listen. But then his voice rose. He
spoke with the authority of the great Leader of the First World War.
He denounced the way in which the Government had conducted their
negotiations with the Soviet Union :

'We sent a first-class clerk to negotiate with the Prime Minister of
the greatest country of the world, while Germany sent her Foreign Secretary with a splendid retinue. That door is closed. Oil in foreign ships
is now carried across the Black Sea for the aeroplanes of Germany.
Strategically that was an immense victory for the Nazi Government.'

Then he referred to the Prime Minister's speech :

'Hitler does not hold himself answerable to the Whips of the
Patronage Secretary'.

Finally he came to his peroration :

'I was not here when the Rt Hon. Gentleman made the observation,
but he definitely appealed on a question which is the great national,
imperial and world issue. He said "I have my friends". It is not a ques-

tion of who are the Prime Minister's friends. It is a far bigger issue. The Prime Minister must remember that he has met this formidable foe of ours in peace and in war. He has always been worsted. He is not in any position to appeal on the grounds of friendship. He has appealed for sacrifice. The nation is prepared for every sacrifice so long as it has leadership, so long as the Government show clearly what they are aiming at and so long as the nation is confident that those who are leading it are doing their best. I say solemnly that the Prime Minister should give an example of sacrifice, because there is nothing which can contribute more to victory in this war than that he should sacrifice the seals of office.'

Lloyd George sat down at ten minutes past six. At eleven minutes past ten Churchill, as First Lord of the Admiralty, wound up the debate. It was the least effective speech of his whole career. In his memoirs he complained several times that the clamour was such that he could not make himself heard. He goes on to say : 'In all this time it was clear that the anger was not directed at me, but the Prime Minister, who I defended to my utmost ability and without regard to any very strong conviction.' Many of those who heard him formed the impression that he was doing so without conviction.

Then the Division Bell rang. Under the Standing Orders of the House of Commons six minutes were allowed. The bell rang a loud peal. Members, whether they had been in the Chamber or not, rushed to enter one lobby or the other before the six minutes elapsed. On this occasion there was, of course, no doubt that the Labour and Liberal Parties would give an adverse vote. But everything turned upon the Conservative dissentients. There were of course some, like Mr Law (son of Bonar Law), Mr Boothby, Mr Macmillan and Lord Winterton who could be relied upon to vote with the Opposition. But how many others? A group were gathered on the Government back benches below the gangway. They included Mr William Anstruther-Gray, Mr Quintin Hogg and a number of others. They were all in Army uniform. Until the last moment they were undecided. Then Mr William Anstruther-Gray pronounced his verdict. The fate of the nation was at stake and they could not be concerned with the Party Whips. So, with a few seconds to go, they proceeded into the No Lobby. Mr Quintin Hogg was the last of all. He had to force aside the attendant who was locking the door.

The scene in the No Lobby was unique in Parliamentary history. The Liberal and Labour Members, together with the habitual dissidents, were already there. Then, as the doors were about to close, the young Tories marched in. To at least one observer it appeared as if they were marching four abreast. They were all in uniform. The effect was tremendous.

Then, back in the Chamber, the figures were announced : Ayes 281, Noes 200. The Government majority was only 81 votes compared with the normal figure of over 200. On the Opposition side Members were preparing, in accordance with tradition, to shout 'Resign'. But Geoffrey Mander, recalling Amery's Cromwellian speech, on the day before, whispered that they should shout 'Go'. When the figures were announced Chamberlain rose and walked out of the House to shouts from the other side of 'Go, go, go'. It was his last appearance as Prime Minister.

Next day the Germans invaded the Low Countries. This created a new and ominous situation, and for a few hours Neville Chamberlain cherished the hope that he might remain at No 10. But the Labour and Liberal leaders were adamant. In no circumstances would they serve under him. Reluctantly, therefore, he handed over the seals of office and Churchill became Prime Minister. This was Churchill's supreme moment. He had had the most chequered career of any man in public life. Mr Robert Rhodes James has written a book entitled *Churchill: a Study in Failure*. It deals with the years up to 1938. He had been in the public eye ever since, in 1900, he had escaped from a Boer prison camp. He had been involved in every major controversy – often, it might be thought, on the wrong side. He had been responsible for sending British troops to Russia in 1920 to support Denikin and Koltchak and for the wasteful expenditure of £100 million. As Chancellor of the Exchequer he had taken Britain back on to the Gold Standard at the old parity, with disastrous results. As recorded in the last chapter, he had no understanding of, or sympathy with, Indian nationalism.

For many years he was the most distrusted politician in the whole country. Yet he had all the qualities needed in the crisis of May, 1940. He had a bulldog appearance. He had a remarkable command of the English language. His baroque style of oratory, derived from Gibbon and Macaulay, was precisely suited to the hour. It enabled him to make a series of patriotic and defiant speeches which rang through the country and the world.

Above all, he enjoyed making war. Margot Asquith has recorded how, on the night of the 4th August 1914, she looked down the stairs at 10 Downing Street and saw Winston Churchill 'with a happy face' striding towards the door of the Cabinet room. From his earliest days, when he had managed to attach himself to Kitchener's army and taken part in the Battle of Omdurman, his main interest had been in warfare.

Here was the main contrast between the outgoing and incoming Prime Ministers. Chamberlain had been reluctantly constained to go to war and had hated every moment of it. Churchill revelled in it and, so far as it was possible for one man, assumed its whole direction.

Here was the contrast with his predecessor in the First World War. Lloyd George had been full of ideas. But his genius lay in detecting and using the talents of those around him. He could always charm and persuade. Churchill, on the other hand, tended to down-grade his colleagues. The heads of the Service Departments were treated as mere administrators concerned with problems of supply and recruitment. The direction of the war rested with Churchill alone. He was a bad listener. Cabinet meetings tended to consist of a series of outbursts from the Chair. It almost became Government by rhodomomtade[1].

His accession was received with enthusiasm in the country. To use his own phrase about Lloyd George in the First World War, the people had 'an occult sense that he was the man to lead them to victory'. Nevertheless, there was still a sense of deep resentment among Chamberlain's supporters. In the early days Churchill made a series of speeches in Parliament which will never be forgotten. He proclaimed: 'We will fight on the hills. We will fight on the beaches. We will never surrender', and in a hardly less striking passage on 18th June he told the House that the Battle of France was over and the Battle of Britain was about to begin. There followed this passage:

'Upon this Battle depends the survival of christian civilization. Upon it depends our own British life and the long continuity of our institutions and our Empire. The whole fury and might of the enemy must very soon be turned on us. Hitler knows that he will have to break us in this island or lose the war. If we can stand up to him, all Europe may be free, and the life of the world may move forward into broad, sunlit uplands; if we fail, then the whole world, including the United States, and all that we have known and cared for, will sink into the abyss of a new dark age made more sinister and perhaps more prolonged, by the lights of a perverted science. Let us therefore brace ourselves to our duty and so bear ourselves that if the British Commonwealth and Empire lasts for a thousand years, men will still say 'This was their finest hour.'

[1] On one occasion I was summoned to a Cabinet meeting in the evening. I was concerned with Item 3 on the agenda. Mr Churchill had been at Marrakesh and it was not quite certain whether he had yet returned. The attendant at the door said to me 'If the Deputy Prime Minister (Attlee) is presiding, you will be away by half past seven. If the Prime Minister is back you will be fortunate to leave by half past nine.'

These speeches, delivered at such a moment, were in themselves a major contribution to ultimate victory. Their impact was hardly less in the United States than in Britain, and the words are still repeated in oratorical tournaments in American universities. In the House of Commons they were received with enormous enthusiasm by Labour and Liberal Members. But from the Conservative Members there was scarcely a cheer. They still could not overcome the fall of Chamberlain.

His other supreme achievement, which eventually determined the course of the war, was the understanding which he established with Roosevelt. As First Lord of the Admiralty he had been in direct correspondence with the President. Now Roosevelt continued to send his messages to 'Former Naval Person'. This relationship had two consequences of the utmost importance. In the first place the United States, while still technically neutral, agreed to Lend Lease. Without this form of aid it is difficult to see how Britain could have continued at war. Secondly, there was the decision taken after the Japanese attacked at Pearl Harbour. Many Americans were far more concerned with the war in the Pacific than in Europe. Yet Churchill was able to persuade Roosevelt that Europe should have the first priority.

The Government's position was by no means impregnable. The House of Commons had overthrown one Prime Minister : they could overthrow another. And during the next two years there was a series of miscalculations and disasters. It is now clear that after Wavell's early victories in North Africa, the Italians might have been completely driven out from their African territories, and the Germans would have been powerless to rescue them. But the troops were diverted to Greece and Crete, where they met swift and overwhelming defeat. For this Churchill himself must bear the responsibility. He despatched a telegram to Wavell : 'Our major effort must now be to aid Greece and/or Turkey. This rules out any serious effort against Tripoli.'

One disaster followed another. In the Far East Burma was lost; the *Prince of Wales* and the *Repulse*, despatched without air cover, were sunk by Japanese aircraft. On 11th February the German battle cruisers *Scharnhorst* and *Gneisenau*, together with the cruiser *Prinz Eugen*, which had been taking refuge at Brest for nearly a year, steamed up the Channel. Attempts were made to attack them by shore-based aircraft and destroyers. These were wholly unsuccessful and the German warships reached their destination. No-one could help comparing this event with Drake's harrying of the Spanish Armada. *The Times* observed that 'Vice-Admiral Ciliax had succeeded where the Duke of Medonia failed.'

Next, on 15th February, came the fall of Singapore which Churchill privately described as 'the most shameful defeat ever sustained by British arms'. And finally there was, on 21st June, the successful German attack on Tobruk. It fell after twenty-four hours and the Germans took 30,000 prisoners.

In fact the situation was less grim than it appeared. The Japanese had reached the limits of their expansion. They had abandoned any intention of advancing upon India. Their attempted invasion of Ceylon had been beaten off. Abyssinia had been liberated from Italian rule by British troops. The bulk of the German Army was irretrievably committed to the war in Russia. These considerations, however, were not apparent either to Parliament or to the general public. What could not be denied was that, since the Churchill Government had been formed, there had been a record (apart from Abyssinia) of unbroken defeat.

The Press were increasingly hostile. At Westminster the knives were out. It was in these circumstances that the Government had to meet its first and, with one later exception, its only serious challenge. This was the Vote of Censure moved on 1st July 1942. It was in these terms :

'That this House, while paying tribute to the heroism and endurance of the Armed Forces of the Crown in circumstances of exceptional difficulty, has no confidence in the central direction of the War.'

In retrospect it would seem that the Government were never in real danger. There was no alternative to Churchill who would have been acceptable to the House and the country. This, however, did not so clearly appear at the time. There was a general awareness as to the general extent of his personal direction of the war; he must therefore take responsibility for the disasters which had befallen. The House of Commons had overthrown one Prime Minister : they might well overthrow another. The debate began in a mood of tense excitement. Perhaps, after all, the scene of 8th May 1940 was about to be repeated.

The motion was proposed by Sir John Wardlaw-Milne, the Member for Kidderminster. He was a highly respected Conservative backbencher. He had already become a formidable critic of the Government, complaining that our troops in the Western Desert had been 'out-gunned and out-tanked'. His speech was in effect an attack upon Churchill. No-one, he suggested, should endeavour to combine the office of Prime Minister with that of Minister of Defence. In particular he dwelt on the fall of Singapore and the loss of Burma. Then he passed to Libya. He demanded 'an inquiry into what it is that causes us always to be behind the enemy'.

It was indeed a formidable indictment. Nevertheless, the effect was

completely destroyed by one short passage in the speech. He had argued
that we had suffered both on land and on sea from the want of the
closest examination by the Prime Minister of what was going on here
at home, and also by the want of direction which it received from the
Minister of Defence, or other officer, whatever his title might be, in
command of the Armed Forces. Then he continued :

'Incidentally, I hope the House will allow me to make one suggestion
in this connection. I do not know whether Members have thought of it,
but it would be a very desirable move, if His Majesty the King and His
Royal Highness will agree, if His Royal Highness, the Duke of Gloucester
were to be appointed Commander in Chief of the British Army – without
of course, administrative duty. He has experience of all fields of battle
in the present war, and I believe that his appointment would greatly
please all ranks of the Army and give them somebody entirely independent and capable of bringing forward the needs of the Army and views
of the ranks.'

There was a gasp of incredulity, and then a gale of laughter. The
Duke of Gloucester was a respected member of the Royal Establishment. But to suggest, at this time of crisis, that he should be placed at
the head of the Armed Forces was in the realm of fantasy. The debate
never recovered. Sir John had effectively defeated his own motion.

He was followed by Admiral of the Fleet Sir Roger Keyes, who had
intervened with such dramatic effect in the Norway Debate. But now
it was different. Sir John had attacked the Prime Minister for exercising
too much control. Sir Roger bitterly complained that he had exercised
too little – at least in Naval affairs. He said :

'It is hard that three times in the Prime Minister's career he should
have been thwarted – in Gallipoli, In Norway and in the Mediterranean
– in carrying out strategic strokes which might have altered the whole
course of two wars, each time because his constitutional Naval adviser
declined to share the responsibility with him if it entailed any risk.'

The contrast was not lost on the House. It was pointed out in an
intervention by Mr Campbell Stephen.

He was followed by the Minister of Production, Mr Oliver Lyttelton[1].
He was an eminent business man who had been brought into the Government and into the House of Commons when Churchill formed his
Government in 1940. No-one doubted his abilities as an administrator,
but like others who enter Parliament in middle age, he could never
adapt himself to the House of Commons. He began by expressing regret
that the Vote of Censure had been moved at all, and pointed out that

[1] Later Lord Chandos.

it had received wide publicity all over the world. Sir Herbert Williams, an inveterate critic of the administration, intervened to point out that the Government had come into existence on a Vote of Censure.

This speech had one possibly important consequence. Ever since the fall of Chamberlain an element in the Conservative Party had been looking around for an alternative to Churchill. Their resentment over the Norway Debate and its result remained unabated. They would have overthrown Churchill if they could. But who was to take his place? Various names were canvassed, and one of them was Oliver Lyttelton. No more was heard of this suggestion after his speech on the 1st July.

Lord Winterton then spoke, an ex-Minister who had been dropped from the Chamberlain Government. He was a high Tory but of independent mind. During the previous two years on the Opposition Front Bench, he had formed an unlikely alliance with Emanuel Shinwell. They were known as 'Arsenic and Old Lace'. Now he suggested that the Prime Minister should step down and be replaced by one of his colleagues. He did not specify which. The debate proceeded. There was an angry speech from Mr Clement Davies, who declared:

'We have had Norway, Dunkirk, Greece, Crete, North Africa, Hong Kong, Singapore and Malaya, the Dutch East Indies and Burma. How long will it be before the facts come home to the people in this House, as they have come home to the people of the country, that there is no confidence in a Government so closed to the realities of the case that they live in an atmosphere of romance which they themselves have created? I have no hesitation about the course I shall take in the division. Every man must judge for himself, on his own conscience, but if there is one man in this country who, on a two-year record of that kind, can say "I have complete confidence in that Government", I am sorry for that man.'

For personal reasons Mr Davies did not altogether carry conviction. It was true that, in its last stages, he had been a strong critic of the Chamberlain Government and had presided over the Committee which held its meetings upstairs as a focus of discontent. Nevertheless, it was not forgotten that in 1931 he had acceded to the leadership of Sir John Simon and became a Liberal National. Thereafter he had faithfully supported the Government until 1938 and had even voted with them in the Munich Debate. He had undoubtedly expected high office when the Churchill Government was formed. Before 1942 he was in fact offered a position, albeit not in the Government, as Commissioner in charge of Post-War Relief. He had refused unless it carried a seat in the Cabinet – an impossible condition. He was afterwards, in 1945, to become the Leader of the Liberal Party. But in 1942 he did not yet command sufficient authority to carry the House with him.

The debate proceeded to its second day. There was a highly effective speech by Aneurin Bevan. He was already the outstanding figure on the Labour back-benches. He dwelt on the general sense of anger and humiliation. Sebastopol could hold out for four months while Tobruk had collapsed in 26 hours. He appealed in particular for an attack in Europe. 'Get at the enemy where he really is – 21 miles away, not 14,000 miles away. Get him by the throat.' And he suggested that 'some of us' should be sent out with the land troops. It was a very moving appeal, but in substance not an attempt to displace the Government.

The most formidable attack on the second day came from Mr Hore-Belisha. He quoted the appeal made by Churchill on 17th November 1938 that if only fifty Members of the Conservative Party would go into the lobby to vote for the amendment, it would not affect the life of the Government but it would make them act, and he ended :

'Think what is at stake. In 100 days we lost our Empire in the Far East. What will happen in the next 100 days; let every Member vote according to his conscience.'

But Hore-Belisha, for the reasons explained above, had lost credibility. And so the attack petered out. When the division was called the Government was supported by the overwhelming vote of 475 votes to 25. The minority included Clement Davies, Hore-Belisha, Sir Roger Keyes, Sir John Wardlaw-Milne and Sir Herbert Williams.

There could be no greater contrast than with the division of 8th May 1940. The case against the Government for mishandling the war was not less formidable than in the Norway Debate. They had clearly been guilty of the most serious errors of judgment. There were, however, four reasons why the attack so signally failed. The first was Sir John Wardlaw-Milne's proposal regarding the Duke of Gloucester. Secondly, the critics themselves inspired no degree of confidence. Thirdly, they had no agreed target. Were they attacking the Prime Minister or his advisers? Lastly, and most important of all, there was no obvious alternative to Mr Churchill.

The last occasion on which the Government came under attack was on a very different subject. On 10th June 1941 there was appointed an Inter-Departmental Committee on Social Insurance and Allied Services. The Chairman was Sir William Beveridge. The terms of reference were :

To undertake, with special reference to the inter-relation of the schemes, a survey of the existing national schemes of Social Insurance and Allied Services, including Workmen's Compensation, and to make recommendations.

The Committee embarked on a comprehensive review. Its Report was laid on the Table of the House of Commons on the 1st December 1942. It represented a considerable extension of the Social Services, including a National Health Scheme and Children's Allowances. Looking back after thirty years, it does not appear a very sensational document. At the time it had a profound effect, and attracted world-wide attention.

An American commentator stated : 'Sir William, possibly next to Mr Churchill, is the most popular figure in Britain today.' A Gallup Poll, two weeks after publication, reported that 19 in every 20 adults had heard of the Beveridge Report at the time of the survey, and that there was overwhelming agreement that it should be put into effect. In the United States, President Roosevelt considered making it a Congressional document, and having a million copies distributed. The British Government arranged for an American edition to be printed, and this brought in 5,000 dollars.

The effects did not end there. The Beveridge Report, with its emphasis on social justice, became a major theme of British propaganda. The information reaching London showed that it aroused the greatest interest in the occupied countries of Europe.

This universal reaction was one of the strangest phenomena of war-time years. The nations of the world were locked in a conflict of unprecedented dimensions. This was total war on an unprecedented scale. The distinction beween combatant forces and the civilian population had ceased to have any meaning. On both sides everyone was engaged, in a greater or lesser degree, in the greatest struggle of all time. And yet, for vast numbers of people, the focal point of interest was a highly technical report on the future of the Social Services. What is the explanation? One answer suggests itself. A war is an intensely interesting experience for those who have to direct it, whether in Government or in the field. But for the vast majority, whether soldiers or civilians, it is, apart from moments of action or of patriotic fervour, a time of immense boredom. It means years of blackout, rationing and shortages, including a shortage of news. Most people have only a limited appetite for military themes. All this was true in 1942, especially in Britain. The reception given to the Beveridge Report reflected this widespread ennui. Members of Parliament were overwhelmed with correspondence.

The question arose : would the Report be carried into effect? The Government dragged their feet. They were reluctantly constrained to debate the matter in the House of Commons. The debate lasted for three days.

The Government spokesman on the first day (16th February 1943) was the Lord President of the Council, Sir John Anderson. He was a distinguished Civil Servant who had been drafted into the Government by Chamberlain at the beginning of the war. But, like other latecomers, he never mastered the techniques of the House of Commons. His idea of a Parliamentary speech was to read out a departmental memorandum. He approached the Report with extreme caution, emphasizing the cost that would be involved. The House rose in a state of seething unrest. Next day disapproval of the Government and acceptance of the Report came from all sides. Thus Mrs Cazalet Keir from the Conservative benches stated that she ranged herself, as she was sure the vast majority of the people in this country did, on the side of this humane and vital document, and Mr Quintin Hogg, speaking for 'the despised left-wing Conservatives', said : 'If we are to go to the people of this country and say "You have to look forward to a long period of self-sacrifice and restriction," we can do so only if we offer at some time a complete measure of social justice to guarantee that we shall all suffer alike.' And he went on to say '. . . If you do not give the people social reform, they are going to give you social revolution.'

But again the Government disappointed the House. The Chancellor of the Exchequer, Sir Kingsley Wood, was no less cautious than Sir John Anderson on the day before. When the House rose, it appeared once more that there might be a dangerous revolt. On the following afternoon, Mr James Griffiths moved an amendment expressing dissatisfaction with the now declared policy of His Majesty's Government towards the Report. From the Liberal Benches Captain Grey, a young officer in Army uniform, described the debate as 'In many ways . . . the most crucial of the war'. Mr Clement Davies spoke of the intense disapppointment that must be felt throughout the country with the Government's attitude. The situation was retrieved by the Home Secretary, Mr Herbert Morrison, in what was probably the most effective speech of his career. He was a highly skilled Parliamentarian. He pointed out that, with one possible exception, all the fundamental principles of the Beveridge Report were accepted by the Government. No-one had understood this from the speeches of Sir John Anderson and Sir Kingsley Wood. Gradually the temperature subsided. When the division bells rang, 330 Private Members voted for the Government and

119 against. I myself followed Anderson and Ernest Bevin into the division lobby. Bevin, who never concealed his dislike of Morrison was furious. He complained bitterly of the conduct of Labour Members in voting against the Government and declared his intention to resign from the Government. Anderson was endeavouring to dissuade him, saying 'Both you and I came here to do a job'. Apparently he carried conviction. Bevin did not resign.

This was the last occasion before the end of the war in Europe when the Churchill Government was seriously challenged. Thereafter, beginning with the Battle of Alamein, the tide of war began to turn. No-one in Britain was in any real doubt as to what the result would be. And the struggle proceeded with constantly increasing success in Allied planning and operations. Of course the war would not have ended as it did if it had not been for the Russian Armies. But in the West the Allied Commanders showed increasing mastery.

One of the most remarkable operations in the history of the war were the landings in France on D Day. This was made possible by Mulberry Harbour, which was Churchill's original inspiration. He conceived the original plan as early as 1941. At the same time the Germans were completely misled. There has never been a more successful exercise in deception as Operation Royal Flush. Even at the end of the war, there were thousands of German troops in Norway waiting for an attack which never arrived.

Victory, when it came, was complete. But it was only made possible by the vote in the House of Commons on the 8th May 1940.

(*Right*) Neville Chamberlain at No. 10 Downing Street on 10th May 1940

(*Below*) Ministers leaving No. 10 after the Cabinet Meeting of 10th May 1940; L to R Sir Kingsley Wood (Secretary of State for Air), Winston Churchill (First Lord of the Admiralty) and Anthony Eden (Secretary of State for the Dominions)

Mr and Mrs Chamberlain on a walk in St James's Park on the morning of 10th May 1940, when his resignation seemed certain after the debate of Wednesday 8th May

Mr and Mrs Winston Churchill on their way to take up official residence at No. 10 Downing Street, on 28th May 1940

BIOGRAPHICAL NOTES

ADAMS, William George Stewart (1874–1966).
Secretary to the Prime Minister (1916–1919); Gladstone Professor of Political Theory and Institutions, Oxford (1919–1933).

ADDISON, Christopher (1st Viscount) (1869–1951)
Minister of Health (1919–1921); Minister of Agriculture and Fisheries (1930–1931); Lord Privy Seal (1947–1951).

AITKEN, William Maxwell (1st Baron Beaverbrook) (1879–1964).
Newspaper magnate (*Daily Express, Sunday Express, Evening Standard*) and Conservative politician, Minister of Information (1918); Minister for Aircraft Production (1940–41); Minister of Supply); Lend-lease administrator in USA (1942).

AMERY, Leopold Charles Maurice Stannett (1873–1955).
Conservative politician. First Lord of Admiralty (1922); Secretary of State for Colonies (1924–29) and for Dominion Affairs (1925–29); Secretary of State for India (1940–45).

AMPTHILL, Oliver Arthur Villiers (2nd Baron) (1869–1935).
One of the founders of the National Party in 1918.

ANDERSON, Sir John (1st Viscount Waverley) (1882–1958).
Conservative politician; Held various offices including Governor of Bengal (1932–37); Chancellor of the Exchequer (1943).

ARGYLL, George John Douglas, (8th Duke) (1823–1900).
Liberal statesman. Lord Privy Seal (1852–55); Postmaster General (1855–58; Secretary of State for India (1868–74); Lord Privy Seal under Gladstone (1880–81); Opposed Home Rule for Ireland and Irish Land Bill.

ASQUITH, Herbert Henry, (1st Earl of Oxford and Asquith) (1852–1928).
Liberal statesman. Home Secretary (1892–95); Chancellor of the Exchequer (1905–08); Prime Minister (1908–16).

ASTOR, William Waldorf, (2nd Viscount) (1879–1952).

Newspaper owner (*Observer*) and politician. Held various Government appointments.

ATTLEE, Clement Richard, (1st Earl) (1883–1967).
Labour statesman; Held various high offices including Postmaster-General 1931); Secretary of State for Dominions (1942–43); Deputy Prime Minister (1943–45); Prime Minister (1945–51).

BALDWIN, Stanley, (1st Earl Baldwin of Bewdley) (1867–1947).
Conservative statesman. Chancellor of the Exchequer (1922–23); Prime Minister (1923–24, 1924–29, 1935–37); Lord President of the Council (1931–35).

BALFOUR, Arthur James, (1st Earl of Balfour) (1848–1930).
Conservative statesman. Chief Secretary for Ireland (1887–91); First Lord of the Treasury (1892, 1895, 1900) and Government Leader in the Commons (1895); Prime Minister (1902–05); Unionist Leader of Opposition (1906); First Lord of the Admiralty (1915); Foreign Secretary (1916–19).

BANBURY, Sir Frederick (Lord Banbury of Southam) (1850–1936).
Conservative MP, Camberwell (1892–1906); City of London (1906–24).

BARTLETT, Vernon (1894–   ).
Journalist, novelist and broadcaster on foreign affairs.

BEVAN, Aneurin, (1897–1960).
Labour politician; Trades unionist in the coalfields; Minister of Health (1945); introduced National Health Service (1948); Minister of Labour (1951); Labour's Shadow Foreign Secretary (1956).

BEVIN, Ernest (1881–1951.
Labour statesman and trade unionist. Built up and became General Secretary of National Transport and General Workers Union; Minister of Labour (1940–45); Secretary of State for Foreign Affairs (1945–51).

BIRKENHEAD, (see F. E. Smith).

BIRKETT, William Norman (1st Baron) (1883–1962).
Lawyer and Liberal politician. Judge, King's Bench Division (1941–50); British alternate judge at Nuremberg Trials (1945–46); Lord Justice of Appeal (1950–57); MP (1923–24, 1929–31).

BOOTHBY, Sir Robert John Graham, (1st Baron Boothby of Buchan and Rathay Head) (1900–   ).
Scots Conservative politician; Parliamentary Private Secretary to Winston

Churchill (1926–29); Parliamentary Secretary to Ministry of Food (1940–41); Commentator on public affairs.

BOSCAWEN-GRIFFITH, Rt Hon. Sir A. S. T. (1865–1946).
• Minister of Agriculture and Fisheries (1921–22); Minister of Health (1922–23).

BRACKEN, Brendan, (1st Viscount) (1901–58).
Journalist and Conservative politician. Minister of Information (1941–45); First Lord of Admiralty in 'caretaker Government' (1945).

BRIGHT, John, (1811–89).
Radical statesman. MP (almost continuously (1843–99); with Cobden contributed to defeat of corn laws (1838–46); campaigned for free-trade, financial reform, electoral reform, religious freedom; opposed to Crimean War, advocated disestablishment of the Irish Church (1868); President of Board of Trade (1868–70); Chancellor of Duchy of Lancaster (1873, 1881).

BROWN, Ernest, (1881–1962).
Minister of Labour (1935–40); Minister of Health (1941–43); Secretary of State for Scotland (1940–41).

BROCKDORFF-RANTZAU, Count Ulrich von (1869–1928).
German statesman, Minister in Copenhagen (1912–18); Foreign Minister (1919); Opposed Treaty of Versailles and Membership of League of Nations and Locarno Pact; Ambassador to Moscow (1922).

BURNS, The Rt Hon. John (1858–1943).
MP, Battersea (1892–1918); President, Local Government Board (1905–14); Resigned on the declaration of war.

CAMPBELL-BANNERMAN, Sir Henry (1836–1908).
Liberal statesman; Financial Secretary to War Office (1871–74, 1880–82); Chief Secretary for Ireland (1884–85); Secretary of State for War (1886, 1892–95); supported Home Rule for Ireland; Leader of Liberals in Commons (1899); opposed harsh treatment of Boers; Prime Minister (1905–08); advocated arbitration of national disputes limitation of armaments, alliances with naval powers. Attacked House of Lords.

CARSON, Edward Henry, (Baron) (1954–1935).
Conservative politician and lawyer. Solicitor-General for Ireland (1892) and for England (1900–06); Attorney-General (1915); First Lord of the Admiralty (1917); Lord of Appeal (1921–29); Organized the Ulster Volunteers; Opposed Home Rule.

CECIL, Lord Hugh Richard Heathcote Gascoyne- (1st Baron Quickswood) (1869–1956).
Conservative politician. With Winston Churchill headed group of independents in Commons. Opposed tariff reform and Parliament Bill.

CHAMBERLAIN, Arthur Neville, (1869–1940).
Conservative statesman. Son of Joseph Chamberlain. Chancellor of the Exchequer (1923–24, 1931–37); Minister for Health (1924–29); Prime Minister (1937–1940); Lord President of the Council (1940).

CHAMBERLAIN, Sir Austen (1863–1937).
Unionist statesman. Held various high offices including Chancellor of the Exchequer (1903–06, 1919–21); Secretary of State for India (1915–17); Secretary of State for Foreign Affairs (1924–29); First Lord of the Admiralty (1931).

CHAMBERLAIN, Joseph (1836–1914).
Liberal statesman. President of the Board of Trade (1880); opposed Home Rule Bill and Irish Land Purchase Bill; Leader of the Liberal Unionists (1891); Secretary for the Colonies (1895).

CHURCHILL, Lord Randolph Henry Spencer (1849–95).
Father of Sir Winston Churchill. Conservative politician.

CHURCHILL, Sir Winston Leonard Spencer (1874–1965). Conservative statesman. Under Secretary for the Colonies (1906–08); President of Board of Trade (1908–10); Home Secretary (1910–11); First Lord of the Admiralty (1911–15); Minister of Munitions (1917); Secretary of State for War and Air Minister (1918–21); Chancellor of the Exchequer (1924–29); First Lord of the Admiralty (1939); Prime Minister (1940–45, 1951–55).

COBDEN, Richard (1804–65).
Politician and economist, known as 'Apostle of Free Trade'; contributed to defeat of corn laws (1846); campaign in Europe for international arbitration and disarmament (1846–47); opposed to Crimean War; opposed Palmerston's Chinese War policy (1857); declined Cabinet office; negotiated treaty of commerce with France providing mutual reduction of tariffs; believed in minimum of government at home and minimum of intervention abroad.

COLLINGS, Jesse (1831–1920).
Radical MP for Ipswich (1880); sat for Bordeslay as a Unionist (1886–1918); identified with Agricultural Labourers Union; PC (1892); Under-Secretary to the Home Office (1895–1902).

COLLINS, Michael (1890–1922).
Irish politician and Sinn Fein leader. Minister of Finance in Sinn Fein Ministry (1922); Commander in Chief of military forces of Irish. Largely responsible for negotiation of treaty with Great Britain (1921). Killed (1922).

COOPER, Sir Alfred Duff, (1st Viscount Norwich) (1890–1954).
Conservative statesman; Secretary of State for War (1935–37); First Lord of Admiralty (1937–38); Minister of Information (1940–41); Ambassador to France (1944–47).

CREWE, Robert Offley Ashburton Crewe-Milnes, (1st Marquess of Crewe) (1858–1945).
Statesman; Secretary of State for the Colonies (1908–10); Secretary of State for India (1910–15); President, Board of Education (1916); Ambassador to France (1922–28); Secretary of State for War (1931).

CRIPPS, Sir Richard Stafford (1889–1952).
Economist, lawyer and Labour statesman. Solicitor-General (1931); Ambassador to USSR (1940); Minister of Aircraft Production (1942–45); Chancellor of the Exchequer (1947–50).

CURZON, George Nathaniel, (Marquess Curzon of Kedleston) (1859–1925).
Conservative statesman; Viceroy and Governor-General of India (1899–1905); Lord Privy Seal (1915), Secretary of State for Foreign Affairs (1919–24).

DALTON, Edward Hugh John Neil (Baron Dalton of Forast and Frith) (1887–1962).
Labour politician. Minister of Economic Warfare (1940–42); President, Board of Trade (1942–45); Chancellor of the Exchequer (1945–47).

DAVIES, Clement (1884–1962).
Welsh politician. Leader of Liberal Party in Commons (1945–56). Refused all Ministerial offices offered by Conservative Governments.

DAVIES, David, (1st Baron) (1880–1944).
MP (1906–48). Private secretary to Lloyd George.

DAVIES, Sir Joseph, KBE (1866–1954).
Secretary, Prime Minister's Secretariat (1916–20); Member of Parliament (1918–22).

DAWSON, Geoffrey, (1874–1944).
Editor of *The Times* (1912–19) (1923–41).

DERBY, Edward Henry Smith Stanley, (1st Earl) (1826–93).
Conservative statesman; joined Liberal Party 1880; joined Liberal Unionist Party (1886) and was Leader of that Party in Lords (1886–91).

DICEY, Edward James Stephen (1832–1911).
British journalist. Editor of London *Observer* (1870–89).

DILKE, Sir Charles Wentworth (1843–1911).
Radical politician. Widely travelled; MP for Chelsea (1868–86); Under-Secretary of State for Foreign Affairs (1880–82); President of Local Government Board under Mr Gladstone (1882–85); campaigned in support of trades unions and improved conditions for working men; defeated after involvement in divorce scandal (1886); Returned as MP for the Forest of Dean (1892).

DYER, Reginald Edward Henry (1864–1927).
Army Officer. Commanded operations in South Eastern Persia (1916–17); Forced to resign from service (1920) after Amritsar affair.

EDEN, Robert Anthony, KG, (1st Earl of Avon) (1897–).
Conservative statesman. Secretary of State for Foreign Affairs (1935–38, 1940–45, 1951–55); Secretary of State for War (1940); Prime Minister (1955–57).

FINLAY, Robert Bannatyne, (Viscount) (1842–1929).
Lawyer and Unionist politician. Solicitor General (1900–06); Lord Chancellor (1916–19); Member of Hague Permanent Court of Arbitration.

FISHER, Herbert Albert Laurens (1865–1940).
Historian and politician; MP (1916–26); President, Board of Education (1916–22); Warden of New College, Oxford (1925–40).

GARDINER, Alfred George (1865–1946).
Editor of the *Daily News* (1902–19). Wrote under the pseudonym 'Alpha of the Plough'.

GEDDES, Sir Eric Campbell (1875–1937).
Industrialist and politician; Director General of Transportation (1916–17); First Lord of Admiralty (1917–18); Minister of Transport (1919–21).

GLADSTONE, Herbert John, (1st Viscount) 1854–1930). Son of W. E. Gladstone. Liberal politician; Secretary of State for Home Affairs (1905–10); First Governor General of Union of South Africa.

GLADSTONE, William Ewart (1809–1898).
Liberal statesman. Junior Lord of the Treasury (1834); Under-Secretary for the Colonies (1835); Vice-President of the Board of Trade and Master of the Mint (1841); President of the Board of Trade (1843); Secretary of State for Colonies (1845); Chancellor of the Exchequer (1852); Leader of the Liberal Party (1867); Prime Minister (1868–74), 1880–85, 1886, 1892–94).

GORDON, Charles George, (1833–85).
Soldier. Served in China, Egypt, Africa, Mauritius; Governor of Sudan (1877–80); visited India; Palestine; sent to Sudan to relieve the besieged garrisons in Egypt; killed when Khartoum fell to the troops of the Mahdi.

GOSCHEN, George Joachim, (1st Viscount) (1831–1907).
Liberal statesman. Held various high Government appointments. Opposed to Home Rule.

GRANVILLE, George Leveson-Gower, (2nd Earl).
Liberal statesman and free-trader. Secretary of State for Foreign Affairs (1851); President of the Council (1853); Leader of the House of Lords (1855); Joined Lord Palmerston's second administration (1859); Secretary of State for the Colonies (1868–1886); Secretary of State for Foreign Affairs (1870, 1880–85); Supported Gladstone's Home Rule policy.

GRAY, Milner, (1871–1943).
MP Mid-Beds. (1929–31); Parliamentary Secretary, Ministry of Labour (1931).

GREENWOOD, Arthur, (1880–1954).
Labour politician. Held various Government offices. Deputy Leader of Parliamentary Labour Party (1935); Treasurer of the Labour Party; Chairman, National Executive of Labour Party (1953).

GREY, Sir Edward, (1862–1933). (1st Viscount Grey of Fallodon).
Liberal statesman. Under-Secretary of State for Foreign Affairs (1892–95); Secretary of State for Foreign Affairs (1905–16); Ambassador to USA (1919–20).

HALDANE, Richard Burdon, (1st Viscount) (1856–1928). Liberal statesman. Secretary of State for War (1905–12); Lord Chancellor (1912–15); Minister of Labour (1924).

HALIFAX, Edward Frederick Lindley Wood, (1st Earl of Halifax) (1881–1959).

Conservative statesman; Viceroy of India (1926–31); Secretary of State for Foreign Affairs (1938–40); Ambassador to USA (1941–46).

HANKEY, Sir Maurice Pascal Alers (1st Baron) (1877–1963). Secretary, War Cabinet (1916); Imperial War Cabinet (1917–18); Secretary to Cabinet (1919–38); Minister without Portfolio (1939–40); Chancellor of Duchy of Lancaster (1940–41); Paymaster General (1941–42).

HARCOURT, Lewis (1st Viscount) (1863–1922).
Secretary of State for the Colonies (1910–15); First Commissioner of Works 1915–17).

HARCOURT, Sir William Vernon (1827–1904).
Barrister and Liberal politician; Leader of Liberal Party in Commons.

HARMSWORTH, Cecil Bishopp, (1st Baron) (1869–1948).
Liberal politician. Under-Secretary of State Home Office (1912); Under-Secretary of State Foreign Office (1919–22).

HARTINGTON, Spencer Compton (Marquess of Hartington later 8th Duke of Devonshire) (1833–1908). Liberal statesman; Secretary of State for War (1866); Postmaster General under Gladstone; Chief Secretary for Ireland (1870–74); Leader of Liberal Party in Commons (1875–80); Secretary of State for India (1880–82); Secretary of State for War (1882–85); opposed Gladstone's Irish Home Rule policy; founded Liberal Unionists with Joseph Chamberlain; President of Council in Salisbury's Coalition Government (1895–1902) and under Balfour (1902–03); Free trader, opposed tariff reform.

HARVEY, Sir Ernest (1867–1955).
Deputy Governor of the Bank of England (1929–36).

HENDERSON, Arthur (1863–1935).
Labour politician. Chairman of Labour Party (1908–10, 1914–17, 1931–32); Served in Coalition Cabinets (1915–17); Secretary of State for Home Affairs (1824); Secretary of State for Foreign Affairs (1929–31); President of World Disarmament Conference (1932).

HERSCHELL, Farrer, (1st Baron) (1837–1899).
Solicitor General (1880); Lord Chancellor (1886, 1892–95).

HEWART, Gordon, (1st Viscount) (1870–1943).
Lawyer and politician. Solicitor-General (1916–19); Attorney-General (1919–22); Lord Chief Justice (1922–40).

HITLER, Adolf (1889–1945).
German dictator; Chancellor (1933); Established Rome–Berlin Axis with Mussolini (1936); Began Second World War (1939); Committed suicide (1945).

HOARE, Sir Samuel John Gurney, (1st Viscount Templewood) (1880–1959).
Conservative statesman; Secretary of State for Air (1922–29); Secretary of State for India (1931–35); Secretary of State for Foreign Affairs (1935); First Lord of the Admiralty (1936–37); Secretary of State for Home Affairs (1937–39); Ambassador to Spain (1940–44).

HOOVER, Herbert Clark (1874 1964).
31st President of the United States.

HORE-BELISHA, Leslie, (1st Baron Hore-Belisha) (1893–1957).
Liberal politician. First Chairman of the National Liberal Party (1931). Financial Secretary to the Treasury (1932–34); Minister of Transport (1934–37); Secretary of State for War (1937–40); Minister of National Insurance (1945).

HORNE, Robert (1st Viscount, of Slammannan) (1871–1914).
President of the Board of Trade (1920–21); Chancellor of the Exchequer (1921–22).

ISAACS, Rufus (see Reading).

JAMES, Henry, (1st Baron James of Hereford) (1828–1911).
Lawyer and politician.

JOWETT, Frederick William (1864–1944).
Labour politician; First Commissioner of Works in first Labour Cabinet (1924).

JOWITT, William (1st Earl) (1885–1957).
Attorney General (1929–32); Solicitor General (1940–42); Paymaster General (1942); Minister without Portfolio (1942–46); Minister of National Insurance (1943–45); Lord Chancellor (1945–51).

JOYNSON-HICKS, William, (1st Viscount Brentford) (1865–1932).
Conservative politician; Postmaster General and Paymaster General (1923); Minister of Health (1923–24); Secretary of State for Home Affairs (1924–29).

KERR, Philip Henry (11th Marquess of Lothian). (1882–1940).
Diplomat and statesman; Secretary to Prime Minister Lloyd George (1916–

21); Parliamentary Under-Secretary, India Office (1931–32); British Ambassador to USA (1939–40).

KEYES, Sir Roger John Brownlow (1st Baron) (1872–1945).
Naval Officer. Held various appointments including Chief of Staff Eastern Mediterranean (1915); Commander in Chief Mediterranean Station (1925–28); Director of Amphibious Warfare (1940); Admiral of the Fleet (1930).

KEYNES, John Maynard (1st Baron) (1883–1946).
Economist and author. Adviser to Treasury in both World Wars.

LABOUCHÈRE, Henry (1831–1912).
Diplomat, journalist and Liberal MP. Founder and Editor of *Truth*; Advocate of Irish Home Rule and of abolition of House of Lords.

LANSBURY, George (1859–1940).
Labour politician. Founded and edited the *Daily Herald*; First Commissioner of Works (1929–31); Leader of Labour Party (1931–35).

LANSDOWNE, Henry Charles Keith Petty-Fitzmaurice (5th Marquess) (1845–1927).
Liberal statesman. Under-Secretary of State for War (1872–74); Under-Secretary for India (1880); Governor-General of Canada (1883–88); Governor-General of India (1888–94); Secretary of State for War (1895–1900); Secretary of State for Foreign Affairs (1900–05); Unionist leader in Lords from 1903; sat without portfolio in Asquith's Coalition Cabinet (1915–16).

LAVAL, Pierre (1883–1945).
French lawyer and politician. Premier (1931–32, 1935–36); Petain's deputy in Vichy Government (1940); Premier (1942–44) when he collaborated with the Germans; Executed for treason (1945).

LAW, Andrew Bonar (1858–1923).
Unionist politician; Secretary of State for the Colonies (1915–16); Chancellor of the Exchequer (1916–18); Lord Privy Seal (1919–21); Prime Minister (1922–23).

LLEWELLYN-SMITH, Sir Hubert (1864–1945).
General Secretary, Ministry of Munitions (1915).

LLOYD GEORGE, David (1st Earl of Dwyfor) (1863–1945).
Liberal statesman. President of Board of Trade (1905–08); Chancellor of the Exchequer (1908–15); Minister of Munitions (1915–16); Secretary of State for War (1916) Prime Minister (1916–22).

LLOYD GEORGE OF DWYFOR, Frances, Countess (née Frances Stevenson)
Secretary to Rt Hon. David Lloyd George (1st Earl Lloyd George of
Dwyfor) whom she married (1943).

LLOYD GEORGE, Gwilym (1st Viscount Tenby) 1894–1967).
Liberal politician. Son of 1st Earl Lloyd George of Dwyfor; Parliamentary
Secretary to Board of Trade (1939–41); Minister of Fuel and Power (1942–
45); Minister of Food (1951–54); Minister of Welsh Affairs (1954–57).

LLOYD GEORGE, Lady Megan (1902–66).
MP (Liberal) for Anglesey (1929–50) and (Labour) for Carmarthen from
1957. Youngest daughter of Earl Lloyd George.

LONG, Walter Hume (1st Viscount Long of Wraxhall) (1854–1924).
Politician. Held various offices including Chief Secretary to Ireland (1905–
06); Secretary of State for the Colonies (1916–18); First Lord of Admiralty
(1919–21).

LOTHIAN, Philip Henry Kerr (11th Marquess of Lothian) (1882–1940) (see
P. H. Kerr).

LYTTELTON, Oliver (1st Viscount Chandos) (1893–1972).
Industrialist and Conservative statesman. Held various high offices including Minister of State, Cairo (1941–42); Secretary of State for Colonies
(1951–54).

McCURDY, The Rt Hon. Charles Albert
Food Controller (1920–21); Coalition Liberal Chief Whip (1921–22).

MacDONALD, James Ramsay (1866–1937).
Labour statesman. Leader of the Labour Party (1911–14); Leader of the
Opposition (1922); Prime Minister and Foreign Secretary (1924) of Britain's first Labour Government; Prime Minister (1929–35); Lord President
of the Council (1935–37).

MacDONALD, Malcolm (1901–   ).
Son of Ramsay MacDonald. Statesman. Secretary of State for Colonies
(1935, 1938–41); Secretary of State for Dominion Affairs (1935–38, 1938–
39); High Commisioner for the UK in Canada (1941–46).

McKENNA, Reginald (1853–1943).
First Lord of the Admiralty (1908–11); Home Secretary (1911–15); Chancellor of the Exchequer (1915–16); Chairman, Midland Bank (1919).

MACMILLAN, Harold (1894–).
Publisher and Conservative statesman. Minister Resident at Allied HQ in North-West Africa (1942–45); Prime Minister and First Lord of the Treasury (1957–63).

McNEILL, Weir L. (1877–1939).
MP (Labour) Clackmannan and East Stirlingshire (1922–31 and 1935–39); Parliamentary Private Secretary to Ramsay MacDonald (1924–31).

MASSINGHAM, Henry William (1860–1924).
Journalist; Editor *Daily Chronicle* (1895–99); Editor the *Nation* (1907–23).

MASTERMAN, Charles Frederick Gurney (1873–1927).
MP (Liberal) West Ham North (1906–11); Financial Secretary to the Treasury (1912–14); Chancellor of the Duchy of Lancaster (1914–15).

MAXTON, James (1885–1946).
Labour politician; Chairman of Independent Labour Party (1926–31, 1934–39); Conscientious objector in First World War.

MINNEY, Rubeigh James (1895–).
Editor, journalist, novelist, playwright.

MONTAGU, Edwin Samuel (1879–1924).
Financial Secretary to the Treasury (1914–16); Minister of Munitions (1916); Secretary of State for India (1917–22).

MOORE-BRABAZON, John Theodore Cuthbert (1st Baron Brabazon of Tara) (1884–1964). Aviator and Conservative politician; Parliamentary Private Secretary to Winston Churchill at War Office (1918); Parliamentary Secretary to Ministry of Transport; Minister of Transport (1940); Minister of Aircraft Production (1941).

MORLEY, John (1st Viscount) (1838–1923).
Author and Radical politician. Supported Home Rule. Irish Secretary (1886, 1892–95). Secretary for India (1905–10).

MORRISON, Herbert Stanley (Baron Morrison of Lambeth) (1888–1965).
Labour politician; Chairman, National Labour Party (1928–29); Held various Government offices including Secretary of State for Home Affairs and Minister of Home Security (1940–45); Lord President of Council and Leader of Commons (1945–51).

MOSLEY, Sir Oswald Ernald (6th Bart.) (1896–   ).
Successively Conservative, Independent and Labour MP; Leader British
Union of Fascists; Detained under Defence Regulations during Second
World War; Founded a new 'Union' Movement in 1948.

MUIR, Ramsay, 1872–1941).
MP Mid-Beds. (1929–31); Parliamentary Secretary, Ministry of Labour,
(1931).

MUSSOLINI, Benito (1883–1945).
Italian dictator (1922); Resigned (1943); killed by Italian partisans (1945).

MUSTAFA, Kemal Ataturk (c. 1880–1938).
Turkish general and statesman. Leader of Turkish nationalist movement
from 1909; President of Turkey (1923–38).

NICOLSON, Sir Harold George (1886–1948).
Diplomat and author. National Liberal MP (1935–45).

NORTHBROOK, Thomas George Baring (2nd Baron) (1826–1904).
Statesman; Governor-General of India (1872–76).

OLIVER, Frederick Scott (1864–1934).
Author of *Alexander Hamilton* and *Endless Adventure*.

ORMSBY-GORE, William George Arthur (4th Baron Harlech) (1885–1964).
Secretary of State for Colonies (1936–38).

PERCY, Eustace (1st Baron of Newcastle) (1887–1958).
Politician. President of Board of Education (1924–29); Minister without
Portfolio (1935–36).

READING, Rufus Daniel Isaacs (1st Marquess of Reading) (1860–1935).
Liberal statesman and eminent advocate. First Attorney General to join
Cabinet (1912); Lord Chief Justice (1913); special envoy to United States
in First World War; British Ambassador in Washington (1918–2); Viceroy
of India (1921–26); Secretary of State for Foreign Affairs (1931).

RIDDELL, George Allardice (1st Baron) (1865–1934).
Lawyer and newspaper proprietor. Chairman of *News of the World*;
Chairman of George Newnes Ltd.

ROSEBERY, Archibald Philip Primrose (5th Earl of Rosebery) (1847–1929).
Liberal statesman. Secretary of State for Foreign Affairs (1886, 1892–94);
Prime Minister (1894–95).

ROWNTREE, Benjamin Seebohm (1871–1954).
Manufacturer, philanthropist and author.

RUNCIMAN, Walter (1st Viscount) (1870–1949).
Politician. Held various ministerial posts. President of Board of Trade (1914–16, 1931–37).

SALISBURY, Robert Arthur Talbot Gascoyne (3rd Marquess of Salisbury) (1830–1903).
Conservative statesman. Secretary for India (1866–67), (1874–78); Secretary of State for Foreign Affairs (1878); Leader of Conservative Opposition in House of Lords (1881); opposed Gladstone's Home Rule Bill; Prime Minister and Secretary of State for Foreign Affairs (1885–86, 1886–92, 1895–1902); Resigned the Foreign Secretaryship in 1900; Retired from public life (1902).

SALTER, Sir James Arthur (1st Baron) (1881–1975).
Economist and politician. Head of British Merchant Shipping, Washington (1941–43); Minister of State for Economic Affairs (1951–52).

SAMUEL, Herbert Louis (1st Viscount) (1870–1963).
Liberal statesman. Held various offices including Postmaster-General (1910, 1915); Secretary of State for Home Affairs (1916, 1931–32); High Commissioner for Palestine (1920–25).

SANDYS, Duncan (1908–   ).
Conservative statesman; Minister of Supply (1951–54); Minister of Housing (1954–57); Minister of Defence (1957–59).

SANKEY, John (1st Viscount) (1866–1948).
Judge, King's Bench Division (1914–28); Lord Chancellor (1929–35).

SCRYMGEOUR, E. (1866–1947).
Prohibitionist MP for Dundee (1922–31).

SEELY, John Edward Barnard (1st Baron Mottistone) (1868–1947).
Conservative MP (1900–06); Liberal MP (1906); Secretary of State for War (1912–14); Deputy Minister of Munitions (1918); Under Secretary of State for Air and President of Air Council (1919).

SELBORNE, Roundell Palmer (1st Earl) (1812–95).
Solicitor General (1861); Attorney General (1863–66); Lord Chancellor (1872–74, 1880–85).

SELBORNE, Roundell Cecil Palmer (3rd Earl) (1887–1971).
Conservative politician. Assistant Director War Trade (1916–18); Parliamentary Secretary, Board of Trade (1922–24); Assistant Postmaster-General (1924–29); Director of Cement, Ministry of Works and Buildings (1940–42); Minister of Economic Warfare (1942–45).

SHARP, Granville (1894–1968).
QC (1948); Judge of the Supreme Court in Ghana.

SIMON, Ernest Darwin (Lord Simon of Wythenshawe) (1879–1960).
MP (Liberal) Withington (1923–24) and 1929–31); Parliamentary Secretary, Ministry of Health (1931); Chairman, BBC (1947–52).

SIMON, John Allsebrook (1st Viscount) (1873–1954).
Liberal statesman and lawyer. Solicitor General (1910); Attorney General (1913–15); Secretary of State for Home Affairs (1915–16, 1935–37); Secretary of State for Foreign Affairs (1931); Chancellor of the Exchequer (1937–40); Lord Chancellor (1940–45).

SINCLAIR, Sir Archibald Henry MacDonald (1st Viscount Thurso) (1890–1970).
Liberal politician. Chief Whip of Liberal Party (1930–31); Secretary of State for Scotland (1931–32); Leader of the Liberal Party (1935–45); Secretary of State for Air (1940–45).

SINHA, Sir Satyendra Prasanno (1st Baron of Raipar) (1864–1928).
Indian lawyer and statesman. Representative of India at Imperial War Conference in London (1917). Under Secretary of State for India (1919–20); Governor of Bihar and Orissa (1920–21); First Indian member of Viceroy's Executive Council.

SMITH, Frederick Edwin (1st Earl of Birkenhead) (1872–1930).
Conservative politician and eminent advocate. Attorney General (1915); Lord Chancellor (1919–22); Secretary of State for India (1924–28).

SNOWDEN, Philip (1st Viscount) (1864–1937).
Labour politician. Chairman of Independent Labour Party (1903–06, 1917–20); Chancellor of the Exchequer (1924, 1929–31); Lord Privy Seal (1931–32).

SPENDER, John Alfred (1862–1942).
Journalist and biographer. Editor of Liberal *Westminster Gazette* (1896–1922).

STAMFORDHAM, Arthur J. B. (1st Baron) (1849–1931).
Private Secretary to the King from 1906.

STEVENSON, Frances (see Countess Lloyd George of Dwyfor).

STONEHAVEN, John Lawrence Baird (1st Baron) (1874–1941).
Diplomat and politician; Governor-General of Australia (1925–30).

SYKES, Sir Mark (1879–1919).
Politician, traveller and Foreign Office adviser, especially on Near Eastern
Affairs.

TAYLOR, Alan John Percivale (1906–   ).
Historian and journalist.

THOMAS, James Henry (1874–1949).
Labour politician and trades unionist. General Secretary National Union
of Railwaymen (1917–24, 1925–31); Secretary of State for Colonies (1924,
1931, 1935–36). Lord Privy Seal and Minister of Employment (1929–30);
Secretary of State for the Dominions (1930–35).

THOMSON, Christopher Birdwood (1st Baron) (1875–1930).
Soldier and statesman. Secretary of State for Air (1924, 1929–30); Killed
in crash of R101 (1930).

TREVELYAN, Sir George Otto (2nd Bart.) (1838–1928).
Liberal statesman; A Lord of the Admiralty (1868–70); Parliamentary Sec-
retary to the Admiralty (1880–82); Chief Secretary for Ireland (1882–84);
Secretary for Scotland (1886, 1892–95).

VENIZELOS, Elentherios (1864–1936).
Greek statesman. Greek Prime Minister (1910–15, 1924, 1928–32, 1933);
established rival Government at Salonika and forced abdication of King
Constantine (1917); Instigated unsuccessful revolt and fled into exile (1935).

WARING, Samuel (1st Baron) (1860–1940).
Organised factories for production of aeroplane engines during first war.

WEDGWOOD, Josiah Clement (1872–1943).
Naval architect and Labour politician; Vice-Chairman Labour Party
(1921–24); Chancellor of Duchy of Lancaster in first Labour Cabinet
(1924).

WIGRAM, Clive (1st Baron) (1873–1960).
Permanent Lord in Waiting and Extra Equerry to George VI (1936–52); and to the Queen after 1952.

WILKINSON, Ellen Cicely (1891–1947).
Labour politician; Early member of Independent Labour Party; Joined Communist Party (1920), resigned (1924); Minister of Education (1945), the first woman to hold such an appointment.

WOOD, Sir Kingsley (1881–1943).
Conservative politician. Held various ministerial offices including Postmaster-General (1931–35); Chancellor of the Exchequer (1940–43).

YOUNGER, Sir George (1st Viscount Younger of Leckie) (1851–1929).
Chairman of the Unionist Party Organisation (1916–23).

SELECTED BIBLIOGRAPHY

Aitken, Max (Lord Beaverbrook): *The Decline and Fall of Lloyd George*, Collins, 1963.

Amery, Leo: *My Political Life*, Hutchinson, 1953.

Asquith, H. H.: *Memories and Reflections, 1852–1927*, Cassell & Co., 1928. *Letters of the Earl of Oxford and Asquith to a Friend*, Geoffrey Bles, 1933.

Basset, Reginald: *Nineteen Thirty-One: Political Crisis:* Macmillan, 1958.

Birrell, Francis; *Gladstone*, Duckworth, 1944.

Blake, Robert; *The Unknown Prime Minister*, The Life and Times of Andrew Bonar Law, 1858–1923, Eyre & Spottiswoode, 1955.

Boothby, Lord: *I Fight to Live*, Victor Gollancz, 1947.

Churchill, Sir Winston: *The World Crisis: The Aftermath,* Thornton Butterworth, 1929. *The Second World War: The Gathering Storm*, Cassell, 1948. *Great Contemporaries,* Thornton Butterworth, 1937. *Lord Randolph Churchill*, Macmillan, 1906.

Davidson, J. C. C.: *Memoirs of a Conservative*, edited by Robert Rhodes James, Weidenfeld & Nicolson, 1969.

Gardiner, A. G. *Prophets, Priests and Kings*, Wayfarers' Library, J. M. Dent, 1914. *The War Lords*, Wayfarers' Library, 1915.

Garvin, J. L.: *The Life of Joseph Chamberlain*, Macmillan, 1932.

Gaunt, Admiral Sir Guy: *The Yield of the Years*, Hutchinson, 1940.

George, David Lloyd; *The War Memoirs of David Lloyd George*, Nicholson & Watson, 1933–36.

Gilbert, Martin: *Churchill*, Heinemann, 1971.

Hankey, Lord: *The Supreme Command 1914–18*, Allen & Unwin, 1961.

Hoare, Sir Samuel: *Nine Troubled Years*, Collins 1954.

Hyde, Harford M.: *Norman Birkett: The Life of Lord Birkett of Ulveston*, Hamish Hamilton, 1964.

James, Robert Rhodes: *Churchill: A Study in Failure*, Weidenfeld & Nicolson, 1970.

Jenkins, Roy: *Asquith*, Collins, 1964.

Keynes, J. M.: *Economic Consequences of the Peace*, Macmillan, 1919. *Economic Consequences of Mr Churchill*, L. & V. Woolf, 1925.

McNeill Weir, L.: *The Tragedy of Ramsay MacDonald*, Secker & Warburg, 1938.

Magnus, Sir Philip: *Gladstone: A Biography*, John Murray, 1954.

Max, of Baden: *Memoirs of Prince Max of Baden*, Constable, 1928.

McKenna, Stephen: *Reginald McKenna – a Memoir*, Eyre & Spottiswoode, 1948.

Middlemas, Robert, & Barnes, Anthony: *Baldwin: A Biography*, Weidenfeld & Nicolson, 1969.

Minney, R. J.: *The Private Papers of Hore-Belisha*, Collins, 1960.

Morley, John: *The Life of William Ewart Gladstone*, Macmillan, 1903.

Mowat, Professor Charles: *Britain between the Wars*, Methuen, 1955.

Nicolson, Sir Harold: *Diaries and Letters* edited by Nigel Nicolson, Collins, 1966–68.

Riddell, Lord: *Lord Riddell's War Diary 1914–18*, Nicolson & Watson, 1933.

Roskill, Steven W.: *Hankey, Man of Secrets*, Collins, 1970–74.

Samuel, Sir Herbert: *Memoirs*, Cresset Press, 1945.

Scott, C. P.: *Political Diaries 1911–28*, edited by Trevor Wilson, Collins, 1970.

Spender, Edward H.: *David Lloyd George*, Hodder & Stoughton, 1922.

Spender, John A., and Cyril Asquith: *Life of Herbert Henry Asquith, Lord Oxford and Asquith*, Hutchinson, 1932.

Stevenson, Frances (Countess Lloyd George): *The Years that are Past*, Hutchinson, 1967.

Wilson, Trevor: *The Downfall of the Liberal Party, 1914–35*, Collins, 1966.

Index

INDEX

Aberdeen, 75, 173
Aberdeen, Lord, 20
Abyssinia, 148, 149, 150, 154, 162, 179, 186
Acland, Sir Francis, 78, 79
Adams, W. G. S., 57
Addison, Christopher, 76
Agadir, 55
Aitken, Max, *see* Beaverbrook, Lord
Aix-les-Bains, 112
Alsace-Lorraine, 87
Amery, Leo, 57, 92, 108, 139, 142, 143, 150, 163, 169, 179, 180, 183
Ammon, C. G., 98
Ampthill, Lord, 91
Amritsar, 88, 89, 99
Anderson, Sir John, 172, 191, 192
Argyll, Duke of, 29, 37
Anstruther-Gray, William, 182
Asquith, H. H., 9, 10, 45, 46, 47, 48, 49, 50, 51, 52, 53, 54, 55, 58, 59, 60, 61, 62, 63, 64, 65, 66, 67, 68, 71, 72, 74, 75, 76, 77, 78, 79, 80, 81, 85, 92, 94, 96, 97, 104, 125.
Asquith, Margot, 183
Asquith, Raymond, 52, 53
Astor, Lord, 57, 102
Attlee, Clement, 138, 140, 142, 177, 178, 184
Australia, 143
Austria, 176
Bagehot, 16
Baldwin, Stanley, 77, 85, 99, 107, 110, 111, 112, 113, 114, 118, 119, 120, 132, 137, 139, 142, 144, 148,

149, 151, 156, 157, 158, 163, 168
Balfour, Lord, 21, 46, 59, 64, 65, 72, 92, 103, 107
Balkans, 20, 23, 29
Banbury, Sir Frederick, 105
Barnes, Anthony, 144, 157
Barthou, M., 101
Bartlett, Vernon, 161
Basset, Reginald, 130
Beaverbrook, Lord, 54, 61, 62, 63, 94, 95, 103, 106, 109, 110, 119
Belfast, 50
Belgium, 71
Bennett, Arnold, 38
Bennett, Richard, 143, 144
Berchtesgaden, 56, 163
Bevan, Aneurin, 153, 161, 189
Beveridge, Sir William, 189, 190
Bevin, Ernest, 177, 192
Birkenhead, Lord, 46, 50, 54, 90, 92, 93, 94, 95, 98, 103, 107, 108, 114
Birkett, Lord, 135, 136
Birmingham, 23, 24, 33, 55, 165, 168
Birrell, Francis, 18
Blake, Lord, 62, 92, 109
Bodmin, 9, 98, 152
Boer War, 21, 22
Bonar Law, Andrew, 46, 54, 58, 59, 60, 61, 62, 64, 65, 73, 77, 91, 92, 102, 106, 109, 111, 114, 182
Bonham Carter, Sir Maurice, 60, 62
Bonham-Carter, Lady Violet, 81
Bonomi, Signor, 100
Boothby, Lord, 87, 140, 154, 161, 182

Boscawen-Griffith, Sir A. S. T., 114
Boulogne, 105
Bowen, W. J., 112
Bracken, Brendan, 161
Brest, 185
Briand, M., 100, 101
Bright, John, 15, 30, 37, 56, 75, 166
Brockdorff-Rantzau, Count, 87
Brougham, 30
Brown, Ernest, 124, 135, 140
Brown, George, 161
Buckle, 17
Buckmaster, Lord, 80, 96, 97
Burma, 185, 186, 188
Burns, John, 46, 57
Buxton, 126, 135
Buxton, Lord, 80
Caithness, 158
Cambridge, 85, 100
Campbell-Bannerman, Sir Henry, 22, 48, 51
Canada, 58, 143, 144
Cannes, 95, 100, 107
Caradon, Lord, *see* Foot, Hugh
Carlingford, Lord, 37
Carlton Club, 9, 84, 86, 91, 94, 98, 99, 110, 112, 114
Carnarvon, 80
Carson, Sir Edward, 59, 69, 93
Cartland, Ronald, 163, 167, 168
Cazalet Keir, Mrs, 191
Cecil, Lord Hugh, 50, 56, 58
Cecil, Lord Robert, 58, 114
Chamberlain, Sir Austen, 46, 92, 94, 95, 97, 99, 100, 103, 106, 107, 108, 110, 113, 114, 142
Chamberlain, Joseph, 15, 19, 20, 21, 23, 24, 25, 26, 27, 29, 30, 31, 32, 33, 36, 37, 38, 41, 42, 43, 44, 47, 51, 55, 137. 143
Chamberlain, Neville, 10, 57, 86, 125, 130, 131, 141, 142, 143, 145, 147, 149, 151, 153, 154, 156, 164, 165, 166, 167, 168, 169, 170, 174, 175, 177, 178, 180, 181, 182, 183, 184, 185, 188

Chandos, Lord, *see* Lyttelton, Oliver
Chile, 106
Churchill, Lord Randolph, 36, 37, 40
Churchill, Winston, 11, 12, 22, 35, 46, 48, 54, 55, 57, 58, 72, 75, 76, 79, 82, 84, 85, 88, 90, 92, 93, 94, 95, 99, 108, 109, 119, 128, 140, 141, 147, 148, 154, 155, 157, 158, 159, 160, 162, 163, 169, 178, 183, 184, 186, 189, 190, 192
Citrine, Walter, 160
Clarke, Sir Andrew, 18
Clarry, Reginald, 112
Clayton, 98
Cobden, Richard, 15, 30, 75
Collings, Jesse, 19, 22, 31, 36
Collins, Sir Godfrey, 80
Collins, Michael, 93
Constantinople, 109
Cooper, Sir Alfred Duff, 119, 154, 173
Courtney, Leonard, 152
Cowdray, Lord, 80
Cranborne, Lord, 154, 161, 162, 163
Crewe, Lord, 62
Cripps, Sir Stafford, 140, 143, 153, 160, 161
Cross, Ronald, 174
Crossley, Anthony, 163
Curzon, Lord, 61, 64, 107
Czechoslovakia, 87, 151, 161, 165, 176
Dalton, Hugh, 12, 140, 159, 160
Davidson, J. C. C., 102, 111, 122
Davies, Clement, 137, 173, 189, 190
Davies, David, 57, 188
Davies, Sir Joseph, 57, 73
Dawson, Geoffrey, 63, 144
Denmark, 177
Derby, Lord, 37, 61, 99
Devonport, 125, 126
Dicey, Edward, 30
Dilke, Sir Charles, 20, 21, 25, 29, 30, 36, 37, 44

Disraeli, Benjamin, 17, 19, 22, 37, 40, 84
Douglas-Home, Sir Alec, 163
Dublin, 15, 38, 41, 94
Duggan, Hubert, 163
Dundee, 11, 22, 118, 146
Dunglass, Lord, *see* Douglas-Home, Sir Alec
Dunkirk, 105
Durham, 140
Dyer, General, 88, 89, 90, 91
Eden, Anthony, 154, 161, 162, 163, 167, 169
Edinburgh, 42
Edward VII, King, 49
Edward VIII, King, 158
Epping, 154, 159
Esher, Lord, 49
Evans, Emrys, 163
Farquhar, Lord, 102, 103
Fermanagh, 50
Fife, 47, 76
Finland, 176, 177
Finlay, Lord, 90, 91
Fisher, H. A. L., 86, 100
FitzRoy, Edward, 156
Foot, Hugh, 10
Foot, Isaac, 10, 11, 98, 149, 150
Fox, Charles, 30, 51
France, 70, 73, 87, 117, 128, 130, 162, 165, 168, 174, 192
Franco, General, 162, 165
Fraser, Lovat, 97
French, Sir John, 53
Gardiner, A. G., 21, 51
Garvin, J. L., 22, 25, 31, 32
Gaunt, Ad. Sir Guy, 68
Geddes, Sir Eric, 85
Geneva, 148, 157
Genoa, 100, 101, 107
George V, King, 9, 63, 65, 102, 103, 132
George VI, King, 187
Germany, 56, 69, 70, 74, 101, 109, 129, 151, 156ff
Ghandi, Mahatma, 119

Gilbert, Martin, 54
Gilbert, W. S., 152
Gilmour, Sir John, 169
Gladstone, Lord, 32, 35, 46
Gladstone, Sir John, 17
Gladstone, William Ewart, 16, 17, 18, 19, 20, 21, 22, 24, 25, 27, 28, 29, 30, 31, 32, 33, 34, 35, 36, 37, 38, 39, 40, 41, 42, 43, 44, 45, 47, 51, 75, 93, 116, 124.
Glasgow, 140, 146
Gloucester, Duke of, 187
Godesberg, 163
Goebbels, Dr, 167
Gordon, General, 19
Goschen, G. J., 36, 37, 42
Grandi, Signor, 162
Granville, Lord, 18, 31, 37
Gray, Milner, 139
Greece, 185, 188
Greenock, 81
Greenwood, Arthur, 140, 167, 169
Grenville, Lord, 44
Grey, Captain, 191
Grey, Lord, 10, 46, 63, 79, 80, 81, 96, 97, 98
Griffith, Arthur, 94
Griffiths, James, 191
Grigg, Edward, 57
Guest, Captain, 103
Gunston, Derrick, 163
Haldane, Lord, 46
Halifax, Lord, 119, 166
Hankey, Lord, 51, 57, 59, 60, 113, 169
Hannon, Sir Patrick, 168
Hanson, Sir Charles, 98
Harcourt, Sir William, 36, 43, 63
Harmsworth, Cecil, 57
Harrison, Mrs, 80
Hartington, Lord, 30, 31, 33, 36, 37, 42, 43
Hartshorn, Vernon, 128
Harvey, Sir Ernest, 130, 132
Heath, Edward, 54
Henderson, Commander, 69

Henderson, Arthur, 59, 65, 112, 118, 140, 153, 160
Henderson, H. D., 78, 82
Herbert, Sidney, 163
Herschell, Farrer, 43
Hewart, Sir Gordon Hewart, 88, 97
Hines, Lord, 91
Hitler, Adolf, 56, 149, 155, 163, 164, 165, 166, 168, 181, 184
Hoare, Sir Samuel, 131, 148, 149, 151, 165, 166, 172, 180
Hobhouse, L. T., 66
Hogg, Quintin, 182, 191
Hoover, President, 130
Hore-Belisha, Leslie, 11, 124, 125, 126, 127, 135, 136, 140, 174, 175, 176, 189
Horne, Sir Robert, 95, 103, 107
Horsbrugh, Florence, 11
Howard, Geoffrey, 66, 80
Hull, 24, 25
Hungary, 130
India, 88, 89, 90, 99, 119, 123
Ipswich, 158
Ireland, 15ff, 93, 94, 95, 107
Isaacs, Rufus, *see* Reading, Lord
Italy, 29, 152
James, Sir Henry, 36, 37
Japan, 185
Jarrow, 118
Jenkins, Roy, 80
Jones, Dr Thomas, 92
Joynson-Hicks, Sir William, 90
Jowett, F. W., 153
Jowitt, Sir William, 115, 176
Kemal, Mustapha, 108, 109
Kerr, Philip, 57, 82
Keynes, Sir Roger, 179, 180, 187, 189
Keynes, J. M., 56, 81, 82, 86, 87, 120, 124, 145
Kidderminster, 186
Kinloch-Cook, Sir Clement, 125, 126
Kitchener, Lord, 53, 183
Labouchère, Henry, 27, 31, 32, 44

Lansbury, George, 128, 140, 180
Lansdowne, Lord, 28, 70, 71
Laval, Pierre, 148, 149
Layton, Walter, 78
Leeds, 29
Lennox-Boyd, Alan, 139
Lesley, Norman, 69
Lincoln, Abraham, 16
Lincolnshire, Lord, 80
Llandudno, 116, 117
Llewellyn Smith, Sir Hubert, 58
Lloyd George, Countess *see* Stevenson, Frances
Lloyd George, David, 9, 10, 16, 17, 21, 44, 45, 47, 48, 50, 53, 54, 55, 56, 57, 58, 59, 60, 61, 62, 63, 64, 65, 66, 67, 68, 69, 70, 71, 72, 73, 74, 75, 76, 77, 78, 79, 80, 81, 82, 83, 84, 85, 86, 88, 91, 92, 94, 95, 96, 97, 99, 100, 101, 102, 103, 104, 106, 107, 108, 110, 111, 112, 113, 114, 115, 120, 121, 122, 124, 125, 126, 127, 128, 129, 133, 134, 135, 142, 146, 150, 152, 158, 163, 165, 173, 178, 179, 180, 181, 184
Lloyd George, Gwilym, 158
Lloyd George, Megan, 77, 142, 158, 180
Long, Walter, 46, 92
Lothian, Lord, 128
Loughborough, 99
Lyndon Moore, W., 112
Lyttelton, Oliver, 187, 188
Macarthy, Justin, 29
McCurdy, Charles, 88, 94
MacDonald, Malcolm, 134
MacDonald, Ramsay, 9, 46, 116, 118, 127, 128, 129, 131, 132, 133, 134, 135, 136, 137, 138, 140, 141, 148, 153
McKenna, Reginald, 9, 46, 55, 63, 64, 88
McKenna, Stephen, 64
Maclay, Sir Joseph, 70
Maclean, Sir Donald, 76, 80, 81, 96, 139

Macmillan, Harold, 140, 150, 151, 154, 174, 177, 182
Macmillan, Lord, 170
Macnamara, T. G., 94
Macneill, Ronald, 105, 106
McNeill Weir, L., 116, 130, 133
Magnus, Sir Philip, 18, 19, 39
Malaya, 188
Mallalieu, E. L., 139
Manchester, 18, 22
Manchuria, 151
Mander, Geoffrey, 183
Massingham, H. W., 97
Masterman, C. F. G., 10, 46, 48, 58, 76
Maurice, General, 73, 75
Max of Baden, Prince, 71
Maxton, James, 116
Middlemas, Robert, 144, 157
Midlothian, 18, 30, 33, 116
Minney, R. J., 176
Montagu, E. S., 52, 62, 66, 88, 89, 90, 99, 100
Moore-Brabazon, Colonel, 119
Morley, John, 17, 19, 34, 37, 40, 43, 57
Morrison, Herbert, 140, 180 191
Moscow, 22, 166
Mosley, Sir Oswald, 116, 118
Mowat, Prof. Charles, 84, 114
Muir, Ramsay, 77, 78, 138
Munich, 150, 151, 152, 154, 159, 164, 167, 188
Mussolini, Benito, 148, 149, 150, 151, 154, 155, 162, 165, 179
Naples, 20
Narvik, 178
Newark, 17
Newcastle, 53
Newport, 33, 110, 112
New Zealand, 143, 144
Nicoll, Robertson, 72
Nicolson, Harold, 132, 163, 167
Norman, Montagu, 129, 130
North Africa, 185, 188

Northbrook, Lord, 37
Northcliffe, Lord, 101
Northumberland, Duke of, 103, 104
Norway, 169, 176, 178, 187, 188; debate, 12, 40, 156ff
O'Connor, Lt, 180
Oliver, F. S., 58
Ormsby Gore, William, 57
O'Shea, Captain, 29
Ottawa, 11, 143, 144
Owen, Goronwy, 158
Oxford, 17, 18, 53, 99, 116, 125
Page Croft, Sir Henry, 179
Paisley, 52, 77, 78, 81, 94, 96
Paris, 181
Parnell, Charles, 15, 29, 34, 35, 43, 47, 93
Peacock, E. R., 130
Peel, Sir Robert, 30
Percy, Lord Eustace, 107, 111
Phillips, Vivian, 80
Plymouth, 77, 126
Poincaré, Raymond, 101
Poland, 87, 160, 165, 166, 168, 176
Ponsonby, Sir Henry, 39
Pool, Maj.-Gen. Sir Frederick, 98
Pringle, W. M. R., 74, 80
Probin, Sir Dighton, 39
Punjab, The, 88, 89
Rathbone, Eleanor, 173
Reading, Lord, 46, 48, 60, 62, 67
Rhodes James, Robert, 111, 183
Riddell, Lord, 50, 54, 72
Robey, George, 55
Robinson, Sir Joseph, 103
Rome, 152
Roosevelt, President, 78, 82, 120, 162, 185, 190
Rosebery, Lord, 45, 152
Rowntree, Seebohm, 82, 128
Rowton, Lord, 19
Rumania, 61, 130, 166
Runciman, Walter, 9, 46, 63, 72, 76, 78, 80, 81, 122, 123, 124, 135, 140
Russell, George, 31, 33
Russell, Lord John, 44

Russia, 100, 101, 166, 176, 181, 183, 186, 192
St Ives, 150
St Omer, 54
Salisbury, Lord, 19, 24, 25, 33, 35, 36, 91
Salter, Sir Arthur, 149
Salvidge, Sir Archibald, 94
Samuel, Sir Herbert, 46, 63, 115, 121, 122, 128, 129, 131, 132, 134, 135, 136, 137, 140, 141, 142, 146, 147, 158
Sandys, Duncan, 161
Sankey, Lord, 132, 134
Schnadhorst, Joseph, 23
Scott, C. P., 65, 66, 77
Scrymgeour, Edwin, 138
Seely, Colonel, 50
Selborne, Lord (1st Earl), 37
Selborne, Lord (3rd Earl) 12
Shaftesbury, Lord, 124
Shakespeare, Rev. Dr J. H., 96
Sharpe, Granville, 159
Shinwell, Emanuel, 188
Shortt, Edward, 100
Sicily, 19
Sikorski, General, 160
Simon, E. D., 77
Simon, Sir John, 72, 76, 79, 80, 81, 122, 123, 127, 135, 137, 140, 148, 151, 164, 166, 176, 180, 188
Simpson, Mrs, 158
Sinclair, Sir Archibald, 11, 12, 16, 158, 163, 172, 177, 178
Singapore, 186, 188
Sinha, Lord, 90
Smith, Adam, 86
Smith, F. E. *see* Birkenhead, Lord
Snowden, Lord, 118, 121, 128, 130, 131, 132, 133, 139, 141, 144
South Africa, 144
Spain, 71
Spears, Sir Edwin, 163
Spencer, Lord, 40
Spender, J. A., 59
Stamfordham, Lord, 65, 122

Stanley, Venetia, 52, 80
Steed, Wickham, 101, 111, 149
Stephen, Campbell, 187
Stevenson, Frances, (Countess Lloyd George), 54, 73, 80, 128
Stonehaven, Lord, 133
Strang, William, 166
Strauss, George, 153, 161
Stresa, 148
Sudan, 19, 29
Sutherland, 158
Sweden, 23, 176
Swindon, Sir Ernest, 57
Swinton, Lord, 164, 165
Sykes, Sir Mark, 57
Talbot, Lord Edmund, 102
Thomas, J. H., 123, 132
Thomson, Lord, 117
Tobruk, 186, 189
Trevelyan, Sir George, 38, 42, 57
Tripoli, 185
Trollope, Anthony, 30, 152
Trondheim, 178, 179
Turkey, 108, 109, 185
Tyrone, 50
United States, 128, 185
Venizelos, Elentherios, 108
Versailles, 86, 87, 88, 101
Vestey, Lord, 105
Victoria, Queen, 19, 24, 26, 35, 39, 43, 44
Wardlaw-Milne, Sir John, 186, 187, 189
Waring, Lord, 105
Washington, 68, 96
Watson, William, 21
Wavell, General, 185
Wedgwood, Colonel, 179
Wedgwood, Josiah, 153
Wells, H. G., 18
Wigram, Sir Clive, 132
Wilhelm, Kaiser, 68, 70, 71, 74
Wilkinson, Ellen, 169
Williams, Sir Herbert, 188, 189
Williamson, Sir Archibald, 105, 106
Wilson, Harold, 54

Wilson, Sir Leslie, 110
Wilson, Dr Trevor, 76, 99
Winterton, Lord, 143, 182, 188
Wolseley, Lord, 19
Wood, Sir Kingsley, 191

Worthington-Evans, Sir Llaming, 94, 95, 114
Younger, Sir George, 95, 102, 107
Zeebrugge, 179